P9-BZT-135

KAIZEN

(Ky'zen)

The Key to Japan's Competitive Success

KAIZEN

(Ky'zen)

The Key to Japan's Competitive Success

MASAAKI   IMAI

McGRAW-HILL PUBLISHING COMPANY
New York St. Louis San Francisco Auckland Bogotá Caracas
Hamburg Lisbon London Madrid Mexico Milan Montreal
New Delhi Oklahoma City Paris San Juan São Paulo Singapore
Sydney Tokyo Toronto

First Edition

20 AGMAGM 9 9 8 7

Copyright © 1986 by The KAIZEN Institute, Ltd. (KAIZEN is a trademark of The KAIZEN Institute, Ltd.)

All rights reserved.
Printed in the United States of America. Except as permitted under the United States Copyright Act of 1976, no part of this publication may be reproduced or distributed in any form or by any means, or stored in a data base or retrieval system, without the prior written permission of the publisher. Distributed by McGraw-Hill, Inc.

Library of Congress Cataloging-in-Publication Data

Imai, Masaaki, 1930–
    Kaizen, the key to Japan's competitive success.

    Includes index.
    1. Industrial management—Japan.   2. Comparative
management.   I. Title.
HD70.J3I547   1986   658′.00952   85-30015
ISBN 0-07-554332-X

Permissions Acknowledgments

*G*rateful acknowledgment is made to the following for permission to reprint previously published materials:

excerpt from an article by Jeremy Main, *Fortune.* April 2, 1984. © 1984 Time Inc., All rights reserved.

excerpt from *Quality Progress,* October, 1983, copyright American Society for Quality Control, Inc. reprinted by permission.

Portions of this book originally appeared in the Japan Economic Journal (Nihon Keizai Shimbun) and *When in Japan* (Hotel Okura).

To Kenichi Nakaya, Professor Emeritus of Tokyo University, who opened up new horizons for me when I was a student.

Acknowledgments

I must admit that I cannot take credit for all the ideas expressed in this book. I have merely brought together the management philosophies, theories, and tools that have been developed and used over the years in Japan. If I have contributed anything, it is in organizing them under a single and readily understandable concept: KAIZEN.

In the course of writing this book, I have benefited from the help of many businesspeople, experts, and academics, both in Japan and abroad. Although I have tried to credit them by name in the text, giving all the names each time would be impossible.

Particular thanks go to Musashi Institute of Technology president Kaoru Ishikawa, one of the gurus of Total Quality Control (TQC) in Japan, and former Toyota vice president Taiichi Ohno, who initiated *kamban* and the "just-in-time" system. Ishikawa and Ohno consistently supported the Cambridge Corporation's efforts to explain KAIZEN to Western management and participated generously in the many seminars and workshops the Cambridge Corporation has held.

Other people who have provided assistance include professors Masao Kogure and Yoji Akao of Tamagawa University; president Masashi Nishimura and executive vice president Shuzo Moroto of Aisin-Warner; president Naohiko Yagi of Japan Steel Works; executive managing director Kaisaku Asano of Kayaba Industry; president Kenzo Sasaoka of Yokogawa-Hewlett-Packard, and president Yotaro Kobayashi of Fuji Xerox.

I have also benefited from the help of many executives actively engaged in implementing company-wide QC in Japan, among them Zenzaburo Katayama of Toyota; Zenji Shimada of Pentel; Hisashi Takasu of Kobayashi Kose; Motomu Baba, Ken Yonekura, and Kaoru Shimoyamada of Komatsu; Hidekazu Sadoya of Canon; Takeomi Nagafuchi and Haruo Kamimoto of Ricoh; Kenji Watabe of Japan Steel Works; and Yoshiki Iwata of Toyoda Gosei.

Beginning in 1957, I had the good fortune to start a five-year stint at the Japan Productivity Center in Washington, D.C., studying American management practices and helping to introduce them to Japan. This experience gave me valuable insights into management theory and practice and prepared me for a long and fruitful career as a management consultant. The man who organized the Japan Productivity Center 30 years ago and heads the organization as chairman today is Kohei Goshi. Not only did I find him most supportive during my formative years, I have enjoyed his continuing tutorship since returning to Japan in 1961.

Various publications by such organizations as the Union of Japanese Scientists and Engineers (JUSE), the Japan Productivity Center, the Japan Standards Association, the Central Japan Quality Control Association, and the Japan Management Association have been valuable resources for the writing of this book. In fact, I have often felt overwhelmed by the enormous amount of information available in Japan.

Others who assisted me in writing this book are Philips senior consultant S. Subramanian; Dynamic Management International director Ross Matheson; Japan Research president Fred Uleman; John Powers of the Academy for Educational Development; Educational Systems and Designs vice president Emmett Wallace; and Alberto Galgano, managing director of Alberto Galgano & Associati. I must also thank Allan Austin and Robert Zenowich of Austin & Lindberg, whose introduction to Random House made the publication of this book possible, as well as Patricia C. Haskell and Paul S. Donnelly of Random House for seeing it through to fruition.

Individuals cited in the text are identified by the positions they held at the time the interview took place or the quoted text was written. Likewise, conversion into U.S. dollars is based on the exchange rate prevailing at the time and is for reference only.

Last but not least, my thanks go to my secretary, Noriko Igarashi, who has consistently assisted me in searching out and putting together the materials for the book, patiently typed, retyped, and re-retyped the manuscript, and put in long hours above and beyond the call of duty.

Yet despite my considerable debt to all of these people, it goes without saying that none of them should be held in any way responsible for my own inability to benefit fully from their assistance and to make this a better book than it is.

Masaaki Imai

Contents

4. *KAIZEN—The Practice* 81

5. *KAIZEN Management* 125

6. *The KAIZEN Approach to Problem Solving* 163

7. *Changing the Corporate Culture* 207

List of Illustrations

Glossary

Definitions of key KAIZEN terminology and concepts.

Analytical approach (to management improvement):   an approach based on learning from the evaluation of past experience.

Autonomation (Jidohka):   a word coined to describe a feature of the Toyota production system whereby a machine is designed to stop automatically whenever a defective part is produced.

Check Points and Control Points: both check points and control points are used in measuring the progress of improvement-related activities between different managerial levels. Check points represent process-oriented criteria. Control points represent result-oriented criteria. What is the check point to the manager becomes a control point to the next-level manager. For this reason, check points and control points are also used in policy deployment.

Cross-Functional Management: the interdepartmental coordination required to realize the policy goals of a KAIZEN and a Total Quality Control program. After corporate strategy and planning are determined, top management sets objectives for cross-functional efforts that cut laterally throughout the organization.

Cross-functional management is the major organizational tool for realizing TQC improvement goals. (While cross-functional management may resemble certain Western managerial techniques, it is distinguished from them by an intensive focus on the follow-through to achieve the success of goals and measures.)

Deming Cycle: the concept of a continuously rotating wheel used by W. E. Deming to emphasize the necessity of constant interaction among research, design, production, and sales so as to arrive at an improved quality that satisfies customers (see PDCA Cycle).

Design Approach (to management improvement):   tries to build a better approach through predetermined goals. The design approach should receive greater attention in future applications of the management process.

Five Management Objectives of Factory Management: (see Chapter 4). Five key points of factory management set forth by Graham Spurling, Director of Mitsubishi Motors Australia.

Goals and Measures (in Japanese management):   (see Policy).

Improvement: improvement as a part of a successful KAIZEN strategy goes beyond the dictionary definition of the word. Improvement is a mind-set inextricably linked to maintaining and improving standards. In a still broader sense, improvement can be defined as KAIZEN and innovation, where a KAIZEN strategy maintains and improves the working standard through small, gradual improvements, and innovation calls forth radical improvements as a result of large investments in technology and/or equipment.

A successful KAIZEN strategy clearly delineates responsibility for maintaining standards to the worker, with management's role being the improvement of standards. The Japanese perception of management boils down to one precept: maintain and improve standards.

Jidohka: (see Auto*no*mation).

Just-in-Time: a production and inventory control technique that is part of the Toyota production system. It was designed and perfected at Toyota by Taiichi Ohno specifically to cut waste in production.

KAIZEN: KAIZEN means improvement. Moreover it means continuing improvement in personal life, home life, social life, and working life. When applied to the workplace KAIZEN means continuing improvement involving everyone—managers and workers alike.

Kamban: a communication tool in the "just-in-time" production and inventory control system developed by Taiichi Ohno at Toyota. A kamban, or signboard, is attached to specific parts in the production line signifying the delivery of a given quantity. When the parts have all been used, the same sign is returned to its origin where it becomes an order for more.

The kamban system is only one of many elements in a fully integrated system of Total Quality Control and cannot be inserted into a production process apart from these other TQC elements.

Maintenance: maintenance refers to activities that are directed to maintaining current technological, managerial, and operating standards.

Manageable Margin: the acceptable limits in a production process. When the check points indicate that the process has exceeded control limits, management must immediately determine the factors responsible and correct them.

There is a second phase to the manageable margin that is subtle and somewhat more difficult to manage. When a production process proceeds within the control limits but nonetheless establishes a pattern, such a pattern may be the first indication of forthcoming trouble and must be evaluated accordingly. Developing skills to manage at this level of subtlety is the ultimate challenge to any management system.

PDCA Cycle: The PDCA Cycle — plan, do, check, action — is an adaptation of the Deming wheel. Where the Deming wheel stresses the need for constant interaction among research, design, production, and sales, the PDCA Cycle asserts that every managerial action can be improved by careful application of the sequence: plan, do, check, action (see also SDCA Cycle and Deming wheel).

Policy (in Japanese management): in Japan the term is used to describe long- and medium-range management orientations as well as annual goals or targets. Another aspect of policy is that it is composed of both goals and measures, that is, both ends and means.

Goals are usually quantitative figures established by top management, such as sales, profit, and market share targets. Measures, on the other hand, are the specific action programs to achieve these goals. A goal that is not expressed in terms of such specific measures is merely a slogan. It is imperative that top management determine both the goals and the measures and then "deploy" them down throughout the organization.

Policy Deployment: the process of implementing the policies of a KAIZEN program directly through line managers and indirectly through cross-functional organization.

Policy Prioritization: a technique to ensure maximum utilization of resources at all levels of management in the process of policy deployment. Top management's policy statement must be restated at all management levels in increasingly specific and action-oriented goals, eventually becoming precise quantitative values.

Process-Oriented Management: a style of management that is also people oriented in contrast to one that is oriented solely toward results. In process-oriented management a manager must support and stimulate efforts to improve the way employees do their jobs. Such a style of management calls for a long-term outlook and usually requires behavioral change.

Some criteria for meriting rewards in this style are: discipline, time management, skill development, participation and involvement, morale, and communication. In a KAIZEN strategy these criteria are referred to as: *P Criteria*. KAIZEN strategy asserts that a conscious effort to establish a system which encourages P Criteria can produce significant competitive advantages for the company.

QC (Quality Control):   according to the Japanese Industrial Standards (Z8101-1981) definition, quality control is a "system of means to economically produce goods or services that satisfy customer requirements."

When QC was first introduced to Japan by W. E. Deming in 1950, the main emphasis was on improving product quality by applying statistical tools in the production processes.

In 1954, J. M. Juran brought the concept of QC as a vital management tool for improving managerial performance. Today, QC is used as a tool to build a system of continuing interaction among all elements responsible for the conduct of a company's business so as to achieve the improved quality that satisfies the customer's demand.

Thus, the term QC as used in Japan is almost synonymous with KAIZEN, and although the use of statistics still remains the mainstay of QC, it has come to add many other tools, such as New Seven tools for improvement.

QC (Quality Control) Circles: a small group that voluntarily performs quality control activities within the workplace, carrying out its work continuously as part of a company-wide program of quality control, self-development, mutual education, flow control, and improvement within the workplace.

QCS (Quality, Cost, Scheduling): in the construct of a hierarchy of overall company goals as described by Shigeru Aoki, senior managing director at Toyota Motors, the ultimate goal being "to make profits . . . is self-evident," . . . the "next superordinate goal should be . . . quality, cost, and scheduling (quantity and delivery). . . . Therefore we should regard all other management functions as existing to serve the three super-ordinate goals of QCS."

Quality: there is very little agreement on what constitutes quality. In its broadest sense, quality is anything that can be improved. When speaking of "quality" one tends to think first in terms of product quality. When discussed in the context of KAIZEN strategy nothing could be further off the mark. The foremost concern here is with the *quality of people*.

The three building blocks of a business are hardware, software, and "humanware." Only after humanware is squarely in place should the hardware and software aspects of a business be considered. Building quality into people means helping them become KAIZEN conscious.

Quality Assurance (at Toyota): quality assurance means assuring that the quality of the product is satisfactory, reliable, and yet economical for the customer.

Quality Deployment: a technique to deploy customer requirements (known as "true quality characteristics") into designing characteristics (known as "counterpart characteristics") and deploy them into such subsystems as components, parts, and production processes. Quality deployment is regarded as the most significant development to come out of TQC in the last thirty years in Japan.

Q Seven and the New Seven: the seven statistical tools (commonly referred to as the Q Seven) and seven additional tools (the New Seven) that have made an indispensable contribution to the constant evolution and improvement of the Total Quality Control movement. (See listing in Appendix E.)

Results-Oriented Management: this style of management is well established in the West and emphasizes controls, performance, results, rewards (usually financial), or the denial of rewards and even penalties. Criteria, or *R Criteria,* are easily quantifiable and short term. Western style management emphasizes R Criteria almost exclusively.

SDCA Cycle (Standardize, Do, Check, Action):   a refinement of the PDCA Cycle wherein management decides first to establish the standard *before* performing the regular PDCA function.

Seven-up Campaign: a slogan for an improvement campaign as part of a KAIZEN program at Nissan Motors in 1975 (see Chapter 2).

Standardized Work: as defined at Toyota this is the optimum combination of workers, machines, and materials.

Standards: a set of policies, rules, directives, and procedures established by management for all major operations, which serves as guidelines that enable all employees to perform their jobs successfully.

Suggestion System: in Japan the suggestion system is a highly integrated part of individual-oriented KAIZEN. Its design is as carefully plotted, implemented, and communicated as a company's strategic plan. Scrupulous attention is paid to top management responsiveness, and developing a system of feedback and rewards.
  Japanese-style suggestion systems emphasize morale-boosting

benefits and positive employee participation over the economic and financial incentives that are stressed in the American-style systems. (The dimension of Japanese suggestion systems is illustrated by the number of suggestions submitted annually. In 1985 Matushita was the Japanese company whose employees submitted the highest number of suggestions. The total number of suggestions exceeded *6 million*!)

TPM (Total Productive Maintenance): total productive maintenance aims at maximizing equipment effectiveness throughout the entire life of the equipment. TPM involves everyone in all departments and at all levels; it motivates people for plant maintenance through small-group and voluntary activities, and involves such basic elements as developing a maintenance system, education in basic housekeeping, problem-solving skills, and activities to achieve zero breakdowns.

Top management must design a system that recognizes and rewards everyone's ability and responsibility for TPM.

TQC (Total Quality Control): organized KAIZEN activities involving everyone in a company—managers and workers—in a totally integrated effort toward improving performance at every level. This improved performance is directed toward satisfying such cross-functional goals as quality, cost, scheduling, manpower development, and new product development. It is assumed that these activities ultimately lead to increased customer satisfaction. (Also referred to as CWQC—Company-Wide Quality Control.)

University of Labor: the Japan Productivity Center has a program for educating union executives in the sound concepts of business management so that they can better negotiate with management.

Visible Management: the technique of providing information and instruction about the elements of a job in a clearly visible manner so that the worker can maximize his productivity. (The kamban, or card, system is an example of this technique.)

Warusa-kagen: a term in TQC that refers to things that are not yet problems, but are still not quite right. Left untended they may develop into serious problems. Warusa-kagen is often the starting point of improvement activities. In the workplace, it is usually the worker who notices warusa-kagen, and, hence, the worker becomes the first echelon of maintenance and improvement.

Foreword

*I*f we look back over the forty years follow-
ing the Second World War, we have seen Japan attain the status of a
world economic power, going through five phases of adaptation to
become a formidable competitor in various product areas. These
phases are:

- Large-scale absorption of technology imported from the United
  States and Europe
- A productivity drive of hitherto unseen dimensions
- A country-wide quality improvement programme inspired by the
  ideas of Dr. Deming and Dr. Juran of the United States
- A great degree of manufacturing flexibility, and finally
- Multinationality

After successfully assimilating foreign technology and then achieving very high productivity and top quality, Japanese industries are
now focusing on flexible manufacturing technologies. This means
having the capability to adapt manufacturing in a very short time to
changing customer and market requirements. The key words are
mechanisation, automation, robotisation and related systems.

There are many interesting things which Western companies can
learn from the Japanese industrial environment. As you will read in
this book, Philips has introduced a Company-Wide Quality Improvement programme. Like most Western companies, Philips has learnt
some lessons too. The programme we have instituted is directed

towards "Total Improvement" and is not restricted to product quality alone. The aim is to improve *everything* Philips does.

Mr. Masaaki Imai, who participated in the initial stages of this process in Philips, embraced the slogan and entitled his book *KAIZEN*. From this angle he has reviewed the Japanese strategy of the past three decades of improvements in productivity, quality and flexibility. He does this with vivid examples and also looks at the tools and systems used. As such, this book can also be most illuminating for non-Japanese managers.

The world is going through a period of transition from fragmented markets to a more or less global one. Doing business in such an environment calls for unique characteristics of multinationality. To survive in a highly competitive world, it is imperative for multinationals to acquire the finesse which will enable them to be identified with and integrate into the business environment or country in which business is being done. However successful Japanese companies have been up until now, the real challenge they continue to face lies in becoming truly multinational. Having spent six years of my career in Japan, it became increasingly clear to me that there is a problem area in doing business on a global scale which the Japanese have not yet tackled properly, namely multinationality.

In their search for a model for the conduct of multinational business, the Japanese would do well to study the Dutch example. Sharing as these countries do, a relative smallness, the ability to adapt to the cultures, as well as the business practices, of other countries becomes a necessity. Such multinational behaviour has become second nature to the Dutch and has been exemplified by Philips for nearly 100 years.

One must not be discouraged by cultural differences. Manufacturing is definitely a global activity and, as such, good practices, wherever they come from, deserve our attention. However, Japanese top management, especially in our branch of industry, has to understand that one of the yardsticks used to measure their managerial qualities will be the degree to which they consider the world, including their home country, Japan, to be their battleground. Reciprocity is the key to our joint survival.

Dr. W. Dekker
Chairman of the Supervisory Board
N. V. Philips' Gloeilampenfabrieken

The KAIZEN Challenge

KAIZEN strategy is the single most important concept in Japanese management—the key to Japanese competitive success. KAIZEN means improvement. In the context of this book, KAIZEN means *ongoing* improvement involving *everyone*— top management, managers, and workers. In Japan, many systems have been developed to make management and workers KAIZEN-conscious.

KAIZEN is everybody's business. The KAIZEN concept is crucial to understanding the differences between the Japanese and Western approaches to management. If asked to name the most important difference between Japanese and Western management concepts, I would unhesitatingly say, "Japanese KAIZEN and its process-oriented way of thinking versus the West's innovation- and results-oriented thinking."

KAIZEN is one of the most commonly used words in Japan. In the newspapers and on radio and TV, we are bombarded daily with statements by government officials and politicians regarding the KAIZEN of our trade balance with the United States, the KAIZEN of diplomatic relations with country X, and the KAIZEN of the social welfare system. Both labor and management speak of the KAIZEN of industrial relations.

In business, the concept of KAIZEN is so deeply ingrained in the minds of both managers and workers that they often *do not even realize* that they are thinking KAIZEN.

During the two decades preceding the oil crises, the world

economy enjoyed unprecedented growth and experienced insatiable demand for new technologies and new products. It was a period in which innovation strategy paid off handsomely. Innovation strategy is technology driven and thrives on fast growth and high profit margins. It flourishes in a climate featuring:

- Rapidly expanding markets
- Consumers oriented more toward quantity rather than quality
- Abundant and low-cost resources
- A belief that success with innovative products could offset sluggish performance in traditional operations
- Management more concerned with increasing sales than with reducing costs

Those days are gone. The oil crises of the 1970s have radically and irrevocably altered the international business environment. The new situation is characterized by:

- Sharp increases in the costs of material, energy, and labor
- Overcapacity of production facilities
- Increased competition among companies in saturated or dwindling markets
- Changing consumer values and more exacting quality requirements
- A need to introduce new products more rapidly
- A need to lower the breakeven point

Despite these changes, however, many executives still subscribe to the innovation strategy and refuse to develop a strategy suited to the new era.

Numerous warnings have been issued about the increased cost of resources, stiffer competition to win customer acceptance through quality, and the need to develop more customer-oriented products and services faster than ever before. Yet after having ignored these warnings for so long, Western business now "suddenly" finds Japanese companies emerging as formidable competitors.

In today's competitive business environment, any delay in adopting the latest technology is costly. Delays in adopting improved management techniques are no less costly. Yet Western management has been slow to take advantage of KAIZEN tools developed by Japanese companies. Even worse, many Western managers *are not even aware* that a KAIZEN strategy is available and could work to their competitive advantage.

This book is about such a strategy—a strategy to cope with the challenges of the 1980s, the 1990s, and beyond.

Successful companies have shown that it is possible to anticipate change and to meet the challenges while they are still manageable. Japanese companies, for example, have successfully designed, manufactured, and marketed competitive products using KAIZEN strategy. Many Western businesspeople are asking how the Japanese have done it; yet, for some reason, scholars attempting to answer this crucial question have ignored KAIZEN strategy. While numerous cultural, social, and political factors have been pointed out, very few observers of Japanese management practices have examined the strategy actually employed by Japanese management over the last 30 years.

This book explains why KAIZEN strategy is so indispensable to meeting the challenges of the 1980s and 1990s. Yet this emphasis on KAIZEN does not mean that innovation can or should be forgotten. Both innovation and KAIZEN are needed if a company is to survive and grow.

Most of the articles written on Japanese management have just promoted confusion. Each scholar has had his exclusive explanation of the secret of Japan's management success—often implying that such success is impossible in the West. Even more confusing has been the semantics. Words like quality, productivity, and all the other jargon, while illuminating for the specialist, tend to leave the lay reader in the dark.

I do not intend to refute the explanations of Japanese management put forth by other writers. KAIZEN is the basic philosophical underpinning for the best in Japanese management. Thus, just as first-time readers will find this a solid basis for their future studies, managers who have studied Japanese management will find KAIZEN pulling together the many outwardly unrelated and disparate observations made by other writers.

Many Japanese management practices succeed simply because they are good management practices. This success has little to do with cultural factors. And the lack of cultural bias means that these practices can be—and are—just as successfully employed elsewhere.

Just as Japan has its plodding companies destined to fall by the way-side of progress, so does the United States have excellent companies setting new standards for product and service quality. The distinction is not one of nationality. It is one of mentality.

I would like here to propose KAIZEN as the overriding concept behind good management. It is the unifying thread running through the philosophy, the systems, and the problem-solving tools developed in Japan over the last 30 years. Its message is one of improvement and trying to do better.

Since KAIZEN starts with the recognition that any corporation has problems, KAIZEN solves problems by establishing a corporate culture in which everyone can freely admit these problems. Problems can be both unifunctional and cross-functional. For instance, developing a new product is a typical cross-functional situation in that it involves collaboration and joint efforts of people from marketing, engineering, and production.

In the West, cross-functional problems are often seen in terms of conflict-resolution, while KAIZEN strategy has enabled Japanese management to take a systematic and collaborative approach to cross-functional problem-solving. Herein lies one of the secrets of Japanese management's competitive edge.

Underlying the KAIZEN strategy is the recognition that management must seek to satisfy the customer and serve customer needs if it is to stay in business and make a profit. Improvements in such areas as quality, cost, and scheduling (meeting volume and delivery requirements) are essential. KAIZEN is a customer-driven strategy for improvement. In KAIZEN, it is assumed that all activities should eventually lead to increased customer satisfaction.

Soichiro Honda of Honda Motor says that, as far as customers are concerned, quality is something a product either has or it does not have. There is no middle ground. He asserts that management's role is to make a constant effort to provide better products at lower prices. The KAIZEN strategy has produced a systems approach and problem-solving tools that can be applied to realizing this goal.

KAIZEN movements are going on all the time in most Japanese companies, and most companies contend that management should devote at least 50 percent of its attention to KAIZEN. Japanese managers are constantly looking for ways to improve in-house systems and procedures, and their involvement in KAIZEN extends even to such fields as labor–management relations, marketing practices, and supplier relations. Middle managers, supervisors, and workers are also actively involved in KAIZEN. Engineers at Japanese plants are often warned, "There will be no progress if you keep on doing things exactly the same way all the time."

Another important aspect of KAIZEN has been its emphasis on process. KAIZEN has generated a process-oriented way of thinking, and a management system that supports and acknowledges people's process-oriented efforts for improvement. This is in sharp contrast to the Western management practice of reviewing people's performance strictly on the basis of results and not rewarding the effort made.

In this book, I have tried to explain what is going on at some Japanese companies and what the concepts are behind KAIZEN strategy. Although the theory is explained, the main focus is on implementation. I have tried to provide as many case studies and examples as possible. Since KAIZEN is everybody's business, the thoughtful readers will soon realize that KAIZEN strategy is relevant to their own work—and that many of these KAIZEN practices can be readily implemented to considerable advantage.

This book also explains the important part KAIZEN has played in enabling Japanese companies to compete internationally. Basically, there are only two kinds of companies: those that subscribe to KAIZEN and those that do not. While many Japanese companies have succeeded with KAIZEN, most Western managers have failed to realize the tremendous competitive opportunity KAIZEN offers. Partly this is because nobody has explained KAIZEN strategy and all of its ramifications. Partly it is because KAIZEN strategy was still aborning. Yet Japanese companies now have thirty years' experience with KAIZEN, and the KAIZEN strategy has been fleshed out to the point where it can be explained and applied at any company. That is what this book is all about.

Masaaki Imai, 1986

KAIZEN

(Ky'zen)

The Key to Japan's Competitive Success

1

KAIZEN, The Concept

KAIZEN Values

Back in the 1950s, I was working with the Japan Productivity Center in Washington, D.C. My job mainly consisted of escorting groups of Japanese businessmen who were visiting American companies to study "the secret of American industrial productivity."

Toshiro Yamada, now Professor Emeritus of the Faculty of Engineering at Kyoto University, was a member of one such study team visiting the United States to study the industrial-vehicle industry. Recently, the members of his team gathered to celebrate the silver anniversary of their trip.

At the banquet table, Yamada said he had recently been back to the United States in a "sentimental journey" to some of the plants he had visited, among them the River Rouge steelworks in Dearborn, Michigan. Shaking his head in disbelief, he said, "You know, the plant was exactly the same as it had been 25 years ago."

He also spoke of his recent visit to Europe, where he had led a group of businessmen on a study of European tile-manufacturing plants. As they roamed from one plant to another, the group members became increasingly restless and dismayed at the "archaic" facilities.

The group was surprised to find that these plants were still using belt conveyors, and that not only the workers but even visitors had to walk over or under them, indicating a general lack of safety precautions. One member said, "There is no management if they don't care about the workers' safety." It is rather rare to see belt conveyors

1

in modern Japan. Even if they are still used, they are designed so that people do not have to walk over or under them.

In spite of these observations, Yamada also noted that he had found the facilities at Western universities and research institutions far more advanced, and Western research projects rich in originality and creativity.

I was recently traveling in the United States with Fujio Umibe, chief specialist at Toshiba's Research and Development Center. Umibe told me of a recent encounter with a co-worker from one of Toshiba's outlying plants in Japan. Upon hearing that Umibe had not set foot in the plant for over ten years, the man chided him: "You really should come out and see the plant. You won't recognize it today!" By way of substantiation, I have been told that a quarter of the production lines at one Toshiba plant were changed while the plant was shut down for the week-long summer holiday in 1984.

These conversations set me to thinking about the great differences in the ways Japanese and Western managers approach their work. It is inconceivable that a Japanese plant would remain virtually unchanged for over a quarter of a century.

I had long been looking for a key concept to explain these two very different management approaches, one that might also help explain why many Japanese companies have come to gain their increasingly conspicuous competitive edge. For instance, how do we explain the fact that while most new ideas come from the West and some of the most advanced plants, institutions, and technologies are found there, there are also many plants there that have changed little since the 1950s?

Change is something which everybody takes for granted. Recently, an American executive at a large multinational firm told me his company chairman had said at the start of an executive committee meeting: "Gentlemen, our job is to manage change. If we fail, we must change management." The executive smiled and said, "We all got the message!"

In Japan, change is a way of life, too. But are we talking about the same change when we talk about managing change or else changing management? It dawned on me that there might be different kinds of change: gradual and abrupt. While we can easily observe both gradual and abrupt changes in Japan, gradual change is not so obvious a part of the Western way of life. How are we to explain this difference?

This question led me to consider the question of values. Could it be that differences between the value systems in Japan and the West account for their different attitudes toward gradual change and abrupt change? Abrupt changes are easily grasped by everyone concerned, and people are usually elated to see them. This is generally true in both Japan and the West. Yet what about the gradual changes? My earlier statement that it is inconceivable that a Japanese plant would remain unchanged for years refers to gradual change as well as abrupt change.

Thinking all this over, I came to the conclusion that the key difference between how change is understood in Japan and how it is viewed in the West lies in the KAIZEN concept—a concept that is so natural and obvious to many Japanese managers that they often do not even realize that they possess it! The KAIZEN concept explains why companies cannot remain the same for long in Japan. Moreover, after many years of studying Western business practices, I have reached the conclusion that this KAIZEN concept is nonexistent, or at least very weak, in most Western companies today. Worse yet, they reject it without knowing what it really entails. It's the old "not invented here" syndrome. And this lack of KAIZEN helps explain why an American or European factory can remain exactly the same for a quarter of a century.

The essence of KAIZEN is simple and straightforward: KAIZEN means improvement. Moreover, KAIZEN means ongoing improvement involving everyone, including both managers and workers. The KAIZEN philosophy assumes that our way of life—be it our working life, our social life, or our home life—deserves to be constantly improved.

In trying to understand Japan's postwar "economic miracle," scholars, journalists, and businesspeople alike have dutifully studied such factors as the productivity movement, total quality control (TQC), small-group activities, the suggestion system, automation, industrial robots, and labor relations. They have given much attention to some of Japan's unique management practices, among them the lifetime employment system, seniority-based wages, and enterprise unions. Yet I feel they have failed to grasp the very simple truth that lies behind the many myths concerning Japanese management.

The essence of most "uniquely Japanese" management practices—be they productivity improvement, TQC (Total Quality Control) activities, QC (Quality Control) circles, or labor relations—can be

* Customer orientation
* TQC (total quality control)
* Robotics
* QC circles
* Suggestion system
* Automation
* Discipline in the workplace
* TPM
  (total productive maintenance)

* *Kamban*
* Quality improvement
* Just–in–time
* Zero defects
* Small–group activities
* Cooperative labor-
  management relations
* Productivity improvement
* New–product development

FIGURE 1.1　*The KAIZEN Umbrella*

reduced to one word: KAIZEN. Using the term KAIZEN in place of such words as productivity, TQC, ZD (Zero Defects), *kamban,** and the suggestion system paints a far clearer picture of what has been going on in Japanese industry. KAIZEN is an umbrella concept covering most of those "uniquely Japanese" practices that have recently achieved such worldwide fame. (See Figure 1.1.)

The implications of TQC or CWQC (Company-Wide Quality Control) in Japan have been that these concepts have helped Japanese companies generate a *process-oriented* way of thinking and develop strategies that assure continuous improvement involving people at all

---

*Kamban as a word simply means signboards, cards, or chits. With just-in-time production, a worker from the following process goes to collect parts from the previous process leaving a *kamban* signifying the delivery of a given quantity of specific parts. When all the parts have all been used, the same *kamban* is sent back, at which point it becomes an order for more. Because this is such an important tool for just-in-time production, *kamban* has become synonymous with the just-in-time production system. The just-in-time system was first employed by Toyota Motor Corp. to minimize inventory and hence cut waste. The underlying principle is that the necessary parts should be received "just in time" for the manufacturing process.

levels of the organizational hierarchy. The message of the KAIZEN strategy is that not a day should go by without some kind of improvement being made somewhere in the company.

The belief that there should be unending improvement is deeply ingrained in the Japanese mentality. As the old Japanese saying goes, "If a man has not been seen for three days, his friends should take a good look at him to see what changes have befallen him." The implication is that he must have changed in three days, so his friends should be attentive enough to notice the changes.

After World War II, most Japanese companies had to start literally from the ground up. Every day brought new challenges to managers and workers alike, and every day meant progress. Simply staying in business required unending progress, and KAIZEN has become a way of life. It was also fortunate that the various tools that helped elevate this KAIZEN concept to new heights were introduced to Japan in the late 1950s and early 1960s by such experts as W. E. Deming and J. M. Juran. However, most new concepts, systems, and tools that are widely used in Japan today have subsequently been developed in Japan and represent qualitative improvements upon the statistical quality control and total quality control of the 1960s.

KAIZEN and Management

Figure 1.2 shows how job functions are perceived in Japan. As indicated, management has two major components: maintenance and improvement. Maintenance refers to activities directed toward maintaining current technological, managerial, and operating standards; improvement refers to those directed toward improving current standards.

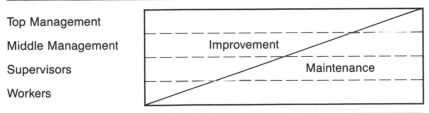

FIGURE 1.2 *Japanese Perceptions of Job Functions (1)*

Under its maintenance functions, management performs its assigned tasks so that everybody in the company can follow the established SOP (Standard Operating Procedure). This means that management must first establish policies, rules, directives, and procedures for all major operations and then see to it that everybody follows SOP. If people are able to follow the standard but do not, management must introduce discipline. If people are *unable* to follow the standard, management must either provide training or review and revise the standard so that people can follow it.

In any business, an employee's work is based on existing standards, either explicit or implicit, imposed by management. Maintenance refers to maintaining such standards through training and discipline. By contrast, improvement refers to improving the standards. The Japanese perception of management boils down to one precept: maintain and improve standards.

The higher up the manager is, the more he is concerned with improvement. At the bottom level, an unskilled worker working at a machine may spend all his time following instructions. However, as he becomes more proficient at his work, he begins to think about improvement. He begins to contribute to improvements in the way his work is done, either through individual suggestions or through group suggestions.

Ask any manager at a successful Japanese company what top management is pressing for, and the answer will be, "KAIZEN" (improvement).

Improving standards means establishing higher standards. Once this is done, it becomes management's maintenance job to see that the new standards are observed. Lasting improvement is achieved only when people work to higher standards. Maintenance and improvement have thus become inseparable for most Japanese managers.

What is improvement? Improvement can be broken down between KAIZEN and innovation. KAIZEN signifies small improvements made in the status quo as a result of ongoing efforts. Innovation involves a drastic improvement in the status quo as a result of a large investment in new technology and/or equipment. Figure 1.3 shows the breakdown among maintenance, KAIZEN, and innovation as perceived by Japanese management.

On the other hand, most Western managers' perceptions of job functions are as shown in Figure 1.4. There is little room in Western management for the KAIZEN concept.

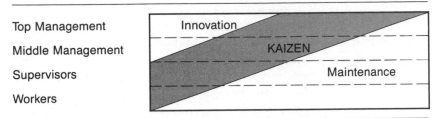

FIGURE 1.3 *Japanese Perceptions of Job Functions (2)*

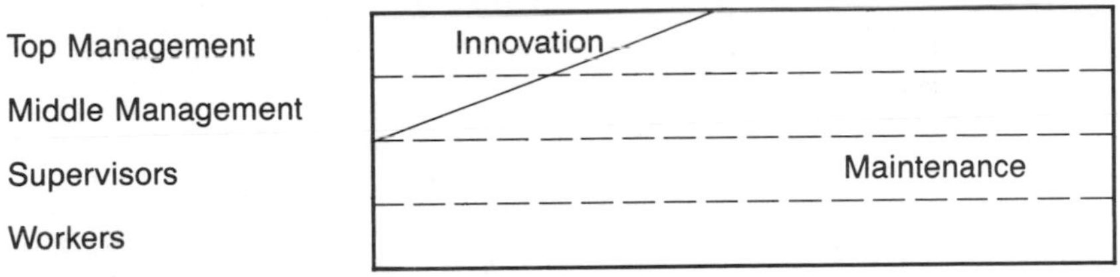

Top Management
Middle Management
Supervisors
Workers

Innovation
Maintenance

FIGURE 1.4 *Western Perceptions of Job Functions*

Sometimes, another type of management is found in the high-technology industries as shown in Figure 1.5. These are the companies that are born running, grow rapidly, and then disappear just as rapidly when their initial success wanes or markets change.

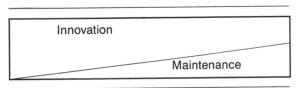

FIGURE 1.5 *Innovation-Centered Job Functions*

The worst companies are those which do nothing but maintenance, meaning there is no internal drive for KAIZEN or innovation, change is forced on management by market conditions and competition, and management does not know where it wants to go.

Since KAIZEN is an ongoing process and involves everyone in the organization, everyone in the management hierarchy is involved in some aspects of KAIZEN, as shown in Figure 1.6.

Top Management	Middle Management and Staff	Supervisors	Workers
Be determined to introduce KAIZEN as a corporate strategy	Deploy and implement KAIZEN goals as directed by top management through policy deployment and cross-functional management	Use KAIZEN in functional roles	Engage in KAIZEN through the suggestion system and small-group activities
Provide support and direction for KAIZEN by allocating resources		Formulate plans for KAIZEN and provide guidance to workers	
		Improve communication with workers and sustain high morale	Practice discipline in the workshop
Establish policy for KAIZEN and cross-functional goals	Use KAIZEN in functional capabilities		Engage in continuous self-development to become better problem solvers
Realize KAIZEN goals through policy deployment and audits	Establish, maintain, and upgrade standards	Support small-group activities (such as quality circles) and the individual suggestion system	
	Make employees KAIZEN-conscious through intensive training programs		Enhance skills and job-performance expertise with cross-education
Build systems, procedures, and structures conducive to KAIZEN		Introduce discipline in the workshop	
	Help employees develop skills and tools for problem solving	Provide KAIZEN suggestions	

FIGURE 1.6   *Hierarchy of KAIZEN Involvement*

Implications of QC for KAIZEN

While management is usually concerned with such issues as productivity and quality, the thrust of this book is to look at the other side of the picture—at KAIZEN.

Any serious discussion of quality, for instance, soon finds itself entangled in such issues as how to define quality, how to measure it, and how to relate it to benefits. There are as many definitions of quality as there are people defining it, and there is no agreement on what quality is or should be. The same is true of productivity.

Productivity means different things to different people. Perceptions of productivity are miles apart, and management and labor are often at odds over this very issue.

Yet no matter what the substance of quality and productivity, the other side of the coin has always been KAIZEN. Thus, the moment we start talking about KAIZEN, the whole issue becomes breathtakingly simple. First of all, nobody can dispute the value of improvement, since it is generic and good in its own right. It is good by definition. Whenever and wherever improvements are made in business, these improvements are eventually going to lead to improvements in such areas as quality and productivity.

The starting point for improvement is to recognize the need. This comes from recognition of a problem. If no problem is recognized, there is no recognition of the need for improvement. Complacency is the archenemy of KAIZEN. Therefore, KAIZEN emphasizes problem-awareness and provides clues for identifying problems.

Once identified, problems must be solved. Thus KAIZEN is also a problem-solving process. In fact, KAIZEN requires the use of various problem-solving tools. Improvement reaches new heights with every problem that is solved. In order to consolidate the new level, however, the improvement must be standardized. Thus KAIZEN also requires standardization.

Such terms as QC (Quality Control), SQC (Statistical Quality Control), QC circles, and TQC (or CWQC) often appear in connection with KAIZEN. To avoid unnecessary confusion, it may be helpful to clarify these terms here.

As already mentioned, the word *quality* has been interpreted in many different ways, and there is no agreement on what actually constitutes quality. In its broadest sense, quality is anything that can be improved. In this context, quality is associated not only with products and services but also with the way people work, the way machines are operated, and the way systems and procedures are dealt with. It includes all aspects of human behavior. This is why it is more useful to talk about KAIZEN than about quality or productivity.

The English term *improvement* as used in the Western context more often than not means improvement in equipment, thus excluding the human elements. By contrast, KAIZEN is generic and can be applied to every aspect of everybody's activities. This said, however, it must be admitted that such terms as quality and quality control have played a vital role in the development of KAIZEN in Japan.

In the years immediately following Japan's wartime defeat, Hajime Karatsu, Technical Advisor to Matsushita Electric Industrial, was working with NTT (Nippon Telegraph and Telephone Public Corp.) as a young QC engineer. NTT had problems. "Whenever I tried to call somebody up, I invariably got a wrong number," recalls Karatsu. Seeing the terrible state of affairs at NTT, General MacArthur's staff invited some American quality control experts from Western Electric to help NTT. The American experts told NTT management that the only solution was to apply quality control. Says Karatsu, "In our pride, we told them that we were applying quality control at NTT the Japanese way. But when they asked to see our control charts, we didn't even know what a control chart was!"

It was from such humble beginnings that efforts were begun to improve Japanese quality-control practices in the late 1940s. An example was the establishment of the quality-control subcommittee at the Union of Japanese Scientists and Engineers (JUSE). At about the same time, the Japanese Standards Association started organizing seminars on statistical quality control.

In March 1950, JUSE started publishing its magazine *Statistical Quality Control.* In July of the same year, W. E. Deming was invited to Japan to teach statistical quality control at an eight-day seminar organized by JUSE. Deming visited Japan several times in the 1950s, and it was during one of those visits that he made his famous prediction that Japan would soon be flooding the world market with quality products.

Deming also introduced the "Deming cycle," one of the crucial QC tools for assuring continuous improvement, to Japan. The Deming cycle is also called the Deming wheel or the PDCA (Plan–Do–Check–Action) cycle. (See Figure 1.7.) Deming stressed the importance of constant interaction among research, design, production, and sales in order for a company to arrive at better quality that satisfies customers. He taught that this wheel should be rotated on the ground of quality-first perceptions and quality-first responsibility. With this process, he argued, the company could win consumer confidence and acceptance and prosper.

In July 1954, J. M. Juran was invited to Japan to conduct a JUSE

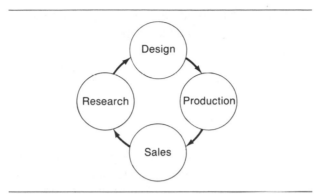

FIGURE 1.7 *Deming Wheel*

seminar on quality-control management. This was the first time QC was dealt with from the overall management perspective.

In 1956, Japan Shortwave Radio included a course on quality control as part of its educational programming. In November 1960, the first national quality month was inaugurated. It was also in 1960 that Q-marks and Q-flags were formally adopted. Then in April 1962 the magazine *Quality Control for the Foreman* was launched by JUSE, and the first QC circle was started that same year.

A QC circle is defined as a small group that *voluntarily* performs quality-control activities within the shop. The small group carries out its work continuously as part of a company-wide program of quality control, self-development, mutual education, and flow-control and improvement within the workshop. The QC circle is only *part* of a company-wide program; it is never the whole of TQC or CWQC.

Those who have followed QC circles in Japan know that they often focus on such areas as cost, safety, and productivity, and that their activities sometimes relate only indirectly to product-quality improvement. For the most part, these activities are aimed at making improvements in the workshop.

There is no doubt that QC circles have played an important part in improving product quality and productivity in Japan. However, their role has often been blown out of proportion by overseas observers who believe that QC circles are the mainstay of TQC activities in Japan. Nothing could be further from the truth, especially when it comes to Japanese management. Efforts related to

QC circles generally account for only 10 percent to 30 percent of the overall TQC effort in Japanese companies.

What is less visible behind these developments is the transformation of the term quality control, or QC, in Japan. As is the case in many Western companies, quality control initially meant quality control applied to the manufacturing process, particularly the inspections for rejecting defective incoming material or defective outgoing products at the end of the production line. But very soon the realization set in that inspection alone does nothing to improve the quality of the product, and that product quality should be built at the production stage. "Build quality into the process" was (and still is) a popular phrase in Japanese quality control. It is at this stage that control charts and the other tools for statistical quality control were introduced after Deming's lectures.

Juran's lectures in 1954 opened up another aspect of quality control: the managerial approach to quality control. This was the first time the term QC was positioned as a vital *management* tool in Japan. From then on, the term QC has been used to mean both quality control and the tools for overall improvement in managerial performance.

Initially, QC was applied in heavy industries such as the steel industry. Since these industries required instrumentation control, the application of SQC tools was vital for maintaining quality. As QC spread to the machinery and automobile industries, where controlling the process was essential in building quality into the product, the need for SQC became even greater.

At a later stage, other industries started to introduce QC for such products as consumer durables and home appliances. In these industries, the interest was in building quality in at the design stage to meet changing and increasingly stringent customer requirements. Today, management has gone beyond the design stage and has begun to stress the importance of quality product development, which means taking customer-related information and market research into account from the very start.

All this while, QC has grown into a full-fledged management tool for KAIZEN involving everyone in the company. Such company-wide activities are often referred to as TQC (Total Quality Control) or CWQC (Company-Wide Quality Control). No matter which name is used, TQC and CWQC mean company-wide KAIZEN activities involving everyone in the company, managers and workers alike. Over the years, QC has been elevated to SQC and then to TQC or CWQC, improving managerial performance at every level. Thus it is that such words as QC and TQC have come to be almost synonymous with KAIZEN. This is also why I constantly refer to QC, TQC, and CWQC in explaining KAIZEN.

On the other hand, the function of quality control in its original sense remains valid. Quality assurance remains a vital part of management, and most companies have a QA (Quality Assurance) department for this. To confuse matters, TQC or CWQC activities are sometimes administered by the QA department and sometimes by a separate TQC office. Thus it is important that these QC-related words be understood in the context in which they appear.

KAIZEN and TQC

Considering the TQC movement in Japan as part of the KAIZEN movement gives us a clearer perspective on the Japanese approach. First of all, it should be pointed out that TQC activities in Japan are not concerned solely with quality control. People have been fooled by the term "quality control" and have often construed it within the narrow discipline of product-quality control. In the West, the term QC is mostly associated with inspection of finished products, and when QC is brought up in discussion, top managers, who generally assume they have very little to do with quality control, lose interest immediately.

It is unfortunate that in the West TQC has been dealt with mainly in technical journals when it is more properly the focus of management journals. Japan has developed an elaborate system of KAIZEN strategies as management tools within the TQC movement. These rank among this century's most outstanding management achievements. Yet because of the limited way in which QC is understood in the West, most Western students of Japanese QC activities have failed to grasp their real significance and challenge. At the same time, new TQC methods and tools are constantly being studied and tested.

TQC undergoes perpetual change and improvement, and it is never quite the same from one day to the next. For instance, the so-called Seven Statistical Tools have been indispensable and have .

been widely used by QC circles, engineers, and management. Recently, the original seven have been supplemented by a "New Seven" used to solve more sophisticated problems such as new-product development, facility improvement, quality improvement, and cost reduction. New applications are being developed almost daily. (See Appendix E for the Seven Statistical Tools and the New Seven.)

TQC in Japan is a movement centered on the improvement of managerial performance at all levels. As such, it has typically dealt with:

1. Quality assurance
2. Cost reduction
3. Meeting production quotas
4. Meeting delivery schedules
5. Safety
6. New-product development
7. Productivity improvement
8. Supplier management

More recently, TQC has come to include marketing, sales, and service as well. Furthermore, TQC has dealt with such crucial management concerns as organizational development, cross-functional management, policy deployment, and quality deployment. In other words, management has been using TQC as a tool for improving overall performance. There will be detailed explanations of these concepts later in the book.

Those who have closely followed QC circles in Japan know that their activities are often focused on such areas as cost, safety, and productivity, and that their activities may only indirectly relate to product-quality improvement. For the most part, these activities are aimed at making improvements in the workplace.

Management efforts for TQC have been directed mostly at such areas as education, systems development, policy deployment, cross-functional management, and, more recently, quality deployment.

The implications of TQC for KAIZEN will be dealt with in detail in Chapter 3.

KAIZEN and the Suggestion System

Japanese management makes a concerted effort to involve employees in KAIZEN through suggestions. Thus, the suggestion system is an integral part of the established management system, and the number of workers' suggestions is regarded as an important criterion in reviewing the performance of these workers' supervisor. The manager of the supervisors is in turn expected to assist them so that they can help workers generate more suggestions.

Most Japanese companies active in KAIZEN programs have a quality-control system and a suggestion system working in concert. The role of QC circles may be better understood if we regard them collectively as a group-oriented suggestion system for making improvements.

One of the outstanding features of Japanese management is that it generates a great number of suggestions from workers and that management works hard to consider these suggestions, often incorporating them into the overall KAIZEN strategy. It is not uncommon for top management of a leading Japanese company to spend a whole day listening to presentations of activities by QC circles, and giving awards based on predetermined criteria. Management is willing to give recognition to employees' efforts for improvements and makes its concern visible wherever possible. Often, the number of suggestions is posted individually on the wall of the workplace in order to encourage competition among workers and among groups.

Another important aspect of the suggestion system is that each suggestion, once implemented, leads to a revised standard. For instance, when a special foolproof device has been installed on a machine at a worker's suggestion, this may require the worker to work differently and, at times, more attentively.

However, inasmuch as the new standard has been set up by the worker's own volition, he takes pride in the new standard and is willing to follow it. If, on the contrary, he is told to follow a standard imposed by management, he may not be as willing to follow it.

Thus, through suggestions, employees can participate in KAIZEN in the workplace and play a vital role in upgrading standards. In a recent interview, Toyota Motor chairman Eiji Toyoda said, "One of the features of the Japanese workers is that they use their brains as well as their hands. Our workers provide 1.5 million suggestions a year, and 95 percent of them are put to practical use. There is an almost tangible concern for improvement in the air at Toyota."

Chapter 4 explains the suggestion system as practiced at Japanese companies.

KAIZEN and Competition

Western managers who have had some business experience in Japan invariably remark on the intense competition among Japanese companies. This intense domestic competition is thought to have been the driving force for Japanese companies in the overseas markets as well. Japanese companies compete for larger market shares through the introduction of new and more competitive products and by using and improving the latest technologies.

Normally, the driving forces for competition are price, quality, and service. In Japan, however, it is safe to say that the ultimate cause of competition has often been competition itself. Japanese companies are now even competing in introducing better and faster KAIZEN programs!

Where profit is the most important criterion for business success, it is conceivable that a company could remain unchanged for more than a quarter of a century. Where companies are vying with each other on the strength of KAIZEN, however, improvement must be an ongoing process. KAIZEN ensures that there will be continuous improvement for improvement's sake. Once the KAIZEN movement has been started, there is no way to reverse the trend.

Process-Oriented Management vs. Result-Oriented Management

KAIZEN generates process-oriented thinking, since processes must be improved before we get improved results. Further, KAIZEN is people-oriented and is directed at people's efforts. This contrasts sharply with the result-oriented thinking of most Western managers.

According to Mayumi Otsubo, manager for tournaments and special-event promotion at Bridgestone Tire Co., Japan is a process-oriented society while the United States is a result-oriented society. For instance, in reviewing the performance of employees, Japanese management tends to emphasize attitudinal factors. When the sales manager evaluates a salesperson's performance, that evaluation must include such process-oriented criteria as the amount of the salesperson's time spent calling on new customers, time spent on outside customer calls versus time devoted to clerical work at the office, and the percentage of new inquiries successfully closed.

By paying attention to these indices, the sales manager hopes to encourage the salesperson to produce improved results sooner or later. In other words, the process is considered just as important as the obviously intended result—sales!

Japan's national sport is sumo. At each sumo tournament, there are three awards besides the tournament championship: an outstanding-performance award, a skill award, and a fighting-spirit award. The fighting-spirit award is given to the wrestler who has fought exceptionally hard throughout the 15-day tournament, even if his won/lost record leaves something to be desired. None of these three awards is based solely on results, that is, how many bouts the wrestler wins. This is a good example of Japan's process-oriented thinking.

This is not to say, however, that winning does not count in sumo. In reality, each wrestler's monthly income is based largely on his record. It is just that winning is neither everything nor the only thing.

Japanese temples and shrines are often built in the mountains, and the most sacred altar is usually in the highest sanctuary. A worshiper wishing to pray at a shrine altar has to walk through dense forest, up steep stone steps, and under many torii (wooden gateways). At the Fushimi Inari Shrine near Kyoto, for example, there are some 15,000 torii along the walkway to the altar! By the time he reaches the altar, the worshiper is steeped in the sacred atmosphere of the shrine and his soul is purified. Getting there is almost as important as the prayer itself.

In the United States, generally speaking, no matter how hard a person works, lack of results will result in a poor personal rating and lower income or status. The individual's contribution is valued only for its concrete results. Only the results count in a result-oriented society.

Bridgestone Tire Co.'s Otsubo maintains that it is process-oriented thinking that has enabled Japanese industry to attain its competitive edge in world markets and that the KAIZEN concept epitomizes Japan's process-oriented thinking. Such management attitudes make a major difference in how an organization achieves change. Top management that is too process-oriented runs the risk of lacking long-term strategy, missing new ideas and innovations, instructing people ad nauseam in minute work processes, and losing sight of the forest for the trees. The result-oriented manager is more flexible in setting targets and can think in strategic terms. However, he tends to slight the mobilization and realignment of his resources for the strategy's implementation.

Otsubo suggests that the result-oriented criteria for evaluating people's performance are probably a legacy of the "mass-production society" and that the process-oriented criteria are gaining momentum in the post-industrial, high-tech, high-touch society.

The difference between process-oriented thinking and result-oriented thinking in business can perhaps best be explained with reference to Figure 1.8.

If we look at the manager's role, we find that the supportive and stimulative role is directed at the improvement of the processes, while the controlling role is directed at the outcome or the result. The KAIZEN concept stresses management's supportive and stimulative role for people's *efforts* to improve the processes. On the one hand, management needs to develop process-oriented criteria. On the other hand, the control-type management looks only at the performance or the result-oriented criteria. For abbreviation, we may call the process-oriented criteria P criteria and the result-oriented criteria R criteria.

P criteria call for a longer-term outlook, since they are directed at people's efforts and often require behavioral change. On the other hand, R criteria are more direct and short term.

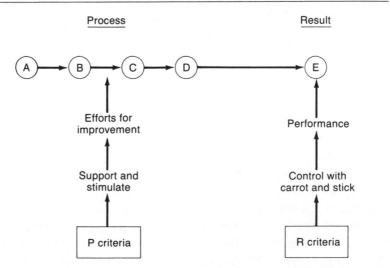

FIGURE 1.8 *Process-Oriented (P) Criteria vs. Result-Oriented (R) Criteria*

The difference between P criteria and R criteria may be better understood by looking at Japanese management's approach to the activities of QC circles.

QC-circle activities are usually directed toward improvements in the workplace, yet the supporting system is crucial. It is reported that QC circles formed in the West are often short-lived. This appears to be attributable mostly to the lack of a system that addresses the real needs of the QC-circle members. If management is interested only in the results, it will be looking only at R criteria for QC-circle activities. The R criteria in this case often mean the money saved as the result of their activities. Accordingly, management's interest and support will be geared directly to the savings made by members of the QC circle.

On the other hand, if management is interested in supporting the QC circle's efforts for improvement, the first thing management has to do is to establish P criteria. What kind of P criteria are available to measure the effort made by QC-circle members?

Some obvious possibilities are the number of meetings held per month, the participation rate, the number of problems solved (note that this is not the same as the amount of money saved), and the number of reports submitted. How do QC-circle members approach their subjects? Do they take the company's current situation into consideration in selecting the subject? Do they consider such factors as safety, quality, and cost in working out the problem? Do their efforts lead to improved work standards? These are among the P criteria to be used in evaluating their efforts and commitment.

If the average QC circle meets twice a month and a particular QC circle averages three meetings a month, this indicates that the members of this group made a greater-than-average effort. The participation (attendance) rate is another measure to check the level of effort and commitment of the QC-circle leader or facilitator.

It is often easy to quantify R criteria. In fact, in most companies, management has only R criteria available, since R criteria typically relate to sales, cost, and profit figures. However, in most cases it is also possible to quantify P criteria. In the case of QC circles, for instance, Japanese management has developed elaborate measures to quantify the effort level. These and other numbers are added together and used as the basis for recognition and awards. (For a more detailed treatment of QC-circle activities, see Chapter 4.)

At one of Matsushita's plants, the waitresses in the cafeteria formed

QC circles and studied the tea consumption during the lunch period. When large tea pots were placed on the tables with no restrictions on use, the waitresses noticed, tea consumption differed greatly from table to table. Therefore, they collected data on the tea-drinking behavior of employees during lunch. For one thing, they found that the same people tended to sit at the same table. After taking and analyzing data for days, they were able to establish an expected consumption level for each table. Using their findings, they started putting out different amounts of tea for each table, with the result that they were able to reduce tea-leaf consumption to half. How much were their activities worth in terms of the actual amount of money saved? Probably very little. However, they were awarded the Presidential Gold Medal for the year.

Most Japanese companies also have a suggestion system, which incorporates incentives. Whenever a suggestion yields savings, management provides rewards in proportion to the savings realized. Such rewards are paid both for suggestions made by individuals and those made by groups such as QC circles.

One of the distinctive features of Japanese management has been that it has made a conscious effort to establish a system that supports and encourages P criteria while giving full recognition to R criteria. At the workers' level, Japanese management has often established separate award systems for P criteria. While the rewards for R criteria are financial rewards directly geared to the savings or profits realized, those for P criteria are more often recognition and honor geared to the effort made.

At Toyota Motor, the most coveted QC award is the Presidential Award, which is not money but a fountain pen presented to each recipient personally by the president. Each recipient is asked to submit the name he wants engraved on the fountain pen. One person might ask for his wife's name to be printed, another his daughter's name. Bachelors sometimes ask for their girlfriends' names. And of course, many recipients ask to have their own names on their pens. The award carries prestige because top management has implemented a carefully planned program to show workers that their active participation in QC projects is important to the company's success. In addition, top executives attend these meetings, showing their active involvement and support. Such clear demonstrations of commitment go beyond the tokens of the awards to bind management and worker together in the program.

The process-oriented way of thinking bridges the gap between process and result, between ends and means, and between goals and measures, and helps people see the whole picture without bias.

Thus, both P criteria and R criteria can be and have been established at every level of management: between top management and division management, between middle managers and supervisors, and between supervisors and workers.

A manager, by definition, must take an interest in the results. However, when we observe the behavior of successful managers at a successful company, we often find that such managers are also process oriented. They ask process-oriented questions. They make decisions based on both P criteria and R criteria, although they may not always be aware of the distinction between the two sorts of criteria.

A process-oriented manager who takes a genuine concern for P criteria will be interested in:

- Discipline
- Time management
- Skill development
- Participation and involvement
- Morale
- Communication

In short, such a manager is people-oriented. Further, the manager will be interested in developing a reward system that corresponds to P criteria. If management makes positive use of the process-oriented way of thinking and further reinforces it with KAIZEN strategy, it will find that the overall corporate competitiveness will be greatly improved in the long term.

This book deals with specific concepts, tools, and systems that are effectively employed in KAIZEN strategy. Readers will find that they can easily apply them in their day-to-day business situations. These concepts and tools work well not because they are Japanese but because they are good management tools. Just as KAIZEN strategy involves everyone in the organization, the message of this book should be extended to everyone, top management, middle management, supervisors, and workers on the shop floor.

2

Improvement
East and West

KAIZEN vs. Innovation (1)

There are two contrasting approaches to progress: the gradualist approach and the great-leap-forward approach. Japanese companies generally favor the gradualist approach and Western companies the great-leap approach—an approach epitomized by the term innovation:

	KAIZEN	Innovation
Japan	Strong	Weak
West	Weak	Strong

Western management worships at the altar of innovation. This innovation is seen as major changes in the wake of technological breakthroughs, or the introduction of the latest management concepts or production techniques. Innovation is dramatic, a real attention-getter. KAIZEN, on the other hand, is often undramatic and subtle, and its results are seldom immediately visible. While KAIZEN is a continuous process, innovation is generally a one-shot phenomenon.

In the West, for example, a middle manager can usually obtain top management support for such projects as CAD (Computer-Aided Design), CAM (Computer-Aided Manufacture), and MRP (Materials Requirements Planning), since these are innovative projects that have a way of revolutionizing existing systems. As such, they offer ROI (Return On Investment) benefits that managers can hardly resist.

However, when a factory manager wishes, for example, to make small changes in the way his workers use the machinery, such as working out multiple job assignments or realigning production processes (both of which may require lengthy discussions with the union as well as reeducation and retraining of workers), obtaining management support can be difficult indeed.

Figure 2.1 compares the main features of KAIZEN and of innovation. One of the beautiful things about KAIZEN is that it does not necessarily require sophisticated technique or state-of-the-art technology. To implement KAIZEN, you need only simple, conventional techniques such as the seven tools of quality control (Pareto

	KAIZEN	Innovation
1. Effect	Long-term and long-lasting but undramatic	Short-term but dramatic
2. Pace	Small steps	Big steps
3. Timeframe	Continuous and incremental	Intermittent and non-incremental
4. Change	Gradual and constant	Abrupt and volatile
5. Involvement	Everybody	Select few "champions"
6. Approach	Collectivism, group efforts, systems approach	Rugged individualism, individual ideas and efforts
7. Mode	Maintenance and improvement	Scrap and rebuild
8. Spark	Conventional know-how and state of the art	Technological breakthroughs, new inventions, new theories
9. Practical requirements	Requires little investment but great effort to maintain it	Requires large investment but little effort to maintain it
10. Effort orientation	People	Technology
11. Evaluation criteria	Process and efforts for better results	Results for profits
12. Advantage	Works well in slow-growth economy	Better suited to fast-growth economy

FIGURE 2.1 *Features of KAIZEN and Innovation*

diagrams, cause-and-effect diagrams, histograms, control charts, scatter diagrams, graphs, and check sheets). Often, common sense is all that is needed. On the other hand, innovation usually requires highly sophisticated technology, as well as a huge investment.

KAIZEN is like a hotbed that nurtures small and ongoing changes, while innovation is like magma that appears in abrupt eruptions from time to time.

One big difference between KAIZEN and innovation is that while KAIZEN does not necessarily call for a large investment to implement it, it does call for a great deal of continuous effort and commitment. The difference between the two opposing concepts may thus be likened to that of a staircase and a slope. The innovation strategy is supposed to bring about progress in a staircase progression, as depicted in Figure 2.2. On the other hand, the KAIZEN strategy brings about gradual progress. I say the innovation strategy "is supposed to" bring about progress in a staircase progression, because it usually does not. Instead of following the staircase pattern of Figure 2.2, the actual progress achieved through innovation will generally follow the pattern shown in Figure 2.3 if it lacks the KAIZEN strategy to go along with it. This happens because a system, once it has been installed as a result of new innovation, is subject to steady deterioration unless continuing efforts are made first to maintain it and then to improve on it.

In reality, there can be no such thing as a static constant. All systems are destined to deteriorate once they have been established. One of the famous Parkinson's Laws is that an organization, once it has built its edifice, begins its decline. In other words, there must be a continuing effort for improvement to even maintain the status quo.

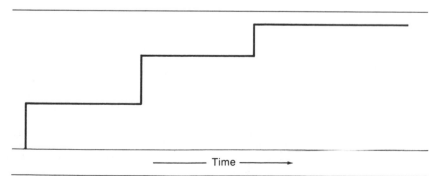

FIGURE 2.2   *Ideal Pattern from Innovation*

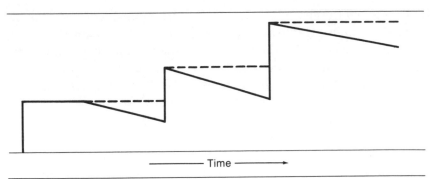

Time

FIGURE 2.3   *Actual Pattern from Innovation*

When such effort is lacking, decline is inevitable. (See Figure 2.4.) Therefore, even when an innovation makes a revolutionary standard of performance attainable, the new performance level will decline unless the standard is constantly challenged and upgraded. Thus, whenever an innovation is achieved, it must be followed by a series of KAIZEN efforts to maintain and improve it. (See Figure 2.5.)

Whereas innovation is a one-shot deal whose effects are gradually eroded by intense competition and deteriorating standards, KAIZEN is an ongoing effort with cumulative effects marking a steady rise as the years go by. If standards exist only in order to maintain the status quo, they will not be challenged so long as the level of performance is acceptable. KAIZEN, on the other hand,

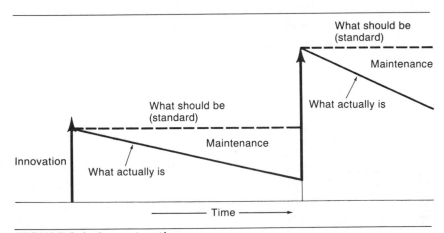

FIGURE 2.4   *Innovation Alone*

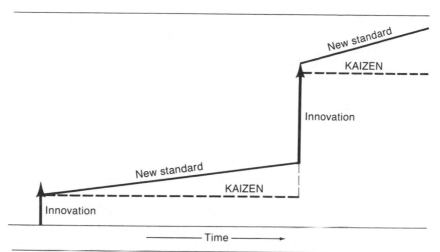

FIGURE 2.5 Innovation plus KAIZEN

means a constant effort not only to maintain but also to upgrade standards. KAIZEN strategists believe that standards are by nature tentative, akin to stepping stones, with one standard leading to another as continuing improvement efforts are made. This is the reason why QC circles no sooner solve one problem than they move on to tackle a new problem. This is also the reason why the so-called PDCA (Plan–Do–Check–Action) cycle receives so much emphasis in Japan's TQC movement. (See Chapter 3 for more discussion on techniques to maintain and raise standards.)

Another feature of KAIZEN is that it requires virtually everyone's personal efforts. In order for the KAIZEN spirit to survive, management must make a conscious and continuous effort to support it. Such support is quite different from the fanfare recognition that management accords to people who have achieved a striking success or breakthrough. KAIZEN is concerned more with the process than with the result. The strength of Japanese management lies in its successful development and implementation of a system that acknowledges the ends while emphasizing the means.

Thus KAIZEN calls for a substantial management commitment of time and effort. Infusions of capital are no substitute for this investment in time and effort. Investing in KAIZEN means investing in people. In short, KAIZEN is people-oriented, whereas innovation is technology- and money-oriented.

Finally, the KAIZEN philosophy is better suited to a slow-growth economy, while innovation is better suited to a fast-growth economy. While KAIZEN advances inch-by-inch on the strength of many small efforts, innovation leaps upward in hopes of landing at a much higher plateau in spite of gravitational inertia and the weight of investment costs. In a slow-growth economy characterized by high costs of energy and materials, overcapacity, and stagnant markets, KAIZEN often has a better payoff than innovation does.

As one Japanese executive recently remarked, "It is extremely difficult to increase sales by 10 percent. But it is not so difficult to cut manufacturing costs by 10 percent to even better effect."

At the beginning of this chapter, I argued that the concept of KAIZEN is nonexistent or at best weak in most Western companies today. However, there was a time, not so long ago, when Western management also placed a high priority on KAIZEN-like improvement-consciousness. Older executives may recall that before the phenomenal economic growth of the late 1950s and early 1960s, management attended assiduously to improving all aspects of the business, particularly the factory. In those days, every small improvement was counted and was seen as effective in terms of building success.

People who worked with small, privately owned companies may recall with a touch of nostalgia that there was a genuine concern for improvement "in the air" before the company was bought out or went public. As soon as that happened, the quarterly P/L (profit/loss) figures suddenly became the most important criterion, and management became obsessed with the bottom line, often at the expense of pressing for constant and unspectacular improvements.

For many other companies, the greatly increased market opportunities and technological innovations that appeared during the first two decades after World War II meant that developing new products based on the new technology was much more attractive or "sexier" than slow, patient efforts for improvement. In trying to catch up with the ever-increasing market demand, managers boldly introduced one innovation after another, and they were content to ignore the seemingly minor benefits of improvement.

Most Western managers who joined the ranks during or after those heady days do not have the slightest concern for improvement. Instead, they take an offensive posture, armed with professional expertise geared toward making big changes in the name of innovation, bringing about immediate gains, and winning instant recognition and promotion. Before they knew it, Western managers had lost sight of improvement and put all their eggs in the innovation basket.

Another factor that has abetted the innovation approach has been the increasing emphasis on financial controls and accounting. By now, the more sophisticated companies have succeeded in establishing elaborate accounting and reporting systems that force managers to account for every action they take and to spell out the precise payout or ROI of every managerial decision. Such a system does not lend itself to building a favorable climate for improvement.

Improvement is by definition slow, gradual, and often invisible, with effects that are felt over the long run. In my opinion, the most glaring and significant shortcoming of Western management today is the lack of improvement philosophy. There is no internal system in Western management to reward efforts for improvement; instead, everyone's job performance is reviewed strictly on the basis of results. Thus it is not uncommon for Western managers to chide people with, "I don't care what you do or how you do it. I want the results—and now!" This emphasis on results has led to the innovation-dominated approach of the West. This is not to say that Japanese management does not care about innovation. But Japanese managers have enthusiastically pursued KAIZEN even when they were involved in innovation, as is evident, for example, in the case of Nissan Motor.

THE CASE OF NISSAN MOTOR

At the No. 2 Body Section at Nissan's Tochigi plant, the first welding robot was introduced around 1973. During the following decade, the section's automation rate was pushed up to 98 percent, and the robotization rate for welding work has been increased to 60 percent. During this period, the standard work time in this section was reduced by 60 percent and production efficiency improved 10 percent to 20 percent.

These improvements in productivity were the combined result of the increased automation and the various KAIZEN efforts made in the workshop during that period.

According to Eiichi Yoshida, who formerly headed this section and is now deputy general manager of the plant's production control and

(Nissan Motor—continued)

engineering department, there have been numerous KAIZEN campaigns implemented in this section.

Each year has its own campaign for improvement programs. In 1975, for instance, the campaign was named the "Seven-up Campaign," and improvements were sought in the seven areas of standard time, efficiency, costs, suggestions, quality assurance, safety, and process utilization. The campaign chosen for 1978 was the "3-K 1, 2, 3 Campaign," the 3-K standing for *kangae* (thought), *kodo* (action), and *kaizen* and the 1, 2, 3 standing for the hop-step-jump sequence of thinking, acting, and improving.

While management makes decisions involving large investment outlays such as for automation and robotics, KAIZEN campaigns involve both management and workers in making small, low-cost improvements in the way work is done.

Reduction in standard time has always been a highly effective way to increase productivity. At the Tochigi plant, efforts in this area included employing the work-factor method and standardizing virtually every motion workers made in performing their tasks.

In terms of each individual's work, the smallest unit of work time considered in a KAIZEN strategy is 1/100th of a minute, or 0.6 seconds. Any suggestion that saves at least 0.6 seconds—the time it takes a worker to stretch out his hand or walk half a step—is seriously considered by management.

Aside from encouraging the QC-circle activities that had been going on in the plant for some time, the section started giving awards and other recognition for workers' KAIZEN efforts in such areas as safety, error reduction, and number of suggestions.

A special KAIZEN sheet is made available to the worker for this purpose, and each suggestion for improvement, whether it is brought by a group (QC circle) or by an individual, is "registered" on the sheet and submitted to the section manager. Most of these suggestions are handled within the same section and by the section manager.

Yoshida says that the majority of the workers' suggestions are for changes that the workers can implement on their own. For instance, a worker may suggest that the height of his tool rack be adjusted to make it easier to use. Such a suggestion can be taken care of within the section, and in fact, the section has bought welding equipment to do just such small repair work. This section has been engaged in continuous KAIZEN all the time that the production processes were being automated and robotized.

Norio Kogure, staff engineer in the section, recalls what his new boss told him when he was transferred into the section: "There will be no progress if you keep on doing the job exactly the same way for six months."

(Nissan Motor—continued)

Thus the SOP in the workplace is subject to constant change and improvement. At the same time, management tells the workers that the SOP is an absolute standard to which they should strictly conform until it is improved.

Both management and workers find room for improvement every day. It typically starts with studying the way workers perform their jobs to see if the standard time can somehow be shortened by 0.6 seconds or more. Next, the search is on for a way to improve the production processes. Sometimes the subassembly work that has previously been conducted off the line can be incorporated in the line so that the few seconds required to move the subassembly to the line can be saved. Kogure says that more than 90 percent of the engineers' work in the manufacturing department is directed at some form of KAIZEN.

Yoshida believes that it is the manager's job to go into the workplace, to encourage the workers to generate ideas for job improvement, and to be genuinely interested in their suggestions. He also believes that these efforts at the grassroots level were behind the plant's success in halving robot breakdowns in 1980 and 1981. ■

KAIZEN vs. Innovation (2)

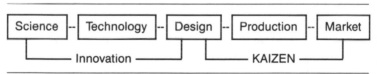

FIGURE 2.6 *Total Manufacturing Chain*

Figure 2.6 represents the sequence from the scientists' laboratories to the marketplace. Scientific theories and experimentation are applied as technology, elaborated as design, materialized in production, and finally sold on the market. The two components of improvement, innovation and KAIZEN, may be applied at every stage in that chain. For instance, KAIZEN has been applied to R&D activities while innovative ideas were applied to marketing to create the supermarkets and discount stores that dominated U.S. distribution in the 1950s. However, KAIZEN's impact is normally more visible closer to production and market, while innovation's impact is more visible closer to science and technology. Figure 2.7 compares innovation and KAIZEN in this sequence.

Innovation	KAIZEN
Creativity	Adaptability
Individualism	Teamwork (systems approach)
Specialist-oriented	Generalist-oriented
Attention to great leaps	Attention to details
Technology-oriented	People-oriented
Information: closed, proprietary	Information: open, shared
Functional (specialist) orientation	Cross-functional orientation
Seek new technology	Build on existing technology
Line + staff	Cross-functional organization
Limited feedback	Comprehensive feedback

FIGURE 2.7   *Another Comparison of Innovation and KAIZEN*

Looking at this list, we find that the West has been stronger on the innovation side and Japan stronger on the KAIZEN side. These differences in emphasis are also reflected in the different social and cultural heritages, such as the Western educational system's stress on individual initiative and creativity as against the Japanese educational system's emphasis on harmony and collectivism.

I was recently talking with a European diplomat posted to Japan, who said that one of the most conspicuous differences between the West and Japan was that between the Western complacency and over-confidence and the Japanese feelings of anxiety and imperfection. The Japanese feeling of imperfection perhaps provides the impetus for KAIZEN.

In looking at the relations between KAIZEN and innovation, we can draw the comparison expressed in Figure 2.8. However, as Japanese industry turns to the high-technology areas, it will lead to the situation depicted in Figure 2.9.

Once perceptions of new products have been changed this way, the Japanese competitive edge will become even greater. This change is already under way. Japanese companies have made major advances in KAIZEN-related development even in the technologically most advanced areas, says Masanori Moritani, senior researcher at Nomura Research Institute.

Moritani points to the semiconductor laser as an example. The goal of semiconductor-laser development was to improve power

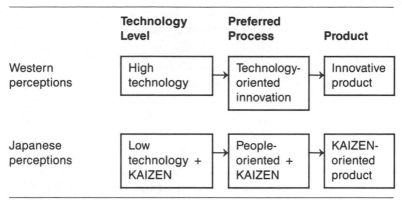

FIGURE 2.8   *Western and Japanese Product Perceptions*

levels and at the same time reduce manufacturing costs. Once this goal was achieved, it became possible to apply the semiconductor laser to mass-produced products such as compact discs and videodiscs.

At one major Japanese electronics company, the semiconductor laser developed for use in compact-disc players cost ¥500,000 in 1978. In 1980, it was down to ¥50,000, and by the fall of 1981, it had been reduced to ¥10,000. In 1982, when the first compact-disc players were put on the market, the semiconductor laser cost only ¥5,000. As of 1984, it was down to the ¥2,000-to-¥3,000 level.

During the same period, the semiconductor laser's useful life was

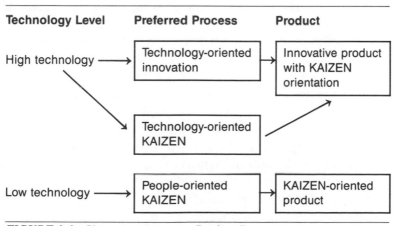

FIGURE 2.9   *Upcoming Japanese Product Perceptions*

extended from 100 hours for some early models to more than 50,000 hours for later models. Most of these developments can be attributed to improvements in materials and production engineering, such as making thinner layers of semiconductors (which requires precision control to the less-than-one-micron level) and adopting the gaseous MOCVD (Molecular Oxidization Chemical Vapor Deposition) method. At the same time, the discs themselves were improved and pit error was reduced.

Reflecting all these efforts, compact disc players themselves underwent many changes for the better during this period. Prices also fell. In 1982, early models were priced around ¥168,000. In 1984, the mass-market model was selling for ¥49,800. During this same two-year period, the size of the player was reduced by five-sixths and the power consumption by nine-tenths. Since the basic technology for the semiconductor laser had been established by the mid-1970s, these developments represent engineering efforts – in R&D, design, and production – to improve on an existing technology.

Super LSI memories, fiber optics, and CCD (Charge-Coupled Devices) also represent high technology that has been successfully applied through the KAIZEN approach. The main thrust of technological development today is shifting from the great-leap-forward approach to the gradual-development approach. Technological breakthroughs in the West are generally thought to take a Ph.D., but there are only three Ph.D.s on the engineering staff at one of Japan's most successfully innovative companies – Honda Motor. One is founder Soichiro Honda, whose Ph.D. is an honorary degree, and the other two are no longer active within the company. At Honda, technological improvement does not seem to require a Ph.D.

There is no doubt about the need for new technology, but it is what happens after the new technology has been developed that makes the difference. A product coming out of an emerging technology starts off very expensive and somewhat shaky in quality. Therefore, once a new technology has been identified, the effort must be increasingly directed at such areas as mass production, cost reduction, yield improvement, and quality improvement – all areas requiring doggedly tenacious efforts.

Moritani says Western researchers typically show enthusiasm in tackling challenging projects and are very good at such work, but they will be at a great disadvantage in meeting the Japanese challenges in mass-produced high-technology products if they concentrate only on the great-leap-forward approach and forget everyday KAIZEN.

An analysis of the semiconductor industries in Japan and the United States reveals the two countries' respective competitive advantages and illustrates the difference between KAIZEN and innovation. Professor Ken'ichi Imai (no relation) and Associate Professor Akimitsu Sakuma at Hitotsubashi University have argued that

> In greatly simplified terms, nearly all major innovations that determine the direction of future product and process development originate in U.S. firms. Japanese firms display their strength in incremental innovations in fields whose general contours have already been established. . . . A dominant design is an authoritative synthesis of individual innovations formerly applied separately in products. The economic value of a dominant design is its ability to impose itself as a standard in the creation of products. By virtue of standardization, economies of scale can be sought in production. This leads to a shift in the nature of competition. While initially the performance characteristics of a product are the deciding factor in competition, mass production leads to a second deciding factor: the cost of the product.
>
> Since a dominant design synthesizes past technologies, after its appearance major innovations no longer occur frequently. From then on, the center stage is occupied by incremental innovations aiming at product refinements and at improvements in the manufacturing process. The innovations conceived by Japanese firms correspond exactly to these incremental innovations. The reputation earned by Japan's 16K RAMs when they captured a large share of the American market was precisely one of high performance and low price.*

Paul H. Aron, vice chairman at Daiwa Securities America and professor of international business at New York University's Graduate School of Business Administration, recently said:

> Americans stress innovation and sophistication, and many companies complain that they cannot retain engineers if they are assigned only to state-of-the-art applications. The dream of the American engineer is to establish an independent company and

---

*Economic Eye, June 1983, published by Keizai Koho Center. Reprinted by permission.

make an important breakthrough. After the breakthrough, the engineer expects his company to be acquired by a large conglomerate. The engineer anticipates receiving an ample financial reward and then, if he is young, to proceed to create another high-technology company and repeat the process. Thus the production engineer often has less prestige, and this field does not attract "the best and the brightest" students.

The Japanese engineer largely expects to remain with the large company. Production engineers in Japanese companies often enjoy at least as much prestige as researchers.

Thus the preference for KAIZEN over innovation may also be explained in terms of management's use of engineering skills, as well as the engineer's own perception of his job.

In the West, the engineer takes pride in doing his job as a theoretical exercise, and he is not necessarily concerned with maintaining rapport with the production site. On visiting an American plant recently, I was told that the machines installed there were designed by engineers at the head office who had never visited the plant. These machines often had to undergo lengthy adjustment and reworking before they were put to use.

In his book *Japanese Technology* (Tokyo, The Simul Press, 1982. Reprinted by permission.), Masanori Moritani states:

Priority on production

A third strength of Japanese technology is the close connection between development, design, and the production line. In Japan this is considered simple common sense, but that is not always the case in the United States and Europe.

In Japan, production runs take off with a bang, quickly reaching yearly outputs of a million units or more. American and European companies are amazed by this. Cautious in their expansion of production, often contenting themselves with simply doubling yearly output over three or four years, these companies are incredulous of the Japanese pace.

The principal element in this rapid expansion is active investment in plant and equipment, but what makes this technologically feasible is the unification of development, design, and production. In the case of home VCRs, development and design were conducted with full appreciation of the need for mass production. Easy mass production was the key design objective, and close consideration was given to parts availability, precision processing, and set assemblage. . . .

Outstanding college-educated engineers are assigned in large numbers to the production line, and many are given an important say in business operations. Many manufacturing-industry executives are engineers by training, and a majority have had extensive first-hand experience on the shop floor. In Japanese firms, the production department has a strong voice in development and design. In addition, engineers involved in development and design always visit the production line and talk things over with their counterparts on the floor.

In Japan, even researchers are more likely to be found on the shop floor than in a research center; the majority of them are assigned to factories and operational divisions. Hitachi has about 8,000 R&D staff, but only 3,000 work at its research center. The remaining 5,000 are distributed among the various factories and operational divisions.

Nippon Electric Company (NEC) employs 5,000 technicians who are engaged either directly or indirectly in research and development. As many as 90 percent work in the factories. What this means is that the connection and understanding between development and production is very smooth indeed. . . .

The shop-floor elite

In certain respects, French television manufacturers outshine their Japanese competitors in the development of top-of-the-line models. Soft-touch and remote control were introduced by the French well before the Japanese began using them. But while France may spend a great deal on producing splendid designs for their deluxe models, the quality of the actual product is inferior to Japanese sets. This is because French designers do not fully understand the problems encountered on the shop floor, and because the design work is not done from the perspective of the person who actually had to put the machine together. In short, there is a serious gap between development and production, a product of gaps between various strata in the company hierarchy itself. . . .

My own career began in shipbuilding, as I worked first for Hitachi Shipbuilding & Engineering Company. Immediately after graduating from the University of Tokyo, I was assigned to the factory, where I took my place on the shop floor and, wearing a uniform like all the other employees, joined them at their work.

At the time, shipyard workers had a distinctive style of dress; they would wrap a towel around their necks and tuck it into the front of their uniforms. In the world of shipbuilding, I suppose it was the fashion equivalent of wearing a scarf or muffler, although it also had the practical function of keeping the sweat from running down one's back and chest. No doubt these sweat-stained towels did not look like the height of fashion to outsiders, but I used to think of that dirty towel around my neck as a proud symbol of my work as an on-site technician.*

Thus one of the strengths of Japanese managers in designing new products is that they can assign capable engineers to both KAIZEN and innovation. In general, the Japanese factory has a far higher ratio of engineers assigned to it than the American or European factory. Even so, the trend in Japan is to transfer more engineering resources to the plant to ensure even better communication with the production people.

Various practical tools, such as quality tables, have also been developed to improve cross-functional communication among customers, engineers, and production people. They have contributed greatly to creating products that meet customer requirements, as shown in Chapter 5 on quality deployment.

KAIZEN and Measurement

Productivity is a measure, not a reality, says Gerald Nadler, professor and chairman of the Industrial and Systems Engineering Department, University of Southern California. And yet we have often sought the "secret" of productivity, as if the key were in defining the measures of productivity. According to Nadler, it is like finding that the room is too cold and looking at the thermometer for the reason. Adjusting the scale on the thermometer itself does not solve the problem. What counts is the effort to improve the situation, such as throwing more logs on the fire or checking the furnace — in other words, invoking the PDCA cycle. Productivity is only a description of the current state of affairs and the past efforts of people.

We might say that quality control, too, is a measure and not reality.

---

*Op cit., pp. 42–43, 46–48.

Quality control was started as a post-mortem inspection of defects produced in the production process. It goes without saying that no matter how hard one may work at inspecting the products, this does not necessarily lead to improvements in the product quality.

One way to improve quality is by improving the production process. Toying with the figures is not going to improve the situation. This is why quality control in Japan was started from the inspection phase, moved back to the phase of building quality in the production processes, and has finally come to mean building quality into the product at the time of its development.

If productivity and quality control are not the reality and serve only as a measure for checking the results, then what is the reality and what has to be done? The answer to this question is that the efforts put in to improve both productivity and quality are the reality. The key words are efforts and improve. This is the time to be liberated from the spell of productivity and quality control, get down to the basics, roll up our sleeves, and start working on improvement. If we define the manager's job as that of managing processes and results, then the manager should have yardsticks or measures for both of them. When Nadler said productivity is only a measure, he actually meant that productivity is a result-oriented index (R criterion). When we deal with improvement, we should be working on process-oriented indices (P criteria).

However, in most Western companies, many executives are not even aware that there are such things as process-oriented indices, because such indices have never been available in the company. The questions that the Western manager asks are always directed at the result-oriented indices, such as monthly sales, monthly expenses, number of products produced, and eventually the profits made. We only have to look at the reporting figures employed by the typical Western company, such as the cost-accounting data, to see how true this is.

When the manager is looking for a specific result, such as quarterly profits, productivity indices, or quality level, his only yardstick is to see whether the goal has been achieved or not. On the other hand, when he uses process-oriented measures to look into the efforts for improvement, his criteria will be more supportive and he may be less critical of the results, since improvement is slow and comes in small steps.

In order to be supportive, management must have rapport with the workers. However, Western management often refuses to establish such rapport. Often, the supervisors in the workplace do not know how to communicate with the workers. They are afraid to talk to them, as if they did not speak the same language (which is literally true in many countries where "guest workers" are employed).

According to Neil Rackham, president of the Huthwaite Research Group, American managers put forward their own ideas nine times for every one time they build on, improve, or support other people's ideas in meetings. The amount of supportive behavior (supportive statements) varies widely but on the average is less than half the level of supportive behavior seen in groups from Singapore, Taiwan, Hong Kong, and Japan. It is essential that Western managers develop a more supportive style in dealing with each other and with workers.

Quite recently, after a day-long discussion on the KAIZEN concept, William Manly, senior vice president of the Cabot Corporation, quipped: "I thought they had two major religions in Japan: Buddhism and Shintoism. Now I find they have a third: KAIZEN!" Facetious though this sounds, one should have a religious zeal in promoting the KAIZEN strategy and not be concerned with the immediate payout. This is a behavioral change requiring missionary zeal, and the proof of its value is in the satisfaction it brings and in its long-term impact. KAIZEN is based on a belief in people's inherent desire for quality and worth, and management has to believe that it is going to "pay" in the long run.

Such things as sharing, caring, and commitment are important in KAIZEN. Just as various rituals are needed in religion, KAIZEN also requires rituals, since people need ways to share their experiences, support one another, and build commitment together. This is why reporting meetings are so important for QC circles. Fortunately, one does not have to wait until the next life before seeing his reward in KAIZEN, as the benefits of KAIZEN may be felt within four or five years, if not immediately. The punishment for not adhering to the KAIZEN creed is to be left out of the enjoyment of the progress every individual and organization must experience to survive.

KAIZEN also requires a different kind of leadership, leadership based on personal experience and conviction and not necessarily on authority, rank, or age. Anybody who has gone through the experience himself can become a leader. For proof, one only has to note how enthusiastically QC circle leaders, young and old, make their presentations at meetings. This is because improvement brings many truly satisfying experiences in life—identifying problems, thinking and learning together, tackling and solving difficult tasks, and thus being elevated to new heights of achievement.

3

KAIZEN by
Total Quality Control

*T*he avenues through which KAIZEN may be pursued are almost endless. However, the "high road" to KAIZEN has been the practice of total quality control (TQC).

As mentioned earlier, the concept of TQC is often understood in the West as part of QC activities, and it has often been thought to be a job for quality control engineers. Given the danger that the name TQC might be misleading and might fail to clearly communicate the scope of Japanese-style TQC, the term *company-wide quality control* (CWQC) was coined as a more precise term to use in explaining Japanese quality control to overseas observers. Within Japan, however, most companies still use the term TQC in referring to their company-wide quality control activities.

Quality Control Deals with the Quality of People

When speaking of "quality," one tends to think first in terms of product quality. Nothing could be further from the truth. In TQC, the first and foremost concern is with the quality of people. Instilling quality into people has always been fundamental to TQC. A company able to build quality into its people is already halfway toward producing quality products.

The three building blocks of business are hardware, software, and "humanware." TQC starts with humanware. Only after the humanware is squarely in place should the hardware and software aspects of business be considered.

Building quality into people means helping them become KAIZEN-conscious. Both functional and cross-functional problems abound in the work environment, and people must be helped to identify these problems. Then they must be trained in the use of problem-solving tools so that they can deal with the problems they have identified. Once a problem has been solved, the results must be standardized to prevent recurrences. By going through this never-ending cycle of improvement, people can become KAIZEN-minded and build the discipline to achieve KAIZEN in their work. Management can change the corporate culture by building quality into people, but this can be done only through training and firm leadership.

The French anthropologist Claude Lévi-Strauss noted at the 1983 International Symposium on Productivity in Japan that

> The concern of this symposium should be less improvement of the productivity of products than improvement of the productivity of systems. We might suggest that productivity nowadays suffers little from a quantitative lack of produced goods and more from the fact that we remain dependent on the old technical system our earliest ancestors relied on: in regard to the exploitation of natural resources, we still are predators.
>
> In order to produce better systems, a society should be less concerned with producing material goods in increasing quantities than with producing people of a better quality—in other words, beings capable of producing these systems.*

According to the Japan Industrial Standards (Z8101-1981) definition, quality control is "a system of means to economically produce goods or services which satisfy customer requirements." The definition is expressed as follows:

> Implementing quality control effectively necessitates the cooperation of all people in the company, including top management, managers, supervisors, and workers in all areas of corporate activities such as market research and development, product planning, design, preparations for production, purchasing, vendor

---

*Brief Report on International Productivity Symposium, Japan Productivity Center, Tokyo, 1983. Reprinted by permission.

management, manufacturing, inspection, sales and after-services, as well as financial control, personnel administration, and training and education. Quality control carried out in this manner is called company-wide quality control or total quality control.

For our purposes, let us consider the two terms CWQC and TQC as interchangeable. No matter which name is employed, the real nature of CWQC or TQC goes far beyond quality control per se. My own definition would be that it is a systematic and statistical approach for KAIZEN and problem solving as a management tool. We will use the term TQC when referring to the broad concept of either CWQC or TQC throughout this chapter.

In 1979, Mankichi Tateno, then president of Japan Steel Works, proclaimed that the company was going to introduce TQC. He formulated three goals:

1. To provide products and services that satisfy customer requirements and earn customer trust.
2. To steer the corporation toward higher profitability through such measures as improved work procedures, fewer defects, lower costs, lower debt service, and more advantageous order filling.
3. To help employees fulfill their potential for achieving the corporate goal, with particular emphasis on such areas as policy deployment and voluntary activities.

He also expressed the hope that TQC thus introduced would help the corporation cope with any severe environmental changes or other external problems, win customer confidence, and secure and improve profitability.

TQC has become an elaborate system of corporate problem solving and improvement activities. Let me briefly outline this TQC system in light of KAIZEN.

TQC signifies a statistical and systematic approach for KAIZEN and problem solving. Its methodological foundation is the statistical application of QC concepts, including the use and analysis of statistical data. This methodology demands that situations and problems under study be quantified as much as possible. As a result, TQC practitioners have acquired the habit of working with hard data, not with hunches or gut feelings. In statistical problem solving, one repeatedly returns to the source of the problem to gather data. This approach has fostered a process-oriented way of thinking.

Process-oriented thinking means that one should check *with* the result and not *by* the result. It is not enough to evaluate people simply in terms of the result of their performance. Instead, management should look at what steps have been followed and work at jointly establishing criteria for improvement. This encourages feedback and constant communication between management and workers. In the process-oriented way of thinking, a distinction is made between process-oriented P criteria and result-oriented R criteria. In TQC, people do not subscribe to the axiom "All's well that ends well." TQC is a way of thinking that says, "Let's improve the processes. If things go well, there must be something in the processes that worked well. Let's find it and build on it!"

These joint efforts often prove to be valuable training experiences for everyone. There are many ways in which processes can be improved, and thus it is necessary to prioritize problem-solving approaches. All these things are taken into account in process-oriented thinking. This introduces an entirely new concept into management science in which the manager's job is basically two-fold. One part of the job is maintenance-related administration: checking the performance (result) of work, R criteria. The other part is improvement-related management: checking the process that has led to a specific result. Here the manager is concerned with P criteria.

Japanese vs. Western Approaches to Quality Control

It is clear that there are some basic differences between the Japanese and the Western approaches to quality control:

1. The job of QC manager in the West is often a technical one with little support from top management for working in the areas of people and organization. The QC manager seldom ranks high enough to have the close and constant contact with top management needed to promote QC as a primary corporate objective in a company-wide program.

2. In the West, the often heterogeneous composition of the work force and the adversarial relations between labor and management may make it difficult for management to introduce changes for improved productivity and quality control. Japan's relatively homogeneous population has a more uniform educational background and social outlook, all of which tends to simplify management–labor relations.

3. Professional knowledge of quality control and other engineering techniques is being spread to engineers in the West, but it is rarely made available to other employees. In Japan, a great deal of effort has been spent on transmitting the necessary knowledge to everyone, including blue-collar workers, so people can solve their own job problems better.

4. Top managers in Japanese companies are committed to TQC, making TQC a company-wide concern rather than the lonely job of a specific QC manager. TQC means that QC efforts must involve people, organization, hardware, and software.

5. There is a Japanese axiom, "Quality control starts with training and ends in training." Training is conducted regularly for top management, middle management, and workers.

6. In Japan, small groups of volunteers within the company engage in quality-control activities, using TQC's special statistical tools. The quality circle is one such small-group activity. Quality-circle activities account for 10 percent to 30 percent of all management efforts in the field of quality control. Quality circles are a very important part of quality control, but their contribution should not be overemphasized, since nothing can substitute for a good, fully integrated TQC management program.

7. In Japan, several organizations actively promote TQC activities on a nationwide basis. Examples are JUSE (The Union of Japanese Scientists and Engineers), the Japan Management Association, Japan Standard Association, Central Japan Quality Control Association, and the Japan Productivity Center. These organizations have few if any counterparts in the West.

Kaoru Ishikawa, president of Musashi Institute of Technology and professor emeritus at Tokyo University, has played a crucial role in developing the QC movement and QC circles in Japan. He has listed six features as characterizing the TQC movement in Japan:

1. Company-wide TQC, with all employees participating
2. Emphasis on education and training
3. QC-circle activities
4. TQC audits, as exemplified by the Deming Prize audit and by the President's audit
5. Application of statistical methods
6. Nationwide TQC promotion

The concept of TQC may be better understood by becoming familiar with certain key phrases that have been developed over the years and are widely quoted among TQC practitioners in Japan. Let's take a look at them.

Speak with Data

TQC emphasizes the use of data. Kaoru Ishikawa writes in his book *Japanese Quality Control* (in Japanese), "We should talk with facts and data." Yet he goes on to say: "When you see data, doubt them! When you see the measuring instrument, doubt it! When you see chemical analysis, doubt it!" He further reminds readers that there are such things as false data, mistaken data, and immeasurables.

Even if accurate data are available, they will be meaningless if they are not used correctly. The skill with which a company collects and uses data can make the difference between success and failure.

In most companies, the job of dealing with customer complaints and reworking the product is assigned to newcomers and regarded as not so important. Says president Kenzo Sasaoka of Yokogawa-Hewlett-Packard, "Actually, this job should be given to the bright young engineers, since it offers a valuable chance to get customer feedback and to improve the product."

The problem is that even if the valuable information is available, few people take the trouble to make good use of it. Obsessed with short-term profits, most managers would much rather forget about customers. To these managers, customer complaints are a nuisance. Such managers thus forfeit a golden opportunity to collect information and get it back to the people who can use it. Information sharing among executives is just as important as information collection and information processing. Where information is properly collected, processed, channeled, and put to practical use, there is always the possibility of improvement. A system of data collection and evaluation is a vital part of a TQC/KAIZEN program.

In order to develop a product that satisfies customers, data on the customers' requirements must first be collected by the sales and marketing people, and, to some extent, by the complaint department staff. These data are next passed along to the design, engineering, and production departments. New-product development requires that TQC be extended through different departments via an effective communication network. TQC in Japan has developed various systems, tools, and formats to facilitate these activities, including crossfunctional organizations, systems diagrams, and quality deployment.

Quality First, Not Profit First

This dictum probably reveals the nature of TQC and KAIZEN better than anything else, for it reflects the belief in quality for quality's sake and KAIZEN for KAIZEN's sake. As mentioned earlier, TQC includes such things as quality assurance, cost reduction, efficiency, meeting delivery schedules, and safety. The "quality" here refers to improvement in all of these areas. Japanese managers have found that seeking improvement for improvement's sake, is the surest way to strengthen their companies' overall competitiveness. If you take care of the quality, the profits will take care of themselves.

Professor Masumasa Imaizumi of Musashi Institute of Technology states that the basic elements to be managed in a company are quality (of products, services, and work), quantity, delivery (time), safety, cost, and employee morale. He continues:

> Managers at every level are responsible for managing these elements properly. An enterprise can prosper only if the customers who purchase the products or services are satisfied. Customers are satisfied or not with the *quality* of products or services. In other words, the only thing an enterprise can offer customers is quality. All other indices relate to internal management. This is the first meaning of quality first.
>
> I do not subscribe to the idea of making top-quality products at low cost and in large quantity from the very beginning. Of course,

such would be the ultimate goal of TQC. However, as a first step, I would suggest making top-quality products first and then moving to faster production and lower costs. In the beginning, we must establish the technologies and systems to make products that can satisfy customers, and at this stage we should disregard such factors as cost, volume, and productivity. Only after the technology has been achieved should we move on to the next phase of making good products at low cost and in large quantity without sacrificing quality. This is the second meaning of quality first.

Manage the Previous Process (Managing Upstream)

Because of its preoccupation with data and processes rather than results, TQC encourages people to go back to the previous process on the production line to seek out a problem's causes. Improvement requires that we always be aware of what comes from the previous process. In the factory, problem solvers are told to ask "why" not once but five times. Often the first answer to the problem is not the root cause. Asking why several times will dig out several causes, one of which is usually the root cause.

Taiichi Ohno, former Toyota Motor vice president, once gave the following example of finding the real cause of a machine stoppage.

Question 1: Why did the machine stop?
  Answer 1: Because the fuse blew due to an overload.

Question 2: Why was there an overload?
  Answer 2: Because the bearing lubrication was inadequate.

Question 3: Why was the lubrication inadequate?
  Answer 3: Because the lubrication pump was not functioning right.

Question 4: Why wasn't the lubricating pump working right?
  Answer 4: Because the pump axle was worn out.

Question 5: Why was it worn out?
  Answer 5: Because sludge got in.

By repeating "why" five times, it was possible to identify the real cause and hence the real solution: attaching a strainer to the lubricating pump. If the workers had not gone through such repetitive questions, they might have settled with an intermediate countermeasure, such as replacing the fuse.

The Next Process Is the Customer

An old-time village basketmaker knew every customer who came to buy his wares. These people were his neighbor's wife, his friends, and his distant relatives. He would not have dreamed of selling them a basket with a hole in the bottom. In today's mass-production age, however, customers have been reduced to the abstract, and the person making the product neither knows nor cares who the customers are. Nor do the customers have any way of knowing who produced the product. The process has been impersonalized. The seller may balk at selling a basket with a big hole in the bottom. But what if it is a small hole? Caveat emptor.

This problem is exacerbated by the fact that the people who make the products and those who sell them are separate people. When an autoworker fails to tighten adequately, the consequences of his work may not be immediately apparent on the assembled car. What does it matter whether the bolt is tight enough or not? However, if the person working next on the car is thought of as a customer, the problem is personalized, and it does make a difference whether the bolt is tight enough or not.

If quality is to be maintained and improved in the production process, there must be smooth communication among all the people at every production stage. We often find strong sectionalism and rivalry among production workers, particularly among those working in neighboring processes. Care must be taken to build cohesion throughout every stage of work.

Thirty years ago, Kaoru Ishikawa encountered this problem head-on while employed as a consultant to Nippon Steel. In one instance, Ishikawa was investigating some surface scratches found on certain steel sheets. When he suggested to the engineer in charge of that particular process that his team review the problems together with the engineers in the following process, the engineer replied, "Do you mean to tell us that we should go examine the problems with our *enemies*?" To this Ishikawa replied, "You must not think of them as your enemies. You must think of the next process as your customer. You should visit your customer every day to make sure he is satisfied with the product." However, the engineer insisted, "How could I do such a thing? If I show up in their workshop, they'll think I've come to spy on them!"

This incident gave Ishikawa the inspiration for his now-famous phrase "The next process is the customer." This concept has helped engineers and shop-floor workers to realize that their customers are not only those in the marketplace who purchase the final product but also the people in the next process who receive work from them. This realization has in turn led to the formal commitment never to send defective parts to those in the following process. This was later institutionalized as the *kamban* system and the just-in-time concept. From the beginning, the challenge of treating next-process workers as customers has required that workers be frank enough to acknowledge their own workplace's problems and do everything within their power to solve them. Today this concept is also applied in clerical work.

For instance, the design engineer's customers are the manufacturing people. Therefore, this dictum calls for the engineer to be attentive to the needs of the manufacturing people when he works on a new product, and to consider such items as the existing equipment's process capabilities and the availability of materials. Similarly, the clerical worker's customers are the people who are on the receiving end of his paper output. The entire concept of quality assurance thus rests on the premise that assuring quality to each customer at each stage will assure quality in the finished product.

Customer-Oriented TQC, Not Manufacturer-Oriented TQC

This concept is also referred to as "market-in" as opposed to "product-out."* As the TQC concept is applied down through the various stages of production, it finally reaches its ultimate beneficiaries — the customers who buy the product. Thus TQC is said to be customer-oriented. This is also why TQC activities have shifted their emphasis from maintaining quality throughout the production process to building quality into the product by developing and designing products that meet customer requirements.

This axiom is probably one of the most fundamental elements of TQC. All TQC-related activities in Japan are conducted with the customers' needs in mind. And yet some managers tend to think in terms of their own requirements. Too often they initiate new-product schemes simply because the financial resources, technology, and

---

*"Product-out," the antonym to "market-in," is used to indicate a priority on producing goods and services without paying sufficient attention to customer requirements.

production capacity are available. These new products satisfy the company's need to increase production, and managers keep their fingers crossed hoping that the customers will like their products.

If the people in the next process are customers, customer-oriented TQC also means that one should never inconvenience them. Whenever a defective product or service is passed on, the people downstream suffer. The effect of a problem is usually recognized not by the people who create it but rather by people downstream, including the ultimate customers.

The customer-oriented nature of TQC is apparent in the way TQC is defined in many Japanese companies. Komatsu, for example, defines its TQC goal as "Satisfying Komatsu's worldwide customers through rational, cost-conscious research, development, sales, and servicing."

Through the application of TQC concepts, Japanese companies have built a system for designing, developing, producing, and servicing products with the ultimate aim of satisfying their customers. This has been the hidden key to Japanese products' acceptance by customers throughout the world. There are still too many companies, both in Japan and abroad, whose top management pays lip service to the concept of satisfying customers but does not have a system to achieve it.

Even today, there are doubts about how attentive most Western salespeople are to their customers' needs. Recently, a European household-appliance retailer was quoted as saying, "Whenever a Japanese salesman comes to visit us, he asks all sorts of questions so that he can learn what we really need. But when a European salesman comes by, all he does is tell us how stupid we are. If we complain, he always tries to win the argument."

Another important aspect is how the customer is defined. For instance, who is the customer for someone who makes automobile tire components? True, he sells the product to the tire manufacturer, and thus he should be attentive to the tire manufacturer's requirements. However, what about the automobile company that buys tires from the tire manufacturer, or the driver who buys an automobile from the auto company? Are these people his customers as well? Often these different customers have different quality requirements.

Thus defining the customer is a top management priority, since this definition determines the quality characteristics that the product needs to satisfy the customer.

The following case illustrates how employees improved telephone reception by paying close attention to customers' needs.

**CASE STUDY:
SHORTENING CUSTOMERS' TELEPHONE
WAITING TIME***

This is the story of a QC program that was implemented in the main office of a large bank. An average of 500 customers call this office every day. Surveys indicated that the callers tended to become irritated if the phone rang more than five times before it was answered, and often would not call the company again. In contrast, a prompt answer after just two rings reassured the customers and made them feel more comfortable doing business by phone.

1. Selection of a Theme. Telephone reception was chosen as a QC theme for the following reasons: (1) Telephone reception is the first impression a customer receives from the company, (2) this theme coincided with the company's telephone reception slogan, "Don't make customers wait, and avoid needless switching from extension to extension," and (3) it also coincided with a company-wide campaign being promoted at that time which advocated being friendly to everyone one met.

First, the staff discussed why the present method of answering calls made callers wait. Figure 3.1 illustrates a frequent situation, where a call from customer B comes in while the operator is talking with customer A. Let's see why the customer has to wait.

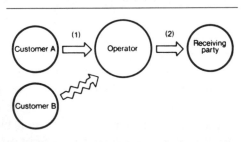

FIGURE 3.1 *Why Customers Had to Wait*

---

*Reprinted with permission from "The Quest for Higher Quality—the Deming Prize and Quality Control," Ricoh Company, Ltd.

(Case Study — continued)

At (1), the operator receives a call from the customer but, due to lack of experience, does not know where to connect the call. At (2), the receiving party cannot answer the phone quickly, perhaps because he is unavailable, and nobody can take the call for him. The result is that the operator must transfer the call to another extension while apologizing for the delay.

2. Cause-and-Effect Diagram and Situation Analysis. In order to fully understand the situation, the circle members decided to conduct a survey regarding the callers who waited for more than five rings. Circle members itemized factors at a brainstorming discussion and arranged them in a cause-and-effect diagram (see Figure 3.2). Operators then kept checksheets on several points to tally the results spanning 12 days from June 4 to 16. (See Figure 3.3.)

3. Results of the Checksheet Situation Analysis. The data recorded on the checksheets unexpectedly revealed that "one operator (partner out of the office)" topped the list by a big margin, occurring a total of 172 times. In this case, the operator on duty had to deal with large numbers of calls when the phones were busy. Customers who had to wait a long time averaged 29.2 daily, which accounted for 6% of the calls received every day. (See Figures 3.4 and 3.5.)

4. Setting the Target. After an intense but productive discussion, the staff decided to set a QC program goal of reducing these waiting callers

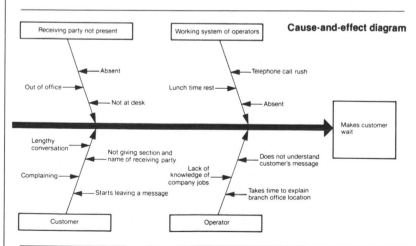

FIGURE 3.2 *What Makes Customers Wait*

FIGURE 3.3 Checksheet—Designed to Identify the Problems

Reason / Date	No one present in the section receiving the call	Receiving party not present	Only one operator (partner out of the office)	～	Total
June 4	|||	正		正 正		～	24
June 5	正	正 |||	正 正 正 ||	～	32
June 6	正		|||	正 ||	～	28
June 15	正	正	正 |||	～	25

FIGURE 3.4 Reasons Why Callers Had to Wait

		Daily average	Total number
A	One operator (partner out of the office)	14.3	172
B	Receiving party not present	6.1	73
C	No one present in the section receiving the call	5.1	61
D	Section and name of receiving party not given	1.6	19
E	Inquiry about branch office locations	1.3	16
F	Other reasons	0.8	10
	Total	29.2	351

Period: 12 days from June 4 to 16, 1980

FIGURE 3.5 Reasons Why Callers Had to Wait (Pareto Diagram)

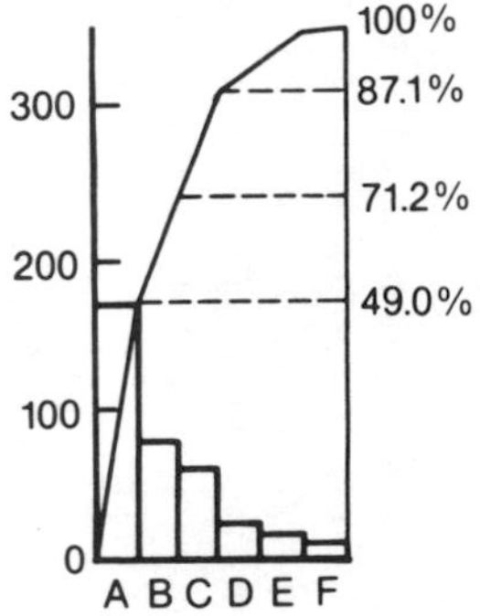

FIGURE 3.6 *Effects of QC (Comparison of Before and After QC)*

	Reasons why callers had to wait	Total number		Daily average	
		Before	After	Before	After
A	One operator (partner out of the office)	172	15	14.5	1.2
B	Receiving party not present	73	17	6.1	1.4
C	No one present in the section receiving the call	61	20	5.1	1.7
D	Section and name of receiving party not given	19	4	1.6	0.3
E	Inquiry about branch office locations	16	3	1.3	0.2
F	Others	10	0	0.8	0
	Total	351	59	29.2	4.8

Period: 12 days from Aug. 17 to 30.

Problems are classified according to cause and presented in order of the amount of time consumed. They are illustrated in a bar graph. 100% indicates the total number of time-consuming calls.

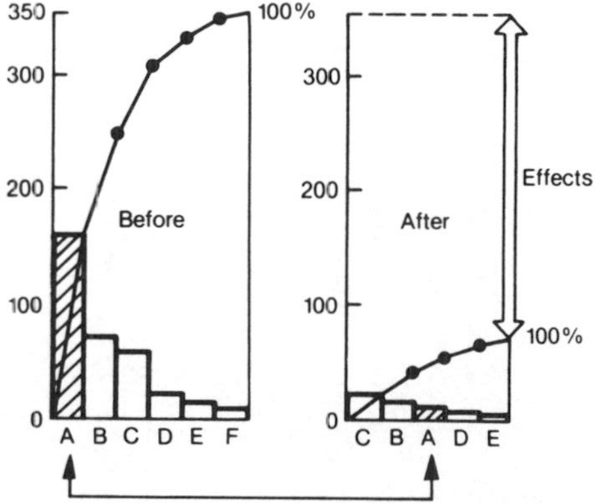

FIGURE 3.7 *Effects of QC (Pareto Diagram)*

(Case Study — continued)

to zero. That is to say that all incoming calls would be handled promptly, without inconveniencing the customer.

5. Measures and Execution. **(1) Taking lunches on three different shifts, leaving at least two operators on the job at all times.**

Up until this resolution was made, a two-shift lunch system had been employed, leaving only one operator on the job while the other was taking her lunch break. However, since the survey revealed that this was a major cause of customers waiting on the line, the company brought in a helper operator from the clerical section.

(2) Asking all employees to leave messages when leaving their desks.

The objective of this rule was to simplify the operator's chores when the receiving party was not at his desk. The new program was explained at the employees' regular morning meetings, and company-wide support was requested. To help implement this practice, posters were placed around the office to publicize the new measures.

(3) Compiling a directory listing the personnel and their respective jobs.

The notebook was specially designed to aid the operators, who could not be expected to know the details of every employee's job or where to connect his incoming calls.

6. Confirming the Results. Although the waiting calls could not be reduced to zero, all items presented showed a marked improvement as shown in Figures 3.6 and 3.7. The major cause of delays, "one operator (partner out of the office)," plummeted from 172 incidents during the control period to 15 in the follow-up survey. ■

TQC Starts with Training and Ends with Training

The introduction of TQC in Japan invariably starts with all-out efforts for training managers and workers. This is a natural follow-up to the concept of building quality into people. When Kajima, one of Japan's leading construction companies, started its TQC activities in 1978, the initial target was to provide educational programs to all 16,000 employees within three years. When the company found that sending managers to public seminars and inviting outside lecturers to speak was not enough to expose all employees to the courses, it developed special TQC video courses to be conducted through 110 in-house video terminals.

The major aim of these various training programs was to instill TQC thinking in all employees—in effect, to spark an "awareness" revolution. Kajima conducted separate courses for the different organizational levels and reached everyone within three years. In the process, the company developed 800 QC leaders and produced its own textbooks to be used within the company.

If TQC regards the next process as the customer, then the scope of TQC by its very nature extends to the adjacent business unit (process) and the next until it reaches the final destination. This is why TQC's sphere extends vertically from top management to middle management, from middle management to supervisors, from supervisors to workers, and from workers to part-time workers. This is also why it extends horizontally from vendors on one end to customers on the other.

In many companies, QC-circle activities are extended to include part-time employees, because in order to solve the company's problems, everyone must be involved. In fact, part-timers often make the most active and enthusiastic members of QC circles and provide many useful suggestions for improvement.

Cross-Functional Management to Facilitate KAIZEN

The concept of managing the previous process means that TQC should be extended to include vendors, suppliers, and subcontractors in order to improve the quality of supplies and materials. As TQC has come to include cost reduction, quality assurance, volume management, and other areas, it has given rise to the concept of cross-functional management. Under this concept, various departments cooperate in cross-functional activities. This is a horizontal extension of TQC.

TQC encompasses various levels of management as well as various functional departments. People are not isolated in TQC. TQC seeks mutual understanding and collaboration. The TQC spirit is contagious.

"Break departmental barriers" is a catch-phrase often used by a company deciding to introduce TQC. This is especially true for companies that have suffered from intense internal strife and know how adversely departmental barriers affect such areas as quality, cost, and scheduling. Thus these companies typically introduce cross-functional management to break departmental barriers. Yet such is not to say that each functional department should be weak. On the contrary, each department should be strong enough to reap the full benefits of cross-functional management.

As TQC spreads from one department to the next, strengthening the horizontal and vertical interrelations among different organizational levels, it facilitates company-wide communication. Among the many benefits of TQC are improved communication and more efficient and effective processing and feedback of information among different organizational strata. TQC not only brings people together around common goals, it underscores the value of information.

Follow the PDCA Cycle (A Continuation of the Deming Wheel)

Deming stressed the importance of constant interaction among research, design, production, and sales in the conduct of a company's business. To arrive at better quality that satisfies customers, the four stages should be rotated constantly, with quality as the top criterion. Later, this concept of turning the Deming wheel constantly for the better was extended to all phases of management, and the four stages of the wheel were seen to correspond to specific managerial actions (see Figure 3.8).

Japanese executives thus recast the Deming wheel and called it the PDCA wheel, to be applied in all phases and situations (see Figure 3.9). The PDCA cycle is a series of activities pursued for

Design → Plan	Product design corresponds to the planning phase of management.
Production → Do	Production corresponds to doing—making, or working on—the product that was designed.
Sales → Check	Sales figures confirm whether the customer is satisfied.
Research → Action	In case a complaint is filed, it has to be incorporated into the planning phase, and positive steps (action) taken for the next round of efforts. Action here refers to action for improvement.

FIGURE 3.8   Correlation Between Deming Wheel and PDCA Cycle

FIGURE 3.9   *Initial PDCA Cycle*

improvement. It begins with a study of the current situation, during which data are gathered to be used in formulating a plan for improvement. Once this plan has been finalized, it is implemented. After that, the implementation is checked to see whether it has brought about the anticipated improvement. When the experiment has been successful, a final action such as methodological standardization is taken to ensure that the new methods introduced will be practiced continuously for sustained improvement.

In the early stages of the application of the wheel, the "check" function meant that inspectors were checking the workers' results, and "action" referred to the corrective actions taken in case errors or defects were found. Thus the concept of PDCA was initially based on a division of labor among supervisors, inspectors, and workers.

In the course of applying this concept in Japan, however, it was soon found that this post-corrective application of PDCA was not enough. As a result, a new concept of PDCA emerged, shown in Figure 3.10.

Unfortunately, the adversarial nature of industrial relations in the United States and Europe has rigidified this role distinction to create what might be called the PDCF cycle (see Figure 3.11).

In too many Western situations, the "F" takes on the extreme of the R criteria, and *firing* of workers or managers becomes a quick solution.

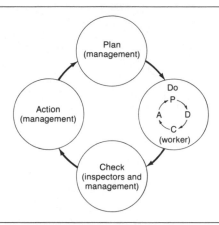

FIGURE 3.10   *Revised PDCA Cycle*

In the revised version of the PDCA cycle as shown in Figure 3.10, "plan" means to plan improvements in present practices by using statistical tools such as the seven tools of QC—Pareto diagrams, cause-and-effect diagrams, histograms, control charts, scatter diagrams, graphs, and checksheets. (See Appendix E for an explanation of these terms.) "Do" means the application of that plan; "check" means seeing if it has brought about the desired improvement, and "action" means preventing recurrence and institutionalizing the improvement as a new practice to improve upon. The

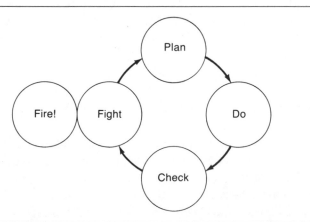

FIGURE 3.11   *Western PDCF Cycle*

PDCA cycle goes round and round. No sooner is an improvement made than it becomes the standard to be challenged with new plans for further improvement. The KAIZEN process has been realized at its maximum.

PDCA is thus understood as a process through which new standards are set only to be challenged, revised, and replaced by newer and better standards. While most Western workers see standards as fixed goals, Japan's PDCA practitioners view standards as the place to start for doing a better job the next time.

In the beginning of Chapter 1, I mentioned that management in Japan can be broken down into the two segments of maintenance and improvement. The PDCA cycle is an essential tool for realizing improvement and ensuring that the benefits of improvement last. Even before the PDCA cycle is employed, it is essential that the current standards be stabilized.

Such a process of stabilization is often called the SDCA (Standardize–Do–Check–Action) cycle. Only when the SDCA cycle is at work can we move on to upgrading the current standards through the PDCA cycle. Management should have both the SDCA and the PDCA cycles working in concert all the time.

Any work process has deviations in the beginning, and it takes effort to stabilize the process. For instance, a production line that is supposed to produce 100 units an hour may actually produce 95 an hour in the morning and 90 in the afternoon. On other days, it may be producing 105 an hour. This happens because of unstable conditions on the production line. At this stage, it is important to stabilize the process so that the hourly production will be closer to 100.

This is done with the SDCA cycle (see Figure 3.12). Only after a standard has been established and stabilized should one move on to the next phase of using the PDCA cycle to raise the standard. As such, SDCA is used for stabilizing and standardizing the conditions and PDCA for improving them.

A group of French executives recently visited a Japanese plant where managers and workers were enthusiastically implementing the PDCA cycle in their TQC efforts. The visiting executives heard a Japanese manager say, "Every time we implement a new measure, we see how it goes, check the results, search out and admit our mistakes on the management end, and then try to do better." One visitor responded, "But you are the manager. Why do you need

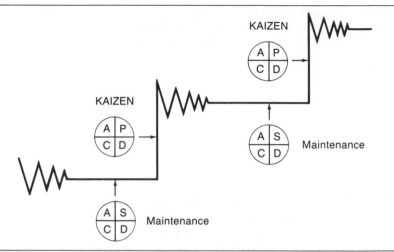

FIGURE 3.12 *Interaction of PDCA and SDCA Cycles with KAIZEN and Maintenance*

to admit anything?" The KAIZEN concept means that everyone, no matter what his title or position, must openly admit any mistakes he has made or any failings that exist in his job, and try to do a better job the next time. Progress is impossible without the ability to admit mistakes.

By turning the PDCA cycle, managers and workers are both constantly challenged to reach new heights of improvement. Yuzuru Itoh, director of Matsushita Electric's QC center, once said in explaining why QC circle members constantly strive for better achievement:

> One of the more interesting QC-related experiences I had involved the soldering workers at a television plant. On the average, each of our solderers soldered 10 points per workpiece, 400 workpieces per day, for a daily total of 4,000 soldering connections. Assuming he works 20 days a month, that's 80,000 soldering connections per month. One color TV set requires about 1,000 soldering connections. Of course, nowadays, most soldering is done automatically, and soldering workers are required to maintain a very low defect rate of no more than one mistake per 500,000 to 1 million connections.
>
> Visitors to our TV factory are usually quite surprised to find

workers doing such a monotonous job without any serious mistakes. But let's consider some of the other monotonous things humans do, like walking, for example. We've walked practically all our lives, repeating the same motion over and over again. It's an extremely monotonous movement, but there are people such as the Olympic athletes who are intensely devoted to walking faster than anyone has ever walked before. This is analogous to how we approach quality control in the factory.

Some jobs can be very monotonous, but if we can give workers a sense of mission or a goal to aim at, interest can be maintained even in a monotonous job.

Use the QC Story to Persuade

TQC employs statistically collected and analyzed data for solving problems. TQC practitioners have found that their suggestions and solutions are persuasive because they are based on a precise analysis of data and not on hunches. Hence the phrase "Use the QC story to persuade."

QC stories typically start with an explanation of the nature of the problem in the workplace and the reason why the QC group chose the particular theme for improvement. The group typically uses a Pareto diagram to plot the key factors contributing to the problem, in order of importance. Having identified these key factors, the group determines the specific goal for its QC activities.

Next, the group employs a cause-and-effect diagram to analyze the causes of the problems. Using this analysis, the group develops solutions to the problems. After the solutions have been implemented, their results are checked and their effectiveness evaluated. Everyone in the group then casts a critical eye inward, tries to prevent any recurrence of the problem by standardizing the result, and starts looking for ways to improve on the improvement. This is the PDCA cycle in action.

QC stories are also effective tools for improving communication among the upper and lower organizational strata on such subjects as quality, cost reduction, and efficiency. Kenzo Sasaoka of Yokogawa-Hewlett-Packard, a Japan-based joint venture between Yokogawa Hokushin Electric Corp. and Hewlett-Packard, once remarked that Japanese YHP managers' letters to Hewlett-Packard for specific information or feedback were not always answered, and when they were it was not always with the information requested. However, when the YHP managers began to frame their inquiries in the context of QC stories, their letters were much better understood. Today, more than 95 percent get the desired responses.

A QC STORY:
REDUCING RESIN-OUTPUT VARIATION
AT RICOH*

This is a story about a dedicated quality-control circle working within Ricoh's Numazu plant. The members of this circle are in charge of the production and inspection of raw materials used to make PPC toner. The circle is composed of six male employees with an average age of 28 years. They carried out a series of QC activities in order to achieve a stable quality of resin through chemical reactions and daily control procedures. Because precise and careful tests to a tolerance of 1/10,000 of a gram must be conducted to control critical chemical reactions, technological expertise and theoretical knowledge are essential for each member. In line with this policy, the circle continually analyzes data from the workplace and reviews test results in a continuing effort to improve the quality of the resin. This QC circle not only studies technical aspects but also directs its attention to safety methods and problem solving. During the implementation period, the circle held 42 meetings, each 90 minutes long. These QC activities also received the Nikkei QC Literature Award in 1980.

1. Selection of a Theme. As shown in Figure 3.13, after the second processing, a lot of material is divided in half, and each half goes through the third and fourth process separately. The average yield was 99.8 percent, but as can be seen in Figure 3.14, the variation was large and 43 percent of the points exceeded the theoretical value. Because output stability is directly linked to resin quality, this circle adopted the theme "how to reduce variation." (Note: **Technical definition,** output = produced amount; yield = the ratio of produced amount to theoretical output.)

2. Understanding the Situation. Based on previous data, a "histogram" (shown in Figure 3.15) was drawn up. Since the graph showed two peaks, the circle members concluded that it included two mixed lots, and furthermore determined that there was a difference of 14kg of element $\bar{\chi}$ between the two. Moreover, the $\bar{\chi}$-R control chart showed

---

*Reprinted with permission from "The Quest for Higher Quality—The Deming Prize and Quality Control," Ricoh Company, Ltd.

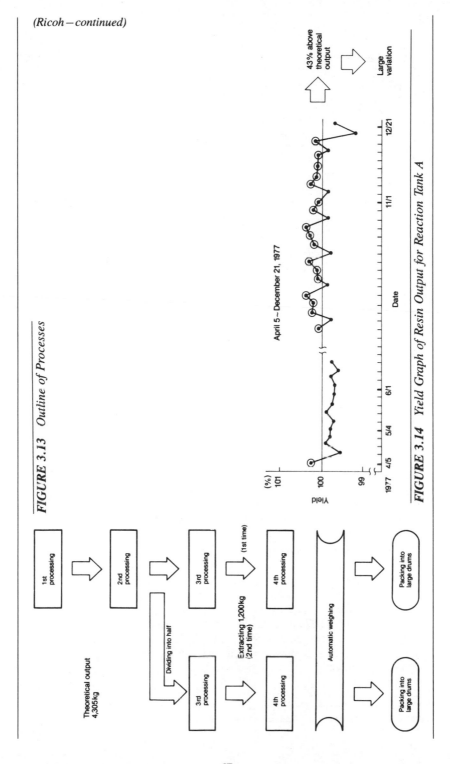

FIGURE 3.13   Outline of Processes

FIGURE 3.14   Yield Graph of Resin Output for Reaction Tank A

(Ricoh — continued)

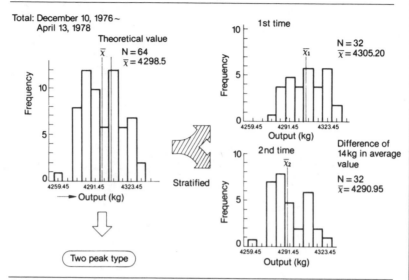

FIGURE 3.15   *Resin-Output Histogram*

variations between the batches (up to 48kg) which had been over-
looked in the yield graphs. Variations of up to 60kg had also occurred
within batches.*

3. Setting the Target.   The data presented some challenging problems
which the QC circle decided to tackle. The group set a target of achieving a stable resin output of 4,300 kg with a variation of ±5kg. This
goal was to be achieved by November 1978.

4. Factors and Measures.   After reducing the variation within the
batch, countermeasures were directed toward reducing the variation
between separate batches. Out of the factors listed in Figure 3.16, three
priority factors were identified: the dividing work after the second processing, the feed ratio, and the automatic weighing process. Next, as
shown in Figures 3.17 and 3.18, analyses were made and countermeasures
were applied that would enable the QC circle to attain its target. Unexpected complications developed during the weighing, but were later
resolved following an on-the-spot check.

---

*In these calculations, R represents the difference between the largest and smallest
value of the group, and $\bar{\chi}$ denotes the average value.

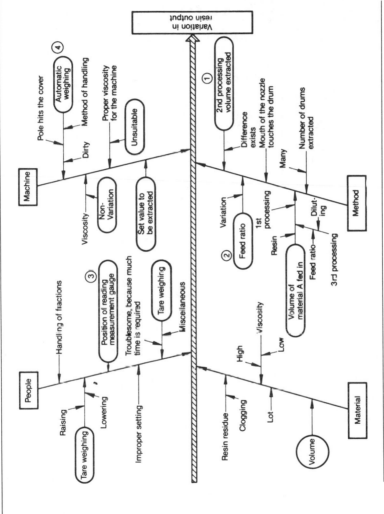

FIGURE 3.16 Cause-and-Effect Diagram

Analysis procedure	Items	Analysis	Analysis results and measures taken
(1) Reduction of deviation within the batch **Countermeasures 1**	Study of the output for 1st and 2nd time	**Sign test for 1st and 2nd output (kg)** — June 24, 1977 — May 17, 1978 No.: 1, 2, 3, 4, 5, 6, 7, ….. , 27, 28, 29, 30 1st Time: 4,303 / 4,291 / 4,306 / 4,346 / 4,326 / 4,332 / 4,307 / …… / 4,319 / 4,336 / 4,296 / 4,279 2nd Time: 4,275 / 4,331 / 4,092 / 4,287 / 4,323 / 4,292 / 4,307 / …… / 4,305 / 4,280 / 4,289 / 4,274 Code: + / − / + / + / + / + / ○ / …… / ○ / + / + / + $n_{n.} = 21$ $n_{n.} = 7$ $○○ = 2$	There was a significant difference of 1% for the 1st output and 2nd output • Review and study of the difference (dividing work) between the 1st time and 2nd time
	One half extracted for the 2nd processing and studied	Total volume extracted at the completion of the 2nd processing Total volume **2,424kg confirmed** ⟹ **1,212kg for one half** A large quantity remained in the reaction tank during the former dividing work — 1,200kg	One half during the 2nd processing was 1,212kg and not 1,200kg • The volume extracted for the 2nd process was changed and confirmed
	Extraction was made for the 2nd processing and an output of 1,212kg confirmed for each	**Sign test for 1st and 2nd output, May 25 — Aug. 26, 1978** No.: 1, 2, 3, 4, 5, 6, 7, 8, 9, 10 1st Time: 4,299 / 4,275 / 4,297 / 4,309 / 4,321 / 4,337 / 4,298 / 4,277 / 4,290 / 4,295 / 4,302 2nd Time: 4,301 / 4,280 / 4,297 / 4,294 / 4,302 / 4,307 / 4,294 / 4,290 / 4,293 / 4,275 / 4,311 Code: − / − / ○ / + / + / + / + / − / − / + / − $n_{.} = 5$ $n_{.} = 5$ $○ = 1$	Through dividing into 1,212kg each, the significant difference between the 1st and 2nd time disappeared • Revision of the work standards • Variation still detected in the output • Review of the cause-and-effect diagram
	Study of the output and the feed ratio	(kg) Scatter diagram for output vs. feed ratio Output: 4350 / 4300 / 4250 Feed ratio: 1/0.95 — 1/1.05 — 1/1.15 — 1/1.25 — 1/1.35 — 1/1.45 — 1/1.55 I $n_1 = 19$ II $n_2 = 10$ III $n_3 = 19$ IV $n_4 = 10$ $n_. = n_1 + n_3 = 38$ $n_. = n_2 + n_4 = 20$	• There was a 5% significant difference for output vs. feed ratio • Review and study of the feed ratio operation

FIGURE 3.17 Analysis of Variation within Batch, and Countermeasures

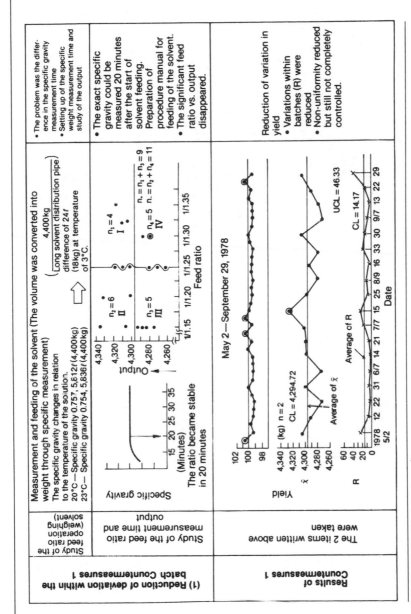

(1) Reduction of deviation within the batch Countermeasures 1	Study of the feed ratio operation (weighing solvent)	Measurement and feeding of the solvent (The volume was converted into weight through specific measurement) The specific gravity changes in relation to the temperature of the soution. 20°C — Specific gravity 0.757, 5,612ℓ (4,400kg) 23°C — Specific gravity 0.754, 5,836ℓ (4,400kg)	• The problem was the difference in the specific gravity measurement time • Setting up of the specific weight measurement time and study of the output
	Study of the feed ratio measurement time and output	The ratio became stable in 20 minutes	• The exact specific gravity could be measured 20 minutes after the start of solvent feeding. Preparation of procedure manual for feeding of the solvent. • The significant feed ratio vs. output disappeared.
Results of Countermeasures 1	The 2 items written above were taken	May 2 — September 29, 1978	Reduction of variation in yield • Variations within batches (R) were reduced • Non-uniformity reduced but still not completely controlled.

FIGURE 3.17 (continued)

Analysis procedure	Items	Analysis	Analysis results and measures taken
(2) Reduction in variation between batches. Counter-measure2	Review of the cause-and-effect diagram	**Work place observation with members and simulated measurement** (1) Weighing (2) Automatic weighing The pole of the scale and the connecting rod touched the cover. Short people look upward and see a deviation in the standard line of the scale.	• As the standard line deviates depending on the person, it was placed at a position where everyone could see the true level. • Improvement of the protective cover.
	The 2 measures written above were taken	Improvement of the standard basic line and the protection cover Yield (%) 101 100 99 (kg) 4,340 4,320 4,300 R 60 40 20 0 Measures: Changes in the extraction volume after completion of the 2nd processing, unification of the solvent processing, specific gravity measurement method. Counter-measure 1 | Counter-measure 2 A lower output than the standard in this case Member B The sensitivity of the weighing was poor Measures taken	• Check made of total number of drum cans. Many contained in excess of 1.21kg to 3.7kg. • Search for the cause of the trouble (lack of sensitivity in the weighing)
(3) Emergency trouble	Emergency meeting of the circle	**New person F stressed the importance of the observation.** Re-checking of the work site The 8 triangular contacts below the conveyor stand were not aligned. The work done the previous week was the cause	• Drop in sensitivity due to the contact points not being in alignment • The contact points were returned to the original position and procedures drawn up for extracting the resin as well as checking the point of the scale.

FIGURE 3.17 (continued)

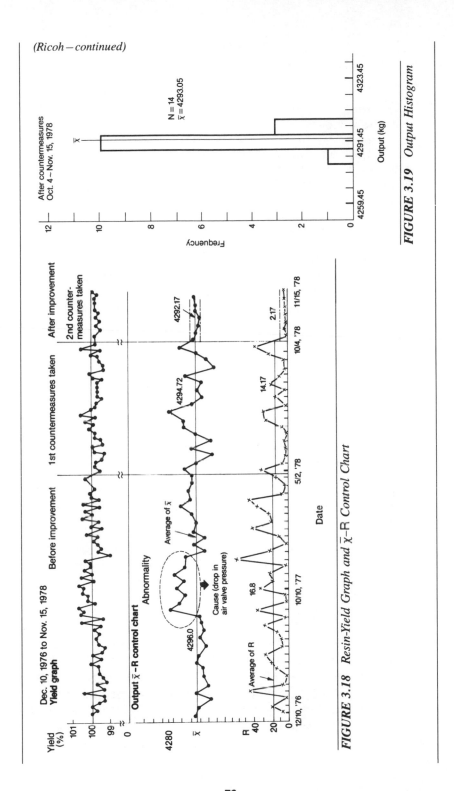

FIGURE 3.19 Output Histogram

FIGURE 3.18 Resin-Yield Graph and $\overline{x}$-R Control Chart

73

(Ricoh — continued)

5. Results.

(1) Tangible results

As shown in Figures 3.18 and 3.19, the variation in resin output decreased substantially. As an added benefit, there was a corresponding reduction in feed-ratio and resin-viscosity variation, which contributed to a stable resin quality.

(2) Intangible results

- Average values can be overemphasized.
  By discovering some of the pitfalls of emphasizing only average values, the members' concepts of variation and data handling have been changed.

- All members came to realize the importance of daily quality controls, thereby increasing yield.

- Daily control methods were improved and implemented through the use of the $\bar{\chi}$-R control chart and by establishing procedures to locate abnormalities.

6. Measures to Prevent Backsliding.

(1) Preparation of resin-extraction-procedure manual
(2) Preparation of solvent-insertion-procedure manual
(3) Revision of manual for synthesizing resin
(4) Periodic regulation of the automatic weighing process

7. Insights and Future Directions.

While keenly appreciating the importance of on-the-spot observation, the members of the circle also realized how easy it is to overlook problems that occur in routine daily work. This experience proved valuable to each member. During the period concerned, there was a change from a two-shift day to a three-shift day, making it difficult for members to plan their meetings. However, this was solved by having the night-shift QC-circle members submit participation papers. Further measures were devised so that QC meetings and related activities would not inconvenience the individual members. ■

Standardize the Result

There can be no improvement where there are no standards. The starting point in any improvement is to know exactly where one stands. There must be a precise standard of measurement for every worker, every machine, and every process. Similarly, there must be a precise standard of measurement for every manager. Even before introducing TQC and the KAIZEN strategy, management must make an effort to understand where the company stands and what the work standards are. This is why standardization is one of the most important pillars of TQC.

As has been noted, the KAIZEN strategy calls for never-ending efforts for improvement. In other words, the KAIZEN strategy is a continuing challenge to prevailing standards. For KAIZEN, standards exist only to be superseded by better standards. Every standard, every specification, and every measurement cries out for constant revision and upgrading.

When we divide the work of an individual into a series of P criteria, we finally reach the ultimate measurable P criteria, or the standard. For example, the job of a machine worker may be broken down into several steps: carrying material, feeding it to the machine, starting the machine, processing the material, stopping the machine, carrying the processed material to the next machine, and so on.

It is neither possible nor necessary to standardize all these operations. However, the crucial elements, such as the cycle time, the work sequence, or the pre-work gauging of the machine, should be measurable and standardized. Sometimes, Japanese factories employ what is called one-point standardization, which means that the worker should have one of his many operations standardized. When a blue-collar worker's work is such that most of it does not have to be standardized, one point is often all that needs to be standardized.

This one-point standard is often displayed at the workplace so that the worker is always mindful of it, and only after observing this standard has become second nature to the worker should management think about adding another standard.

The standard should be binding on everyone, and it is management's job to see that everyone works in accordance with the established standards. This is called discipline.

Each standard carries with it the following characteristics:

1. Individual authorization and responsibility
2. Transmittal of individual experience to the next generation of workers
3. Transmittal of individual experience and know-how to the organization
4. Accumulation of experience (particularly with failures) within the organization

5. Deployment of know-how from one workshop to another

6. Discipline

Every workplace has its own performance standards and SOP for every worker, machine, or process. When people in the workplace encounter a problem, it is analyzed, the causes are identified, and solutions are proposed.

In the PDCA cycle, once a proposed solution has been put into practice, the next step is to check how effective it has been. If the proposed solution is found to be an improvement, it is adopted as a new standard. (See Figure 3.20.) Often this new standard is horizontally deployed to other sections and factories.

Only when subsequent work is conducted in line with the new standard can we say that there has been a real (that is, lasting) improvement. Kenzo Sasaoka defines standardization as a way of spreading the benefits of improvement throughout the organization.

This can perhaps best be illustrated by a case involving a high-technology product manufactured in Japan under license. When production was started in Japan, the Japanese licensee turned down some material from an American supplier because it did not meet

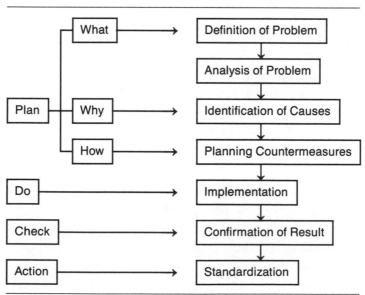

FIGURE 3.20   *Problem-Solving Cycle*

the specifications set by the licensor, another American company. The supplier, however, had been supplying the licensor with the same material for many years. Apparently, the licensor had accepted this supplier's product, even though it was not quite up to specifications, because it had never led to any serious problems. Both licensor and supplier had a very difficult time explaining this to the Japanese licensee, who wanted to know why the standard was not being upheld.

Such a situation could never occur where everyone is TQC-minded. It is common knowledge that engineers design specifications a little high to be on the safe side. However, if more realistic specifications are acceptable, the specifications should be revised rather than being continued at unrealistic levels. Such attention to revision is an improvement of a sort, and management must be sensitive to such a continuing need. A properly functioning KAIZEN program will assure continuing challenges to the prevailing standards.

In the KAIZEN strategy, management must review the current standard and try to improve it. Once the standard has been established, management must make sure all employees observe it strictly. This is people management. If management cannot get people to follow the established rules and standards, nothing else it does will matter.

I have often talked with Japanese engineers who have visited plants in the United States and Europe. One of the most frequent observations these people make is that Western management does not seem to care about this very basic management concern. Discipline is often lacking. One young engineer who recently visited an American plant making plastic components for automobiles commented: "Smoking is strictly prohibited where I work, since we use highly flammable chemicals. This American company uses the same chemicals, and there were 'No Smoking' signs all over. But the manager who showed me around was smoking, and he even threw his cigarette butt on the floor!"

Another engineer told me that when he visited a plant in Italy, a female worker at a machine was eating an apple while she was working, and when she noticed him, she waved in enthusiastic welcome.

By contrast, when Prince Rainier and the late Princess Grace of Monaco visited a Matsushita television plant in April 1981, not a single assembly-line worker so much as looked at them. At the reception held the night before their visit, Chairman Masaharu Matsushita told Prince Rainier and Princess Grace that, even though the workers had been forewarned of their visit, they would probably be too involved in their work to look at the visiting royalty. The next day, when Matsushita showed Prince Rainier and Princess Grace through the television plant, he was probably even prouder of his workers' concentration than he was of the ultramodern equipment.

Lest the reader think that this is typical, I hasten to add that workers at other Japanese companies, where the work does not demand so much concentration, often greet visitors with respectful nods, working all the while.

Management's job is to establish standards and then to introduce discipline so that the standards are maintained. Only then is it qualified to introduce KAIZEN for improving the standards.

In most Western companies, there is a tendency for management to stick to the same "sacred" standard for years. And yet it is often doubtful whether management is doing its best to maintain discipline and make sure that even that standard is being strictly observed.

One of the chief merits of beginning a KAIZEN program is that it prompts management to ponder when the current standards were last challenged. It becomes a good time to check whether discipline is enforced, and whether even the current rules and standards are observed by all employees.

KAIZEN at the Grassroots Level

It is said that 95 percent of all automobile recalls stem from mechanical failures and oversights that could have been avoided if the engineers had been a little more careful in designing the components or the workers a little more attentive in machining or assembling them in the factory. Management is today exposed to an increasing wave of consumerism and product-liability suits, and getting everyone's commitment to maintaining quality is becoming crucial for a company's survival.

Pentel, a manufacturer of stationery products, recently marketed a new mechanical pencil. One of this pencil's distinctive features is that it has a cap on it, since management felt that this would be popular with people who carry pencils in their pockets. When the cap is taken off and put on the other end of the pencil, you can push out the lead by pushing on the cap. In addition, Pentel has made sure that the cap snaps on and off with an audible "click." Pentel does not regard the pencil as market-ready unless it clicks right. Needless to say, whether or not the cap clicks is irrelevant as far as the pencil's performance is concerned. However, the click makes a big difference from the marketing point of view, since it reassures the customer that the cap is on tight.

TQC SLOGANS AT PENTEL

The following is a list of Pentel's slogans for explaining the TQC philosophy to its employees.

1. Subscribe to the market-in (customer-first) concept.
   (People in the next process are your customers. If you stick to the product-out concept, our company's name will not even be listed in the phone book after a while.)
2. Be problem-conscious at all times.
   (Where there is no problem, there can be no improvement.)
3. Management means starting with planning and comparing it with the result.
   (Let's turn the PDCA wheel and change the way we do our job.)
4. You are surrounded by mountains of treasures.
   (There is more to be learned from chronic problems than from problems that suddenly occur.)
5. Manage the process by the result.
   (Rework and adjustments are problems arising from the lack of management. Dealing with them is not management but manipulation.)
6. Look at the factory and manage your work on the basis of facts.
   (Base judgments on data. Do not rely on hunches or gut feelings.)
7. Be attentive to deviations.
   (The priority lies in reducing the deviation rather than improving the average.)
8. Stratify before observation.
   (Classification leads to better understanding.)
9. Improvement starts at home.
   (Become accustomed to classifying problems into those that are your own responsibility and those that are others' responsibilities, and taking care of your own problems first.)
10. Remove the basic cause and prevent recurrence.
    (Do not confuse symptoms with causes.)

(Pentel — continued)

11. Build quality in upstream.
    (Quality must be built into the process. Testing does not make quality.)
12. Never fail to standardize.
    (We need devices to make sure that a good state lasts.)
13. Always consider horizontal deployment.
    (Individual expertise should be extended to company-wide expertise.)
14. Implement TQC involving everybody.
    (A pleasant, meaningful workshop starts with active QC circles for mutual enlightenment and self-development.) ■

Quality demands such as these require painstaking efforts on the part of all production workers. Otherwise the inspection people might end up discarding practically every pencil produced. Such attention to details — even cosmetic details — is becoming increasingly crucial for success in today's highly competitive markets. With the basic technology for something like mechanical pencils broadly available, seldom does the basic design influence customers for or against the product. Minor cosmetic elements can be the determining factor.

Undoubtedly such factors as price, performance, and service are important in gaining customer acceptance for a new product. However, many products today have the same "black box," so their performance is virtually indistinguishable. This being the case, most products in the marketplace, whether it be the industrial or the consumer market, are competing on the strength of purely cosmetic features. Yet these cosmetic features are often discounted by designers, managers, and workers alike as unimportant or immaterial. Managers who are attentive to such "trivial" factors and workers who care about every detail in the workplace can determine success in marketing products that consumers buy. KAIZEN presents a technique for both management and workers to be involved in determining success.

4

KAIZEN–The Practice

We have seen how progress and improve-
ment are approached in Japan and in the West. In particular, we have
contrasted the Japanese KAIZEN philosophy with the Western focus
on innovation as the source of progress. A well-planned program of
KAIZEN can be further broken down into three segments, depending on the complexity and the level of KAIZEN: (1) management-
oriented KAIZEN, (2) group-oriented KAIZEN, and (3) individual-
oriented KAIZEN. (See Figure 4.1.) Let's consider these three
segments in more detail.

	Management-Oriented KAIZEN	Group-Oriented KAIZEN	Individual-Oriented KAIZEN
Tools	Seven Statistical Tools **(see Appendix E)** New Seven Tools Professional skills	Seven Statistical Tools New Seven Tools	Common sense Seven Statistical Tools
Involves	Managers and professionals	QC-circle (group) members	Everybody
Target	Focus on systems and procedures	Within the same workshop	Within one's own work area
Cycle (Period)	Lasts for the dura-tion of the project	Requires four or five months to complete	Anytime

FIGURE 4.1   *Three Segments of KAIZEN (continued next page)*

	Management-Oriented KAIZEN	Group-Oriented KAIZEN	Individual-Oriented KAIZEN
Achievements	As many as management chooses	Two or three per year	Many
Supporting system	Line and staff project team	Small-group activities QC circles Suggestion system	Suggestion system
Implementation cost	Sometimes requires small investment to implement the decision	Mostly inexpensive	Inexpensive
Result	New system and facility improvement	Improved work procedure Revision of standard	On-the-spot improvement
Booster	Improvement in managerial performance	Morale improvement Participation Learning experience	Morale improvement KAIZEN awareness Self-development
Direction	Gradual and visible improvement Marked upgrading of current status	Gradual and visible improvement	Gradual and visible improvement

FIGURE 4.1 *(continued)*

Management-Oriented KAIZEN

The first pillar of KAIZEN is management-oriented KAIZEN. It is the crucial pillar, since management-oriented KAIZEN concentrates on the most important logistic and strategic issues and provides the momentum to keep up progress and morale.

Since KAIZEN is everybody's job, the manager must be engaged in improving his own job. Japanese management generally believes that a manager should spend at least 50 percent of his time on improvement. The types of KAIZEN projects studied by management require sophisticated problem-solving expertise as well as professional and engineering knowledge, although the simple Seven Statistical Tools (see Appendix E) may sometimes be enough. They are clearly a management job, and often involve people from different departments working together on cross-functional problems as project teams.

I recently visited a European electronics manufacturer and talked with the engineers about the opportunities for improvement in the workplace. In the discussion, one of the engineers said that whenever he suggested a new and different method of operation, his boss always asked him to explain the economic benefits that would result. When he was unable to quantify the improvement in financial terms, his boss simply shelved his suggestion.

Opportunities for improvement are everywhere. Quite recently, a Japanese engineer visiting an American steelworks was appalled to see a pile of steel sheets stacked up in the hallway "like the leaning Tower of Pisa." He was appalled for two reasons: first, the leaning tower was a physical threat to the safety of the workers, and second, the money tied up in inventories was a financial threat to the health of the company.

Japanese plants have reference numbers marked out on a grid on the floor so that supplies and work in process can be put at the designated locations. "At our factory, we start our KAIZEN efforts by looking at the way our people do their work," says Toyota's Taiichi Ohno, "because it doesn't cost anything." The starting point of KAIZEN, therefore, is to identify "waste" in the worker's motion. This is, in fact, one of the most difficult problems to identify, since such wasteful movements are an integral part of the work sequence.

Ohno gives the example of a worker mounting an engine block into the press, which is brought on the conveyor. If there is more than one engine block on the conveyor, the worker has to push back the engine blocks, which pile up whenever he falls behind. The worker is quite busy, but this is not productive work. This unproductive work becomes unnecessary if management can identify this waste movement and introduce ways to eliminate it, such as placing only one block on the conveyor at a time.

Similarly, the location and the size of switches are crucial in a continuous operation, and each switch must be located so that the worker can reach it in pace with the flow of his work. Switches are often changed to bar switches for easier operation. At times, switches may be put on the floor so that work-laden workers can simply step on them.

Workers are frequently unmindful of unnecessary motions they make. For instance, a worker taking care of several machines often glances back as he moves from machine to machine. Whenever he saw a worker doing that at Toyota, Ohno would shout "Don't act like a skunk!" (Skunks are known to halt and look back from time to time when chased.) Only after all these unnecessary motions have been identified and eliminated, says Ohno, can we move to the next phase of KAIZEN on machines and systems. Ohno's favorite motto is: "Use your head, not your money."

Management-oriented KAIZEN also takes the form of a group approach such as KAIZEN teams, project teams, and task forces. However, these groups are quite different from the QC circles in that they are composed of management and staff and their activities are regarded as a routine part of management's job.

KAIZEN in Facilities

When we look at management-oriented KAIZEN from the standpoint of facilities, we again find almost endless opportunities for improvement. Although the major emphasis in quality control has shifted to building in quality at the design stage, building in quality at the production stage still remains an indispensable ingredient of quality control. Japanese management assumes that new machinery will need additional improvements. Since most machines are custom-made, this might not seem necessary. But the factory people take it for granted that even the best-designed machinery will need to be reworked and improved upon in practice. As a result, most factories have an in-house capability for repairing and even building such machines.

Daihatsu Motor's Kyoto Plant, for example, has 102 industrial robots in use to build passenger cars. Of these, all but two were either built in-house or purchased from outside manufacturers and remodeled by Daihatsu engineers.

Yotaro Kobayashi, president of Fuji Xerox, recalls the comment by a professor who visited one of Fuji Xerox's assembly plants before the company started TQC. (Later, in 1980, the company received the Deming Application Prize.) On reviewing the production line, the professor remarked, "Gentlemen, this is not a manufacturing plant. What you have here is an assembly line in a warehouse."

Typically, so many parts in process are stacked in the plant that you cannot see from one end of the assembly line to the other. In effect, the warehouse is also used for assembly. Indeed, one of the side benefits of the *kamban* and just-in-time systems is that after their introduction, you can see from one end of the assembly line to the other.

Changing the factory layout for better efficiency has been a top priority, and KAIZEN efforts have always been directed at shortening the belt conveyors or eliminating them altogether. This is why a group of Japanese businessmen was so dismayed to see the old-style belt conveyors still in use in a factory the group visited in Europe.

At the Seminar on *kamban,* quality control, and quality management sponsored by the Cambridge Corporation in Chicago, Illinois, in 1983, Graham Spurling, Managing Director of Mitsubishi Motors Australia, made the following remarks:

> Mitsubishi took over the Chrysler Company in Australia in 1980. In 1977 and 1978, Chrysler Australia lost nearly $50 million. It is now common knowledge that Mitsubishi Motors Australia is profitable and efficient. We believe that we have the highest level of productivity in the Australian car industry and that we make the best quality product.
>
> Whilst it is fair to say that this program of improvement started before the Mitsubishi takeover, and that it has been achieved with a homegrown management team, the continued prosperity of our company is very much due to the management lessons we have learned from our Japanese companies.

According to Spurling, Mitsubishi was able to achieve this with minimum investment by introducing a series of improvements such as reducing inventories and changing the plant layout. For instance, the old layout had been designed to fit the building, but Mitsubishi reversed this concept and designed the building to fit the optimal layout. As a result, it was possible to achieve an 80 percent reduction in stock on the line and a 30 percent increase in worker performance.

Excess inventory hides many problems, and Mitsubishi found that minimizing the inventory level exposed various hidden problems and enabled the company to deal with them one by one.

Says Spurling:

> Plant layout was dictated by containers, so we said, "If we need a store, let's have a store and let's make it a good store. But if we want a factory, let's make it a factory and make it a good factory." That's when we realized that containers should be tailored to suit the layout. Better than that, get rid of them all together if that was possible. The result was dramatic. By eliminating the containers, we were able to shorten the production line and thus achieve another useful step toward minimum inventory.

As a side-benefit, Ping-Pong tables were put in the resulting empty space.

On the basis of his experiences, Spurling believes that factory management should pursue the following five manufacturing objectives.

1. Achieve maximum quality with maximum efficiency
2. Maintain minimum inventory
3. Eliminate hard work
4. Use tools and facilities to maximize quality and efficiency and minimize effort
5. Maintain a questioning and open-minded attitude for constant improvement based on teamwork and cooperation

Adds Spurling:

> I am firmly convinced that the Japanese worker is himself no more subservient or dedicated than his Australian counterpart, but he is better led, better managed. He has experienced better quality management, he expects it, and he respects it. Better management gives him better motivation and better training, from which come better productivity and better product quality.

A group of 12 managers from 3M's Data Recording Products Division listened to Graham Spurling, Taiichi Ohno, and the other lecturers. Recognizing a good thing when they saw it, they decided to put quality control to work at the Weatherford (Oklahoma) plant where 3M processes diskette products. The Weatherford plant team decided to implement a new plant-wide policy of never passing defective work on to the next stage and stopping the line if necessary to maintain quality. Some of the measures introduced at Weatherford included eliminating unnecessary steps, equipment, production, and so on, and moving inspections on-line for faster feedback.

But it was not easy to get support for this effort. When I visited the Weatherford plant in the fall of 1983 and discussed personal involvement and commitment as the key to KAIZEN, the plant manager suddenly stopped me and said, "It is so reassuring for me to talk with you, Mr. Imai. It's almost as if I were talking to my mother, whom I haven't seen for months!"

The efforts for improvement and inventory reduction have led to the following changes at Weatherford.

Refined capacity planning

Layout changes

Changes in planning philosophy

Process consolidation and equipment modification

Line-stop authority

Changes in system philosophy

As a result of these efforts, in-process inventory has been reduced dramatically: to one-quarter of the level 18 months ago overall and to one-sixteenth of the old level on one product line.

Today, spaces for storing in-process stock are sharply defined, and carts carrying in-process stock must stay within the designated areas. If there is no space for another cart, production stops. Instead of using the term *kamban,* the group uses the term "Nip & Tuck" to describe its just-in-time concept.

Weatherford's Quality Improvement Team Leader has been likened to a cheerleader for the way she has been stirring up enthusiasm and involvement to get KAIZEN going. Once people have gone through the excitement of KAIZEN and seen the results, she has found, this enthusiasm is passed on from person to person even without the cheerleader. At Weatherford they use the term "measles" to describe the KAIZEN infection, since you have to get it yourself before you can pass it on to anyone else. By now, practically everyone at Weatherford has had the measles.

When I visited the Weatherford plant again in 1984, the person who was showing me around his workshop introduced me to the person who was going to show me around the next workshop as his "customer." It was clear that he had had the KAIZEN measles. On my last visit to Weatherford in 1985, I found that management had installed a new manufacturing system with the largest clean room in the United States. While the installation of this new system might be regarded as innovation, KAIZEN efforts were also visible everywhere. For instance, the floor was designed so that processing units could be moved when production requirements changed. Workers were encouraged to provide suggestions for optimum layout, and managers told me that the machinery layout was changed for the better almost weekly while they were adding production lines to the new plant.

I also observed a shift in the QC perception at the plant. Today, quality is regarded as everybody's job, and the QC people's job is defined as that of facilitator, informer, trainer, and trust-builder.

Just-in-Time Production: An Example of Management-Oriented KAIZEN

Toyota's Motomachi plant has a long line of trucks waiting outside the plant with full loads of automotive parts and components for the assembly line. As soon as one truck comes out at one end of the plant, another goes inside. There is no warehouse for these parts. Upholstered seats, for example, are fed to the production line directly from the back of the truck.

The Toyota production system is now attracting great attention in Japan and abroad, for Toyota is one of the few companies to have survived the oil crises and still maintained a high level of profitability. There is much evidence supporting Toyota's success. For instance, Toyota is completely debt-free. In fact, Toyota's profits are equivalent to those of a major Japanese bank.

The first to receive the coveted Japan Quality Control Prize in 1966, Toyota is well known for its outstanding quality control systems. To date, only seven other companies have been awarded this prize. Toyota is also famous for its worker-suggestion system. Toyota's production system, sometimes called the *kamban* system, is widely acclaimed as being superior to the Taylor system of scientific management and the Ford system of mass-production assembly lines.

The man who pioneered Toyota's unique system, Taiichi Ohno, claims that it was born out of the need to develop a system for manufacturing small numbers of many different kinds of automobiles. This approach is in direct contrast to the Western practice of producing large numbers of similar vehicles. At the same time, Ohno was determined to eliminate all forms of waste. To do this, he classified the waste incurred in the production process into the following categories:

1. Overproduction
2. Waste time spent at the machine
3. Waste involved in the transportation of units
4. Waste in processing
5. Waste in taking inventory
6. Waste of motion
7. Waste in the form of defective units

Ohno felt that overproduction was the central evil that led to waste in other areas. To eliminate the problem of waste, Ohno devised a production system based on two main structural features: (1) the "just-in-time" concept and (2) *jidohka* (autonomation).

The concept of "just-in-time" means that the exact number of required units is brought to each successive stage of production at the appropriate time. Putting this concept into practice meant a reversal of the normal thinking process. Ordinarily, units are transported to the next production stage as soon as they are ready. Ohno, however, reversed this, so that each stage was required to go back to the previous stage to pick up the exact number of units needed. This resulted in a significant decline in inventory levels.

Even after Ohno came up with the *kamban* concept and initiated it on a trial basis in machining and assembling work in 1952, it took almost 10 years for total adoption in all Toyota plants. Once this concept was well established at Toyota, Ohno began extending it to Toyota subcontractors. In the early days, he invited subcontractors for tours of his plant and sent his engineers out for consultation with subcontractors. The delivery of units that arrive "just in time" for assembling operations is the result of joint efforts by Toyota and its subcontractors.

Kamban, meaning signboard or label, is used as a communication tool in this system. A *kamban* is attached to each box of parts as they go to the assembly line. Because these parts are funneled to the line as needed, the *kamban* can be returned after the parts are used, to serve as both a record of work done and an order for new parts. The beauty of this system is that the *kamban* also coordinates the inflow of parts and components to the assembly line, minimizing the processes and making it possible, for example, for an engine block brought into the plant in the morning to be in a completed automobile on the road by evening. The *kamban* system is thus merely a tool used in Toyota's production system. It is by no means an end in itself.

The just-in-time concept has the following advantages: (1) short-ened lead time, (2) reduced time spent on non-process work, (3) reduced inventory, (4) better balance between different processes, and (5) problem clarification.

The basic structural feature of Toyota's production system is *jidohka* (autonomation—not to be confused with automation). *Jidohka* is a word coined for machines designed to stop automatically whenever a problem occurs. All machines at Toyota are equipped with automatic stop mechanisms. In the Toyota system, each time a defective workpiece is produced, the machine stops and the entire system shuts down. A thorough adjustment must be made to prevent the recurrence of the same mistake; first-aid adjustments are insufficient. Ohno maintains that this has brought about a revolutionary breakthrough in the production concept. The worker does not have to attend the machine when it is functioning properly, only when it has stopped. *Jidohka* enables one worker to take charge of many machines at a time, thus greatly improving his productivity.

Because employees supervise many different machines at once, this system leads to a significant expansion of worker responsibilities and skills. For their part, the workers must be willing to develop such a multiplicity of skills. This approach also provides greater flexibility in the layout of machines and production processes. This concept has been extended to manual assembly work, where the employee is empowered to stop the line whenever he finds something wrong.

The pitfall of modern automation is the overproduction of parts without regard for the requirements of subsequent processes. Furthermore, because ordinary automatic machinery lacks a self-diagnostic mechanism, a single malfunction can result in an entire batch of defective parts. Autostop devices are built into each piece of machinery at Toyota to prevent just such an occurrence.

Throughout the Toyota plants, the visitor will notice large signboards hung from the ceiling. When an individual machine has stopped, the machine's identification number is lit up on the signboard so that the operator knows which machine needs attention.

Toyota's production system is geared to maintain an even flow of production for different units throughout the year, thus avoiding peak loads at any given time, such as the end of the month. It appears that this system is better equipped to cope with the requirements of a changing world characterized by slow growth and diversified consumer demand.

As may be imagined, the Toyota production system is based on KAIZEN and TQC. Unless quality is maintained at the highest level at all stages of production, including subcontractors, the machines will constantly be stopping. It is no coincidence that five of the eight recipients of the Japan Quality Control Prize have been Toyota Group companies.

Toyota has achieved KAIZEN in such areas as plant layout, lot vs. continuous production, frequent setups, and worker posture. To put it another way, the *kamban* and just-in-time concepts represent the results of efforts for improvement in all these areas, efforts that culminated in improvements in inventory. Toyota's efforts for KAIZEN in these vital areas resulted in its achieving a capital turnover ratio up to 10 times that of American car manufacturers.

Zenzaburo Katayama, assistant manager at Toyota Motor's TQC Promotion Department, says:

> The Toyota production system is, in a nutshell, a system which makes sure that the required number of parts and components are manufactured and forwarded to the final assembly line so that final assembly does not stop. It is a system that is still undergoing change and improvement every day.
>
> People sometimes refer to the Toyota production system as a "non-stock system." However, this is not correct. We always have *some* stock at hand, since we do require a certain inventory level in order to produce the necessary number of products at a given time. . . .
>
> A card is attached to the front of the body of each car on the assembly line. Based on numbers and codes on this card, the car

gets different parts and components as it is assembled. You might say that each car has information attached to it which says, "I want to become such and such a car."

For instance, the card may call for a left-side steering wheel or an automatic transmission. The worker on the assembly line then picks up the part based on the instruction on the card. This is sometimes called visible management. In other words, he can control the process of the work by looking at the card.

The workers' know-how and ideas are incorporated into building a better production system. For instance, different colors are used on the card attached on the body of a car on the assembly line in order to avoid mistakes. This idea initially came from the workers. In order for the system to work, you need a trained and disciplined work force.

Another feature of this system is that you will lose money by adopting it unless the parts' quality is satisfactory. Every time a part of inferior quality is forwarded, the line will be stopped.

At Toyota, we stop the entire line when we find a defective part. Since all plant operations are coordinated, it means that when one plant stops, the effect ripples back to the previous processes, and eventually the Kamigo plant, which manufactures engines, stops too. If the stoppage is prolonged, all the plants have to stop operation.

Stopping the plant is a serious blow to management. And yet, we dare to stop it because we believe in quality control. Once we have taken the trouble of stopping the plant operation, we have to make sure that we find the cause of the trouble and adopt a countermeasure so that the same trouble never recurs.

For instance, a worker at the Tsutsumi plant may push the stop button because he finds that the engines which came from the Kamigo plant are defective. He does not have to stop the line, but he is entitled to push the stop button when he finds anything unusual.

If the line is stopped, the engineers and the supervisor will rush to see what is wrong, and they will find that the cause of the stoppage is defective engines. If the engines are really defective, the engineers from the Kamigo plant will hurry to the Tsutsumi plant to study the problem.

In the meantime, all the plants are stopped and no cars are coming out of the plant. However, no matter what happens, we must find the cause. One of the features of Japanese quality control is that it builds good production processes.

Another feature of the Toyota production system is the way information is processed and utilized. Where the computer falls short in production control and scheduling, we utilize such means as *kamban* and cards attached to the body of an automobile in the assembly plant.

Under normal circumstances, the products (parts) and information are separated. At Toyota, each product (part) carries its own information and signals.

We expect our workers to use their brains to read and interpret the information and signals on the *kamban* cards, and we expect them to contribute to refining the system by providing new ideas.

Under this system, even if the worker makes a mistake and assembles a wrong part, it will be a one-time error and the mistake will not be carried forward to subsequent operations.

When you store fruit and meat, you place them in freezers and refrigerators so that they do not rot. In a sense, iron rots, too. Because of technological developments, design changes occur, and a piece of iron in an old design is the same as a rotten piece of fruit. Neither is any good.

I would suggest that information rots, too. Information that is collected but not properly used rots rapidly. Any manager who does not forward the information to the interested parties, and any management that does not have a system to use information, is doing a great disservice to the company and creating massive waste in the form of lost opportunities and wasted executive time.

The trouble with many managers, however, is that they regard information as the source of their authority and try to control their subordinates by monopolizing it. Often they do this at the risk of sacrificing the organization's effectiveness. Managers may be totally ignorant of the value of information and the contribution it can make in the hands of the right people at the right time.

Even when the manager has a genuine interest in sharing information with other executives, this is often difficult because of the geographical separation. This is the problem encountered by many multinationals and U.S. companies. For instance, how do you go about sharing information for new product development if the sales headquarters is in Denver, Colorado, the design engineer's office on Rte. 128 in Massachusetts, and the manufacturing plant in Schaumburg, Illinois? This is not only a problem of physical distance. The psychological resistance of people in these different locations may be an even bigger hurdle, and it must be squarely dealt with by any management that intends to introduce KAIZEN in the way information is gathered, processed, and used.

Systems Improvement

Management should direct its efforts to systems improvement as one of the most important tasks of management-oriented KAIZEN. Systems improvement concerns such crucial areas of management as planning and control, decision-making processes, organization, and information systems. Among the new management concepts that have emerged to meet this need are cross-functional management, policy deployment, and quality deployment. Naturally enough, a "New Seven" group of TQC tools has been used for projects related to systems improvement.

Where management has failed to establish such a system and has instead directed its efforts randomly and in bits and pieces to such areas as suggestions and QC circles, success has often been short-lived. This is why top-management commitment is indispensable when TQC and KAIZEN are introduced.

KAIZEN covers the total spectrum of business, starting with the way the worker works in the shop, moving on to improvements in the machinery and facilities, and finally effecting improvements in systems and procedures. KAIZEN is ubiquitous, and that is why many top Japanese executives believe that KAIZEN is 50 percent of management's job.

Group-Oriented KAIZEN

KAIZEN in group work, as a permanent approach, is represented by QC circles, JK groups, and other small-group activities, that use various statistical tools to solve problems. The permanent approach also calls for the full PDCA cycle and demands that team members not only identify problem areas but also identify the causes, analyze them, implement and test new countermeasures, and establish new standards and/or procedures.

In the permanent approach, the members go through the problem-solving and decision-making processes. This is why the PDCA cycle

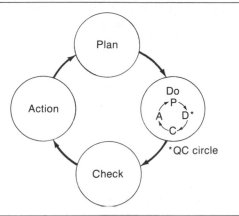

FIGURE 4.2   *PDCA within the PDCA Cycle*

is said to have its own PDCA cycle at the "Do" stage (see Figure 4.2). The activities of QC circles and other groups are confined to problems arising from their own workshop, but morale is improved through KAIZEN activities as everybody masters the art of solving immediate problems.

When group work is the temporary approach, the suggestions are provided by ad hoc groups of employees formed to solve particular tasks. While the members of these ad hoc groups are often trained in the use of statistical and analytical tools, the groups disband when their target is achieved.

In both individual-oriented KAIZEN and group-oriented KAIZEN, it is essential that management properly understand the workers' role in KAIZEN and use every opportunity to support it. In this context, Naomi Yamaki, president of Mitsubishi Space Software, says:

> Today's workers do not seem to be satisfied with conventional repetitive jobs regardless of the monetary compensations they receive. They want their jobs to involve creative areas such as thinking and deciding for themselves how the work should be done.
>
> It is therefore important that management be able to redesign workers' jobs so that workers can feel that their work is worthwhile. People need to work with their minds as well as with their bodies.
>
> Such job design means that it is necessary to revise conventional thinking on the functions of manager and worker. Under the conventional distinction, managers are supposed to plan, administer,

and control, and workers are simply supposed to do. This has meant the manager planned what was to be done and how and gave the workers detailed direction in their work. In turn, workers were expected to mindlessly do exactly as they were told.

However, today's workers want to work with both their minds and their bodies, using their mental as well as their physical capabilities. As a result, under the revised manager–worker distinction, the worker is supposed to plan, do, and control, and management is charged with motivating workers for higher productivity. Management's function thus becomes that of planning, leading, and controlling, and a manager is responsible for leading and supporting his workers.

The basic philosophy behind the new job design is to delegate as much planning and control to workers as possible, thus motivating them to higher productivity and higher quality.

The typical Japanese plant has a space reserved in the corner of every workshop for publicizing activities going on in the workplace, such as the current level of suggestions and recent achievements by small groups. Sometimes, tools that have been improved as a result of workers' suggestions are displayed so that workers in other work areas can adopt the same improvement ideas.

At Mitsubishi Electric, these corners are called KAIZEN Corners, and various tools and machines are placed there for workers to use in implementing improvements generated by either individuals or small groups.

There are several "KAIZEN Men" in each Mitsubishi Electric plant. These are veteran blue-collar workers who have been temporarily released from their routine duties and told to roam around the plant looking for opportunities for improvement. The KAIZEN-Man assignment is rotated among veteran blue-collar workers every six months or so.

Because small-group activities, including QC circles, have played such a vital role in the KAIZEN strategy in Japan, small-group activities and their implications for management will be explained in the following sections.

Small-Group Activities

Small-group activities may be defined as informal, voluntary small groups organized within the company to carry out specific tasks in the workshop. These small-group activities take many forms, depending on their aims: big-brother groups, big-sister groups, QC circles, ZD movements, no-error movements, level-up movements, JK, mini think tanks, suggestion groups, safety groups, workshop involvement movements, productivity committees, management-by-objectives groups, and workshop talk groups. These small groups were often initially formed for the purpose of stimulating cross-development among its members.

Two topics have become the rage in Japan's business community. One is TQC, and the other is small-group activities. These subjects have become so popular among Japanese businessmen that it is said that any book with either of these words in its title is guaranteed to sell at least 5,000 copies. Displays of the latest books on these subjects can be found in virtually any bookstore.

During the last 30 years, Japanese companies have worked feverishly to upgrade quality. They have employed virtually every means available, such as statistical tools, TQC, and quality circles. Japanese businessmen are firmly convinced that the mission of the company is first and foremost to produce quality products that satisfy market requirements.

QC circles, for instance, were started when a new magazine on quality control was established in 1962, enabling foremen and workers to study together and acquire up-to-date knowledge and techniques on quality control. While QC circles began as study groups, they later shifted their emphasis to problem solving in the workshop, using the techniques acquired through earlier study. Departing from the traditional inspection-oriented quality control, Japanese management moved to develop quality control in the areas of production processes and new-product development. The concept has now come to include suppliers and subcontractors. While quality control was initially oriented toward production and engineering processes, an increasing number of companies are directing their efforts at other areas, such as office work, sales, and services.

Probably one of the greatest discoveries made by Japanese managers over the past 30 years is that quality control pays. They have found that it not only improves quality but also increases productivity and lowers costs. And because of the improved quality the products command premium prices. In short, trying to maximize customer satisfaction by improving product quality automatically leads to improved productivity and higher corporate performance. No wonder Japanese management worships at the TQC altar. Today, quality control is not just another engineering and production technique. It has taken the form of a comprehensive management tool involving the whole company, from top management down to rank-and-file workers.

While management's primary concern may be productivity, quality is a concern common to both labor and management. When management asks labor to increase productivity, labor's response is, "Why? Doesn't that just mean we have to work harder? What's in it for us?" However, nobody can object when management asks for labor's cooperation by saying, "Let's talk about quality." After all, quality is the only way to stay competitive and serve the customer. Japanese management has found that efforts to improve quality automatically lead to improved productivity. Without this foundation of superior quality control, it would have been impossible to introduce revolutionary new production concepts such as Toyota's *kamban* production system.

There are two dimensions in industrial relations: (1) confrontation versus cooperation and (2) formal versus informal organization. This is illustrated in Figure 4.3. Small-group activities represent a nonconfrontational, informal way of solving problems and introducing improvements. By contrast, Western-style collective bargaining is confrontational and formal.

The advantages of small-group activities became apparent soon after their initiation:

1. Setting group objectives and working for their attainment strengthens the sense of teamwork

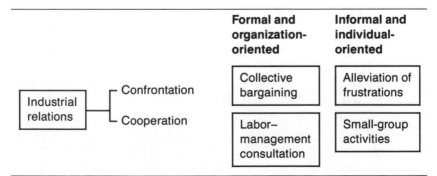

FIGURE 4.3 *Formal and Informal Structures for Corporate Progress*

2. Group members share and coordinate their respective roles better

3. Communication between labor and management, as well as between workers of different ages, is improved

4. Morale is greatly improved

5. Workers acquire new skills and knowledge and develop more cooperative attitudes

6. The group is self-sustaining and solves problems that would otherwise be left to management

7. Labor–management relations are greatly improved

Although small-group activities began as informal, voluntary organizations, they have now come to occupy a respected and legitimate position in the eyes of management and the Japanese company as a whole.

Small-Group Activities: QC Circles

The 19th Annual Conference of QC Circle Leaders was held in Tokyo in November 1980. There were 124 reports on the QC-circle activities at various companies submitted during the three-day conference.

Most reports were related to production. For example, a leader from Kobayashi Kose spoke on how a QC circle dealt with the task of removing pits on the surface of lipstick. But there were also reports involving improvements in office work. For instance, Sanwa Bank, one of Japan's largest banks, has 2,400 QC circles involving 13,000 employees. Since the circles were started in 1977, they have dealt with 10,000 subjects. Being in banking, they define quality as the quality of service and the degree of customer satisfaction. With this as their definition, they are striving to improve the quality of their office work.

Among the subjects they are working on at Sanwa Bank are how to reduce erroneous listings, how to route mail more efficiently, how to remember customers' names, how to save energy, how to save stationery, how to reduce overtime work, how to increase the frequency of customer visits, how to gain new accounts, and how to improve employees' familiarity with the many services the bank provides. All these subjects are being dealt with by the bank's ordinary employees, such as tellers and clerks.

The circle leader from the Kanzanji Royal Hotel, a typical hot-springs inn, explained how the hotel's QC circle approached the problem of how to serve shrimp tempura hot to 500 guests. The QC circle was so successful that hot shrimp tempura has become one of the hotel's main attractions. (Since food has to be prepared hours ahead of time for big groups, it is common for the major resort hotels to serve it cold.)

Sachiko Kamata of Bridgestone Tire reported on how she had formed a "Queen Bee Circle" with four other draftswomen (the youngest one 19 years old) in the engineering department to improve the drafting procedures for tire-making jigs and tools. Holding two-hour meetings every week to obtain and analyze the relevant information, they found that there was much redundancy in their drafting work and that the problem could be solved by resorting to a special application of photocopying machines. "As a result of the new procedure," she said, "we have been able to reduce drafting time by 60 percent. Whereas we used to have an average of two hours of overtime every day, we have been able to eliminate overtime work."

Such tasks as improving lipstick consistency, serving tempura hot, and reducing drafting time are regarded as management tasks in the West and are assigned to production engineers or industrial engineers. However, the outstanding feature of all these reports was that the subjects were thought of and dealt with by workers on their own initiative, albeit with management's blessing, and that the workers arrived at successful solutions yielding improved productivity and quality control.

According to JUSE (The Union of Japanese Scientists and Engineers), an organization coordinating the nationwide QC-circle movement and assisting in its expansion, there are more than 170,000 QC circles officially registered with JUSE and probably twice that many operating independently of JUSE. Since the typical circle has six to ten members, it is estimated that there are at least 3 million workers in Japan directly involved in some kind of official QC-circle activity.

There are eight regional QC-circle chapters in Japan, each of which holds regional meetings where circle leaders report and share their experiences. About 100 such regional meetings are held each year. In addition, there are half a dozen nationwide meetings of various sorts held annually, such as the Annual Conference of QC Circle Leaders.

Thus the QC-circle activities are interconnected in a nationwide network, and QC-circle members have easy access to what other people are doing in other industries. There are more than 1,000 volunteer QC leaders in Japan cooperating in organizing these local and national meetings to promote the flow of information among members.

Today, the QC-circle movement has even been expanded to include employees at subcontractors. This was done in order to solve problems common to the subcontracting company and the subcontractors. Where many housewives are employed part-time, the circles often invite these part-timers to join in working out solutions to problems that affect them. Probably more than half the companies in Japan have introduced QC-circle activities.

QC circles were started in 1962 under JUSE auspices in order to build cheerful and meaningful places of work. QC circles were not formed for the purpose of improving productivity and quality control. On the contrary, the circles were formed by the employees, of their own volition, to make their work more meaningful and worthwhile. When such a group is formed, it takes up an issue immediately at hand, such as how to organize work and maintain safety, and gradually goes on to more challenging tasks. Improved productivity and quality are only two measures of the success of its efforts.

Since QC-circle activities are voluntary, management does not force them on employees. The circles may meet either during regular work hours or after work. When they meet after work, management may or may not pay overtime. In some cases, management allows participants free meals in the company cafeteria.

After QC-circle activities are well under way, management may assist circle members by providing direction and may express its appreciation when the circles' activities bear fruit. In fact, many companies give citations or other awards to QC circles that have made outstanding contributions to the company.

According to the "General Principles of the QC Circle" published by JUSE, the QC circle is defined as a small group that voluntarily performs quality control activities within the shop where its members work, the small group carrying out its work continuously as part of a company-wide program of quality control, self-development, mutual development, and flow-control and improvement within the workshop. By engaging in QC-circle activities, the circle members gain valuable experience in communicating with colleagues, working together to solve problems, and sharing their findings not only among themselves but with other circles at other companies.

**SMALL-GROUP ACTIVITIES
AT KOMATSU**

I recently received a letter from an American business administration student in which he wrote, "Managers in the United States do not seem willing to accept the fact that their employees can introduce productive ideas." This prompted me to think about the manager's role. In the classical definition, the manager's job is to see that a given job gets done. He is supposed to plan, make decisions, tell the workers what to do, and see that they do it. However, as the dimensions of business have become more complex, managers have begun to find that they do not always have the facts and figures necessary to do this planning, instruction, and supervision at the operational level.

Since it is the workers who actually perform the day-to-day operations, they are much closer to these problems and are often better able to find a solution than is the manager. Worker solutions can also have the side effect of enhancing morale. However, management must be receptive to such worker solutions.

Getting productive ideas from employees is not so much a matter of having creative employees as it is one of having supportive management. If a manager cannot get the workers to introduce productive ideas, most likely *he* is the problem, not the workers.

One of the primary features of the Japanese QC movement is that it has involved employees at all levels. Recalling how QC activities were started at Komatsu Ltd., Jisaku Akatsu, general manager of the overseas division, says, "I think we succeeded in introducing the QC movement at Komatsu because it was started at a time when we all recognized that the company was facing a crisis." Komatsu's QC movement was started in 1961 in the wake of Caterpillar's announcement that it was forming a joint venture with Mitsubishi Heavy Industries, Ltd., in Japan. At the time, Komatsu was about one-tenth the size of Caterpillar in terms of annual turnover, and everyone realized that the company could not possibly survive unless its products were competitive in performance and price with those of Caterpillar. To achieve this goal, Komatsu started its Maru-A campaign to be competitive, and TQC was introduced as the heart of the Maru-A campaign.

TQC hinges first of all on involving all employees in QC practices. At Komatsu, five full-time QC instructors report to the QC manager. During the early years, the Komatsu QC staff used to attend JUSE-sponsored QC training seminars. Now, however, these in-house instructors are fully qualified to conduct all QC courses for employees.

(Komatsu—continued)

Everyone at Komatsu must take QC courses. For instance, board members must attend a 16-hour director's course. Department and section managers must take 32-hour courses. New employees must take an 8-hour introductory course. And selected personnel from every technical and clerial work unit must attend basic courses that last from 10 to 20 days. This education is considered essential to the smooth functioning of the QC circles.

Although Komatsu management estimates that QC circles represent only about one-tenth of the entire TQC effort, QC circles have been an effective means of encouraging all employees to come up with productive ideas. Komatsu has a QC staff assisting QC circles at every work unit. All told, there are 300 QC staff people, or one of every 10 in direct labor. They consult, advise, distribute textbooks, and listen to what the workers have to say.

The first QC circle was started at Komatsu in 1963. Today, Komatsu has more than 800 QC circles in manufacturing and 350 in sales and service. Participation is 95 percent in manufacturing and 89 percent in sales and service. Each circle provided an average of 4.2 new ideas per year.

After TQC was well established within the company, Komatsu set out to extend its efforts both vertically and horizontally. Vertically, TQC was extended to Komatsu's subsidiaries, affiliates, and subcontractors, and horizontally, to the overseas network of dealers and manufacturing plants in Brazil and Mexico. Komatsu's QC manager spends more than half his time visiting overseas plants and dealers and helping them introduce TQC. Not unreasonably, Komatsu finds that the best way to get overseas affiliates and dealers to start QC is to convince top management that QC pays financially.

When Komatsu chairman Ryoichi Kawai visited China in 1977, he stressed the importance of TQC to high-ranking Chinese government officials. As a result, a model plant was started in Peking under the guidance of Komatsu engineers. The results have been so encouraging that Deng Xiaoping decided to spread TQC throughout the country, and it is reported that more than 100,000 copies of Komatsu's QC manuals are now in use in China. Quite aside from its benefits for Chinese industry, this can only enhance Komatsu's image in China.

Drawing on the homogeneity of the Japanese people and the affinity between management and labor in Japan, Komatsu has found it possible, although not always easy, to get lower-level workers to participate in QC circles. Komatsu has had somewhat different experiences in other countries, however. For instance, it has found that it is better in many cases overseas to start the QC efforts with middle- and lower-level managers before involving workers. Although workers in Southeast Asia and the Middle East do accept the concept of QC circles fairly positively, it is more difficult to get managers involved in the United States and other

(Komatsu — continued)

industrialized countries, since they often fail to recognize QC as a new management philosophy and assume that it is a technique they already know. Whereas Japanese workers are willing to learn and are interested in acquiring new knowledge and skills, workers elsewhere tend to be more interested in seeing their efforts bear fruit. Other factors that must be considered overseas are the higher worker turnover and the desire for material recognition for improved productivity.

Workers in other countries, however, also find satisfaction in being given a chance to participate and seeing their suggestions put into practice. Some workers have even commented that they look forward to coming to work every day now that they are more deeply involved in their work.

All Komatsu board members attend the annual QC meeting where circle leaders report on their work and compete for prizes. Members from affiliated companies and subcontractors are also invited to report on their progress. Part-time workers at the plants, mostly housewives, often join QC circles, and these women are also given a chance to report at the annual meeting.

Says Akatsu, "QC has . . . become every worker's cause, and we are all searching for new ideas and better ways to satisfy market requirements."

In this age of uncertainty, it seems to me that every company should consider itself at a critical crossroads, and it is hard to see how any manager can be indifferent to the possibilities of this new experiment in management. ∎

SMALL-GROUP ACTIVITIES AT NISSAN CHEMICAL

Can you think of an investment opportunity that will yield an annual ROI of 500 percent? And one in which you do not have to start a new business or introduce a new product? Managers at Nissan Chemical have apparently found just such an investment: small-group activities. Since 1978 they have been practicing a company-wide suggestion system based on small groups, and their aggregate investment of ¥200 million has yielded cost savings of ¥1 billion.

Nissan Chemical employs 2,550 people and manufactures fertilizers, agricultural and industrial pharmaceuticals, and other chemical products. It is a typical chemical company, with heavy investment in plant and equipment. Operators in the plant work on three shifts and are used to working in small groups.

Faced with declining profits in 1977, the company's management decided to "activate" its work force and improve productivity with the

(Nissan Chemical—continued)

introduction of a suggestion system. Within the first six months, the movement produced more than 3,000 ideas from workers. However, most of these ideas were individuals' notions and hints lacking factual substantiation.

As a result, management started a company-wide campaign called the "Ai" movement in 1978. Ai stands for *all* members' *ideas,* but it also means "love" in Japanese and sounds like the English words "eye" and "I." The campaign is intended to encourage everyone to provide ideas in the spirit of brotherly love, meaning that it is a movement by and for the workers themselves, and that they must be alert to new opportunities for exercising this spirit.

In formulating this campaign, management decided that the workers' suggestions ought to be related to their own jobs. Also, instead of being just an idea, each suggestion must include a concrete proposal that can be implemented. Another major feature of the Ai movement is that it is based on group activities. Workers in the same workshop form Ai groups and submit specific suggestions to management that relate to their work and can be applied in the workshop.

The Ai movement's central committee meets at the company's head office and is chaired by the managing director in charge of personnel. The general secretariat for the central committee is placed within the personnel department at the head office. Plant committees are organized at the plants and chaired by the plant managers, and each plant's personnel section serves as secretariat for its committee. Furthermore, each section in the plant has a section committee headed by a section chief.

The central committee promotes company-wide activities, issues the *Ai News,* conducts annual awards ceremonies, and sponsors special seminars for Ai group leaders. The plant-level committees publish their own *Plant Ai News,* solicit suggestions, give out awards, conduct various plant-level seminars, and provide guidance to the various sections. The section-level committees receive and review suggestions and provide assistance to all Ai groups. An *Ai Notebook* is provided in each workshop so that workers can write down any ideas and suggestions they may have while they work.

Generally, each Ai group holds two meetings per week. The leader of the group usually is the most senior member. Engineers at the plant provide consultation whenever the group needs technical advice.

The typical group of five or six members produces a yearly average of three suggestions that are actually implemented at the shop. In some cases, it may take as much as one year to complete a single project. Each formal suggestion must include not only supporting data and statistics but also an implementation plan, complete with cost estimates as well as estimates of the expected productivity improvement and cost savings.

(Nissan Chemical — continued)

The Ai movement has brought about, for one thing, a remarkable improvement in workers' morale. Workers at the plant used to be generally apathetic if not antagonistic, and they seldom tried to improve upon their instructions. At the regular meetings with their section managers, they would often file complaints and submit long lists of requests for improvements to be made by management, thus putting the manager on the defensive. The manager, in turn, always had to explain why certain things could not be done because of budget restraints. Since the Ai movement was started, group activities have nourished a joint commitment among all members.

Before such group activities were started, workers usually passed their break time socializing. Now they are spending much of this time seriously talking about how improvements can be made. Engineers are usually reluctant to touch the machines or make changes, because they do not have a first-hand feel for them. But blue-collar workers who use the machines day in and day out can often make fruitful suggestions that really work. The Ai movement has drastically reduced the number of "passive bystanders" and "armchair critics" in the workshop.

Says Shiro Kashiwagi, deputy personnel manager:

> These workers are, in fact, rewriting the manuals. They constantly come up with new suggestions, and their proposals often lead to a new and different way of using the machines. When suggestions work in one plant, they are adopted in other plants as well. In effect, working procedures and manuals are often rewritten with the help of workers' suggestions.
>
> Engineers do not always know what is really going on in the workshop. The manuals in use are often outdated or at least not practical enough from the workers' standpoint. Even if the manuals are up to date, the workers often resent having to follow them. However, after they have taken the initiative in rewriting the manuals and making them their own, they are happy to follow them.

Special three-day training sessions for group leaders and facilitators are held several times a year. All participants lodge together and talk about such things as how to define themes and how to encourage less active members to participate. In general, they share their personal experiences. The major benefit is that they realize they are all colleagues tackling common objectives and that they are not alone in having problems in the workshop. Managers often join them for such sessions.

Nissan Chemical has been seriously affected by the rising costs of energy and materials. Steam, electricity, and heavy oil have become crucial cost items. As a result of the small-group activities, workers have become profoundly cost-conscious. "Having been heavily involved in various cost-reduction programs," says Kashiwagi, "every worker in the workshop knows the cost of heavy oil, electricity, and water."

(Nissan Chemical—continued)

To cite an example of one such program, there are several thousand high-voltage motors in use at the plant, and the need to maintain insulation resistance meant that a low-level current had to be kept on even when these motors were not in use. Nobody cared about the cost until one Ai group decided to study this problem in search of ways to slow the rapidly rising electricity costs.

The group collected data for one year, taking into consideration all the factors affecting the motors, including insulation, resistance, humidity, and even the weather. After analyzing the data, the group came to the conclusion that the motors would still maintain the necessary level of insulation resistance with an intermittent current. As a result of this discovery, the plant has been able to save ¥3.8 million (U.S. $15,200) a year on electricity. Although the new system required additional work and more frequent inspections by the workers, they are still happy with the change, since it was the result of their own suggestions. As I noted in Chapter 1 when relating the story of the tea saved at lunch time, these QC activities give management a chance to show its appreciation for the spirit as well as the results.

Suggestions are submitted on a form that includes space for an outline, the expected benefits of the improvement, and the estimated cost of implementation. The report attached to the suggestion is sometimes 100 pages long. Some of these suggestions are so fundamental that they should have been thought of by the engineering staff at the head office.

These suggestions are reviewed and appraised according to such factors as their effects, originality, and efforts required. The suggestions implemented fall into three general categories: (1) savings in energy and resources (48 percent), (2) improvement in work procedures and work efficiency (25 percent), and (3) savings in repair and expenses (27 percent).

During its first three years (1978–1980), the Ai movement produced 928 suggestions and yielded total savings of ¥600 million (U.S. $2.4 million). The cost of supporting this campaign has been ¥125 million (U.S. $500,000). In 1981, 987 suggestions were implemented, leading to ¥630 million (U.S. $2.5 million) in cost savings. The cost of the movement in the same year was ¥160 million (U.S. $640,000), including the cost of making improvements based on suggestions. Management's target for 1982 is for savings of ¥1 billion (U.S. $4 million) with an investment of ¥200 million (U.S. $800,000) in the Ai movement. ∎

SMALL-GROUP ACTIVITIES: AD-HOC CAMPAIGNS AT HITACHI

Hitachi Denshi, one of the leading members of the Hitachi group, manufactures such products as video and TV cameras, broadcasting

(Hitachi — continued)

systems, and transmitting and relaying equipment. This company, which employs 1,580 people, has a unique company-wide movement called "Challenge the Top." The movement started in 1979 as a means of activating the organization and improving productivity.

The Challenge-the-Top movement has three pillars: small-group activities, a suggestion system, and in-house campaigns. The more than 100 small groups that have been formed in the company are active in quality control and human resource development, and the company's suggestion system brought forth an average of 22 suggestions per employee in 1980.

In-house campaign activities are conducted in order to grasp the "mood" of the employees and generate better communication and morale. Management feels that it is important that the campaigns be carried out continuously to maintain worker morale and interest. Shigetsugu Yasumoto, the movement's chief secretary, holds monthly meetings with section managers from the major departments in order to discuss the campaign issues.

These campaigns are listed within four broad categories:

1. Creating a pleasant workshop
2. Improving health
3. Savings and cost reduction
4. Finding breakthroughs on existing problems

Unlike small-group activities, which are conducted within separate groups, the Challenge-the-Top campaign activities are open to all employees who wish to participate. Once the subject of the campaign has been determined by the campaign secretariat, it is announced throughout the company at regular weekly meetings. In addition, campaign bulletins are posted on the walls and handouts distributed at the gate. Sometimes, the campaign managers personally give handouts to incoming workers at the gate, standing right alongside union activists who are handing out union flyers.

More than 50 campaigns, covering a wide range of issues, have been carried out since the campaign idea was first started in 1979, and there are usually more than two campaigns per month. The summaries that follow are typical.

1. There are more than 2,000 fluorescent lights in the plant. Each wall switch turns on several lights, yet often only one or two lights are needed. A campaign to install a switch-cord on every light was started to cut down on this waste of electricity. After the switch-cords were installed, members of the campaign formed two-man patrols for the lunch break. Workers were surprised and

(Hitachi—continued)

amused to see the patrolmen wearing sashes that carried slogans urging them to switch off unneeded lights. After repeated patrolling and posting reminders where lights were not turned off, the workers actually became more conservation-minded. As a result of this campaign, some shops were able to bring their electricity consumption down by 30 percent or more.

2. A campaign was started to improve the workers' skill in writing Chinese characters. (In Japan, both Chinese characters and phonetic alphabets are used.) Questions about Chinese characters were posted in "wall bulletins," with the answers covered with a piece of paper that could be lifted up. This quiz proved to be a favorite off-hours pastime for workers.

    Later, many employees willingly accepted the challenge of answering 250 questions about Chinese characters on a special 45-minute test offered to all interested employees. Some of the more amusing incorrect answers were later displayed in the wall bulletin. For instance, there is a Japanese expression "as small as a cat's forehead *(hitai)*," but one worker wrote it "as small as a cat's dead body *(shitai)*."

    At the end of this campaign, the secretariat made arrangements for interested employees to buy dictionaries at a discount, and 648 orders were received (at a factory employing 1,580).

3. Management decided to stretch the budget by cutting down on new stationery orders. A campaign was started to collect unused stationery and recycle it to those in need. More than 3,000 items were collected, among them pencils, letterhead paper, envelopes, file folders, and erasers, with a total worth of ¥100,000. Some managers were pleased with this result, while others were somewhat annoyed to see that so much stationery had been available in the plant to begin with. Yet everyone was happy to see that the campaign got a lot of people to clean out their desks.

4. A campaign was started to get employees to participate in a 43-km walkathon. This campaign was a success, and the campaign secretariat went on to organize a "moonlight hike" one Friday night under a full moon. More than 20 employees came out to walk all night long in the nearby mountains. The hike turned out to be very effective in enhancing group solidarity and helping the members to plan ahead together.

5. Another successful campaign is the garage sale held every summer at the plant. Employees are urged to bring unneeded articles to be put on sale at the plant gate during the plant's summertime *o-bon* dance festival, which is open to the local community. The money from these sales is then donated to local welfare organizations.

(Hitachi — continued)

These campaigns have been rewarded with letters of acknowledgment and other citations, which are posted on company walls.

6. Two of the most effective communication media for campaign activities have been posters and wall newspapers. Various timely subjects of interest are displayed, such as the latest public opinion polls, government statistics, and technical developments explained in layman's language. Some subjects, such as the Chinese character quiz, are run in serials, and cartoons, caricatures, and other illustrations are included to make the papers more entertaining.

7. In one campaign, it was suggested that writing documents succinctly enough to fit on a single piece of paper would save time for both writers and readers, and would also save paper and storage space. The campaign leaders prepared a manual to help workers improve their writing skills. As a result of this campaign, "one-page memo" consciousness has been instilled in every worker.

Campaign leader Shigetsugu Yasumoto says that a successful campaign must have the following qualities:

- Information must be provided regularly through meetings, bulletins, leaflets, and posters. Campaign news must be carried regularly in the company bulletin. The campaign leaders also need to publicize their own activities in a separate news sheet.

- Results of surveys and other campaign activities must be reported immediately. Use lots of photos to make them more interesting.

- The campaign must be carried out in an amusing and pleasant manner. Use cartoons, caricatures, and other illustrations as much as possible.

- Current topics must be included. This means the campaign leaders must always keep current with the news stories, advertisements, and editorials that appear in the mass media. ■

Individual-Oriented KAIZEN

As Figure 4.1 indicates, the third level is individual-oriented KAIZEN, which is manifested in the form of suggestions. The suggestion system is a vehicle for carrying out individual-oriented KAIZEN and to carry out the maxim that one should work smarter, if not harder.

Individual-oriented improvement has almost infinite opportunity. For instance, in offices using party-line telephones, a worker might suggest coloring all the telephones with the same number the same color for convenience. At Canon, a worker who had been using rather expensive cleaning papers to clean lenses found that the cotton swabs sold at the supermarket could do a cheaper and better job. Many of the fool-proofing devices on machines are installed as a result of workers' suggestions. At Hitachi's Tochigi plant, a metal plate with the worker's name and the date of his suggestion is attached to a fool-proofed machine to record the worker's contribution for posterity.

KAIZEN's starting point is for the worker to adopt a positive attitude toward changing and improving the way he works. If a worker who has been doing a job seated at a machine changes his behavior and stands at his machine, it is an improvement, since he gains flexibility and can handle more than one machine.

When Taiichi Ohno, the executive who initiated *kamban* and "just-in-time" at Toyota, became advisor to Toyoda Shokki (a manufacturer of automotive fabrics), he found that the women were doing their jobs seated at their sewing machines. He immediately inaugurated an improvement project and devised special features for each sewing machine so that it would stop automatically as soon as the operation was completed.

Then a cycle was established for each worker so that she could handle several sewing machines in one cycle. This meant the workers' behavior had to be changed so that they stood at their machines and moved from one machine to the next with the work flow. Today, one worker takes care of a dozen sewing machines, walking from one machine to the next, clad in a sporty jogging suit. At Toyota-group companies, one worker may be handling up to 80 different machines in a cycle. Such multiple job assignments are possible because management has succeeded in changing workers' behavior.

Individual-oriented KAIZEN is often regarded as a morale booster, and management does not always ask for immediate economic payback on each suggestion. Management attention and responsiveness are essential if workers are to become "thinking workers" always looking for better ways to do their work.

Suggestion Systems

The suggestion system is an integral part of individual-oriented KAIZEN. Top management must implement a well-designed plan to assure that the suggestion system is dynamic.

It is well known that the initial concepts of statistical quality control and its managerial implications were brought to Japan by such pioneers as Deming and Juran in the postwar years. Less well known is the fact that the suggestion system was brought to Japan about the same time by TWI (Training Within Industries) and the U.S. Air Force. In addition, many Japanese executives who visited the United States right after the war learned about the suggestion system and started it at their companies.

The American-style suggestion system soon gave way to a Japanese-style system. Whereas the American style stressed the suggestion's economic benefits and provided financial incentives, the Japanese style stressed the morale-boosting benefits of positive employee participation. Over the years, the Japanese system has evolved into two segments: individual suggestions and group suggestions, including those generated by QC circles, JK (Jishu Kanri or voluntary management) groups, ZD (Zero Defect) groups, and other group-based activities.

Suggestion systems are currently in operation at most large manufacturing companies and about half of the small and medium-size companies. According to the Japan Human Relations Association, the main subjects for suggestions in Japanese companies' suggestion systems are (in order):

Improvements in one's own work

Savings in energy, material, and other resources

Improvements in the working environment

Improvements in machines and processes

Improvements in jigs and tools

Improvements in office work

Improvements in product quality

Ideas for new products

Customer services and customer relations

Others

Matsushita topped the list of all Japanese companies in number of suggestions with over 6 million suggestions in 1985. The most suggestions made at one company in one year by an individual was 16,821.

Until being dethroned by Matsushita in 1985, Hitachi had been number one for five consecutive years, and it was second in 1985 with 4.6 million suggestions. Far from being dismayed at coming in second, Hitachi says this is because it has shifted its emphasis from number of suggestions to quality of suggestions.

Kenjiro Yamada, managing director of the Japan Human Relations Association, says that the suggestion system should go through three stages. In the first stage, management should make every effort to help the workers provide suggestions, no matter how primitive, for the betterment of the worker's job and the workshop. This will help the workers look at the way they are doing their jobs. In the second stage, management should stress employee education so that employees can provide better suggestions. In order for the workers to provide better suggestions, they should be equipped to analyze problems and the environment. This requires education. Only in the third stage, after the workers are both interested and educated, should management be concerned with the economic impact of the suggestions.

This means that management must think of the suggestion system in terms of a five- to ten-year span. Yamada points out that the difficulties most Western companies encounter stem from the fact that they usually try to skip stages one and two and move straight to the third stage.

According to Yamada, the average number of suggestions per employee hovered around five per year until the mid-1950s. Since then, the number of suggestions has gradually increased. Today the average in the private sector has risen to 19 suggestions per employee per year. This increase in the number of suggestions has been the result of two major developments. First, the suggestion scheme was combined with small-group activities. Second, first-line supervisors were authorized to review and implement workers' suggestions.

Today, most of the suggestions that have economic impact come from groups, while individual-based suggestions serve as morale boosters and educational experiences.

Yamada believes that the number of suggestions is higher where the working instructions are rigidly fixed and where the workers are not stretched to their full capability by the work. In other words, the suggestions serve to fill the gap between the workers' capabilities and the job. Suggestions therefore are a sign that the worker has more skill than the job calls for.

In addition to making employees KAIZEN-conscious, suggestion systems provide an opportunity for the workers to speak out with their supervisors as well as among themselves. At the same time, they provide an opportunity for management to help the workers deal with problems. Thus suggestions are a valuable opportunity for two-way communication in the workshop as well as for worker self-development.

Generally speaking, Japanese managers have more leeway in implementing employee suggestions than their Western counterparts do. Japanese managers are willing to go along with a change if it contributes to any one of the following goals:

Making the job easier
Removing drudgery from the job
Removing nuisance from the job
Making the job safer
Making the job more productive
Improving product quality
Saving time and cost

This is in sharp contrast to the Western manager's almost exclusive concern with the cost of the change and its economic payback.

THE CASE OF AISIN-WARNER

"Positive participation in the suggestion scheme," says Aisin-Warner managing director Haruki Sugihara, "makes each worker problem-conscious and helps him do a better job." According to Sugihara, management should encourage participation by making workers feel free to make all sorts of suggestions that do not cost much to implement. Since most workers are not used to writing down their ideas, they need to be encouraged and trained to put down their ideas on a piece of paper (suggestion form) until it becomes habit. At Aisin-Warner (a manufacturer of automatic transmissions, torque converters, and overdrive systems), the average number of suggestions per worker was 127 in 1982. On a company-wide basis, this means there were 223,986 suggestions. Of these, 99 percent were actually implemented in the workplace. This is well above the national average of 76 percent. In 1982, the suggestions submitted by Aisin-Warner employees concerned:

Reduction in manhours	39.0%
Quality improvement	10.6

(Aisin-Warner—continued)

Safety	10.5
Facility improvement and maintenance	8.4
Environment and hygiene	7.6
Saving materials	3.9
Improving office work	1.7
Others	18.6

When a worker's suggestion cannot be implemented, management promptly explains why. The major categories of "suggestions" that are not considered within the suggestion system framework are grievances or demands directed to management, repetition of subjects that have already been settled or implemented in the workplace, and statements of well-known facts, practices, axioms, and platitudes. Management regards it as the foreman's responsibility to encourage workers to provide suggestions based on the system designed by management. This responsibility then goes up the line to the foreman's supervisor (section chief) and so on. Aisin-Warner management realizes that the system cannot work effectively unless the foreman is committed to helping and motivating the people who work under him. Accordingly, each foreman is held accountable for the number of suggestions his people generate. There is even competition for the most suggestions, and foremen often provide personal consultation for workers with low participation rates.

Management encourages both individual and group suggestions, and individuals account for over half of all suggestions at Aisin-Warner today. Whenever a worker has a suggestion, he writes it down on a form provided at the workplace and drops it in a box. There is no need to submit it to his foreman in person.

Many suggestions go through both primary and secondary reviews on the way to becoming adopted or not. The primary review is conducted by a group of foremen and staff people in the workplace, and the secondary review by a group of department and section managers.

As the number of suggestions soared, management found it increasingly difficult to review them, make decisions on them, and notify each individual promptly. Knowing that prompt attention is essential in keeping employees' interest in the suggestion system, Aisin-Warner moved to computer processing in 1978 when manual processing started taking two or three months.

When a suggestion is provided, it immediately goes through the primary review. For suggestions assessed as worth less than ¥3,000 (approximately U.S. $12), the person who submitted it receives an award within a week after its submission. If a suggestion is assessed as worth more than ¥3,000, it goes to a secondary review, and recognition is provided within a month after the suggestion's submission. All suggestions are processed by computer to calculate award payment. Figure 4.4 shows the suggestion form used at Aisin-Warner.

Individual's name or QC circle's name:	Position: Blue collar, clerical, bench leader, supervisor, foreman or above	Subject of suggestion:

Schematic drawing (before):

Schematic drawing (after):

Method before improvement:

Method after improvement:

Problem:

Effect:

Appraisal:

Appraisal:	Slight	Somewhat	Considerable	Very much	Major
A. Creativity	0 1	2 4 6	8 10 12	14 16	18 20
B. Originality	0 1	2 4 6	8 10 12	14 16	18 20
C. Adaptability	0 1	2 3	4 5	6 7	8 10
D. Indirect effect	0 1	2 3	4 5	6 7	8 10

Calculation of economic effect:

E. Point: _____

F. Position relevance		Blue collar worker	Clerical	Bench leader	Supervisor or above
Own job site	Large	–	0.5	0.5	0.3
	Medium	1.0	0.8	0.7	0.5
	Small	1.0	0.9	0.9	0.7
Other job site		1.1	1.0	1.0	0.9

Total point: (A + B + C + D + E) × F =

Comment by reviewer:

Signature:

FIGURE 4.4 Aisin-Warner Suggestion Form

(Aisin-Warner—continued)

Date	Coding of work site	Coding of name and QC circle
Classification	1. Executed date 2. Not executed (scheduled date)	
Aim of suggestion	1. Reduction in manhours 2. Saving material 3. Improving quality and performance 4. Improving office work 5. Environmental hygiene 6. Safety 7. Facility maintenance and improvement 8. Others	
Self evaluation by individual: ¥ ________		

Total point	Award	Annual economic effect
	¥	¥
Result of review: 1. Adopted 2. Considered 3. Abstained 4. Rejected		
Evaluation: 1. President Award 2. Committee Chairman Award 3. Idea Award 4. A Award 5. B Award 6. C Award		

FIGURE 4.4 (continued)

(Aisin-Warner — continued)

Suggestions are evaluated first by assigning points to each suggestion, in line with the following schedule:

Consideration	Score
Creativity or originality	____ out of 20
Effort in trying out a new method	____ out of 20
Adaptability (Is horizontal deployment feasible?)	____ out of 10
Indirect effect (Contribution to quality improvement, safety, etc.)	____ out of 10
Economic effect (Direct contribution to shortening work processes, saving resources, etc.)	____ out of 40
Total score	____ out of 100

Note that both P criteria and R criteria are used for evaluation purposes and that numerical values are assigned to each item, signifying its importance as seen by management.

This score is then multiplied by the position multiple, which ranges from 1.1 to 0.3, as shown on the suggestion form. Awards are then given out. The following table shows the name, score, and award amount for each ranking.

Award Rank Name	Score	Award (¥)	Award ($)
President's Award	Over 56	30,000–300,000	120–1,200
Committee Chairman's Award	36–56	7,000–20,000	28–80
Idea Award	Creativity + Effort = Over 32	Memento worth 5,000	Memento worth 20
Grade A Award	19–35	1,500–5,000	6–20
Grade B Award	7–18	500–1,000	2–4
Grade C Award	1–6	200–300	0.80–1.20

Assuming that the suggestion has been made by a blue-collar worker, that his total score was 40, and that his suggestion had a medium relevance to his own workplace, his score will be multiplied by 1.0. On the other hand, if this same suggestion has been made by a bench leader, the score will be multiplied by 0.7.

(Aisin-Warner—continued)

At Aisin-Warner, the suggestion system has been extended to include the employees' families as well. From time to time, campaigns are conducted to encourage suggestions from family members regarding improvements at home. Many of these suggestions are delightful ideas for making family life more fun. The suggestions recently presented included one by a four-year-old, rewritten by her mother. Management offers token prizes for these family suggestions felt to be especially deserving, and those suggestions are displayed at the company meeting hall, together with employees' suggestions, so that family ideas can be shared.

Another feature of Aisin-Warner's suggestion system is that the suggestions' results are horizontally deployed to other Aisin-group companies supplying products to Toyota Motor. Aisin-group companies regularly publish *Idea* magazine, which reports on the suggestions made at group companies and gives specific examples of improvements and schedules for promotional campaigns. There are also regular liaison meetings to discuss the suggestion system (for mutual enlightenment), and group-sponsored events such as collecting ideas for posters and slogans (to enhance solidarity among employees). ∎

CANON'S SUGGESTION SYSTEM

As shown in the CPS (Canon Production System) structure chart in Appendix G, the suggestion system, along with small group activities, "clean up your workshop" activities, and conventions and reporting meetings, is an integral instrument for achieving CPS goals. Canon's suggestion system is extended to all employees and temporary workers, exclusive of managers. Joint suggestions and group suggestions are also encouraged.

Any suggestion for improving the workplace is welcome, whether the suggestion relates directly to one's own workshop or not. Only the following kinds of suggestions are rejected:

1. Suggestions for new products (Canon has a different suggestion scheme to handle this)
2. Suggestions about personnel administration and working conditions
3. Complaints and grievances
4. Suggestions on things to be done at the superior's order
5. Suggestions that are too vague or impossible to implement
6. Plagiarism

(Canon — continued)

In 1983, Canon employees submitted a total of 390,000 suggestions with an estimated worth of ¥19.3 billion (U.S. $84 million). Total expenditures on the suggestion system were ¥250 million (U.S. $1.08 million), meaning that the payback was 77-fold. The anticipated total CPS saving was ¥24 billion (U.S. $100 million) in 1983. However, it should be noted that there is some overlap between the effects of the suggestions and CPS savings, since these two systems represent different ways of looking at the savings achieved.

The employee writes down his suggestion on the suggestion form (see Figure 4.5), which has space for up to five suggestions. This simple suggestion form was adopted in 1978 to make it easier for workers to put in suggestions, and the number of suggestions per worker has increased considerably since its adoption.

The foreman reviews the form and immediately takes the necessary measures for implementing ideas below Grade E. Often, the suggestion is made verbally and written down and submitted after it has been implemented. Since the suggestion relates to the workshop, the foreman can easily see the suggestion's implications. The next day, or within three days at the latest, the foreman initials the form and gives it back to the individual who submitted it.

If the idea is ranked as D or above, the employee rewrites it on the form for advanced suggestions (see Figure 4.6) and submits it again for review by the departmental committee and the plantwide committee. Later, the suggestion is forwarded to the central committee for annual appraisal. Grades E and below are handled by the section (department) committee.

The rankings carry cash awards:

Score	Grade	Award (¥)	Award ($)
5	A	50,000	200
4	B	20,000	80
3	C	10,000	40
2	D	5,000	20
1	E	2,000	8
0.33	F	1,000	4
–	G	500	2

Even when the suggestion is rejected, the employee gets back the coupon worth ¥150 (originally set as the price of a pack of cigarettes), which he can use to buy merchandise at the company cooperative. Some employees have managed to buy complete lines of electrical appliances by submitting hundreds of suggestions every year.

(Canon—continued)

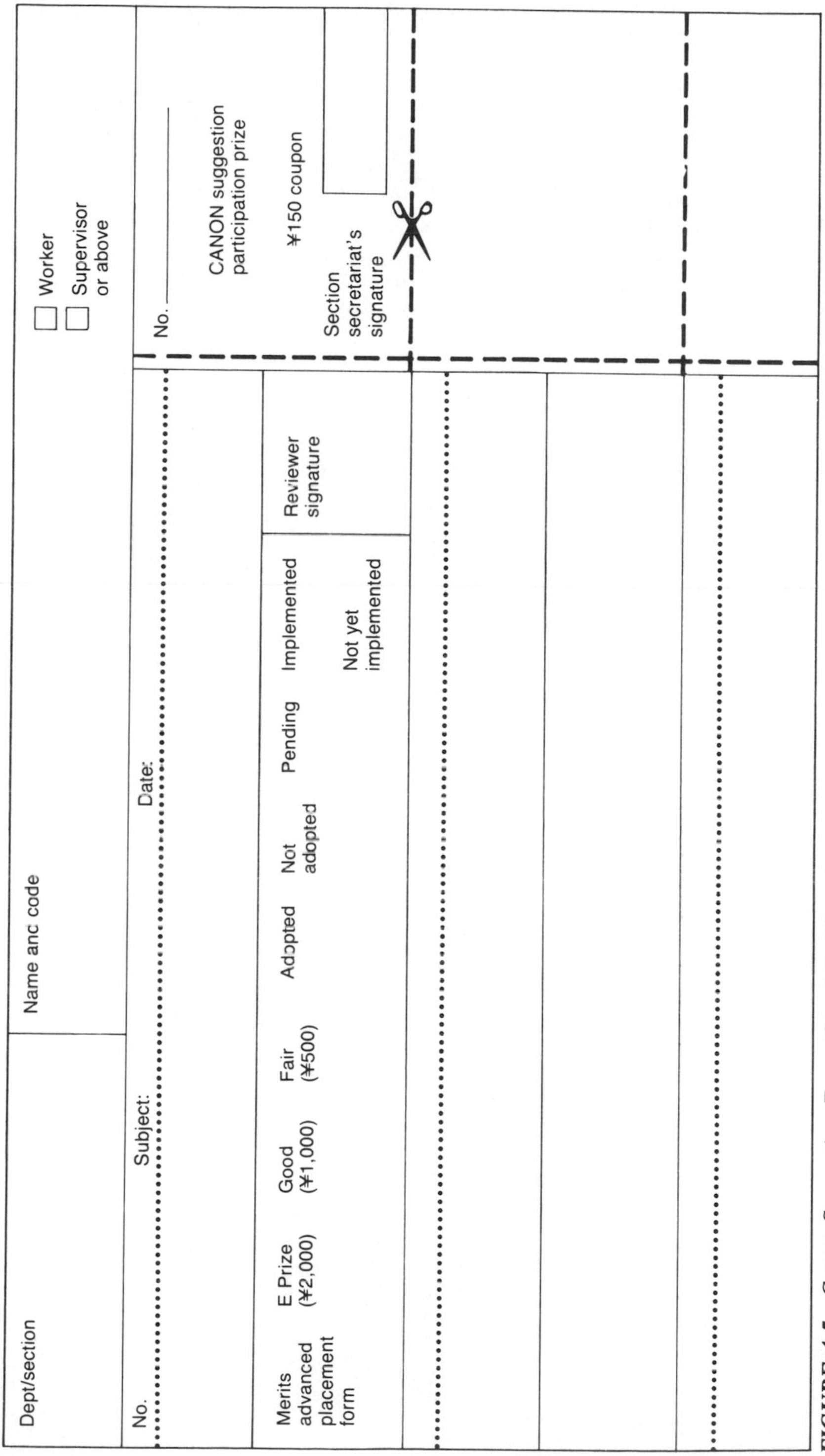

Dept/section

Name anc code

☐ Worker
☐ Supervisor or above

No. ....

Subject:

Date:

No. _____

CANON suggestion participation prize

¥150 coupon

Section secretariat's signature

Merits advanced placement form

	E Prize (¥2,000)	Good (¥1,000)	Fair (¥500)	Adopted	Not adopted	Pending	Implemented	
							Not yet implemented	Reviewer signature

✂

FIGURE 4.5 Canon Suggestion Form (Simplified Form)

121

Annual saved hours: Before improvement (E)   –   After improvement (E)   =   hours

This section to be filled in by person in charge of suggestion system.

1. This suggestion to be implemented as of _____ .
2. Estimated cost of implementing this suggestion: ¥ _____
3. Comments:

Labor-saving budget was used.   Yes ___ No ___

Cost calculation (Engineering and Account Section):

Practicality (Engineering, Machine Design, other sections):

If your suggestion is adopted, the following prize will be awarded:

A Prize (¥50,000)	D Prize (¥5,000)
B Prize (¥20,000)	E Prize (¥2,000)
C Prize (¥10,000)	

FIGURE 4.6 *Canon Suggestion Form — Advanced Placement (for Work Improvement)*

Date:

Section:		Name and Code

Subject:	☐ Worker ☐ Management	

Reason for suggestion (Why is this suggestion required? What is the current procedure?)

Suggestion:

Expected effects of suggestion:

	Category	Before improvement	After improvement
A.	Annual working days	days	days
B.	Manpower/day	persons	persons
C.	Working hours/day	hours	hours
D.	Total working hours (B × C)	hours	hours
E.	Annual working hours (A × D)	hours	hours

* For those items that cannot be expressed in hours, please note quality improvement, prevention of accidents, elimination of parts, etc.

FIGURE 4.6 (continued)

123

(Canon — continued)

In order to promote workers' active participation in the suggestion system, Canon's managers and supervisors follow several guidelines:

1. Always show a positive response to suggestions for improvement.
2. Help workers to write easily and give them helpful suggestions about their work.
3. Try to identify even the slightest inconvenience for the workers. (This requires very good superior-subordinate communication.)
4. Make the target very clear. Example: How many suggestions do we need this month? Which area (quality, safety, etc.) do we need to work on now?
5. Use competition and games to arouse interest, such as displaying individual achievement charts.
6. Implement accepted suggestions as soon as possible. Give awards before payday.

Another unique feature of Canon's suggestion system is the lifetime cumulative award system. Each suggestion is given a certain number of points, and every year President's Awards are given to the 20 people who have accumulated the most points since the system's inception. Each recipient receives ¥300,000 (U.S. $1,350) and a gold medal. Since this can get a bit repetitious, there are also Presidential Awards for the most points in a given year, the top 30 people receiving ¥100,000 (U.S. $450) and silver medals.

Each Canon employee receives a CPS Notebook, a 55-page pocket-size notebook that explains the CPS, how to set KAIZEN targets, and the award system. These CPS Notebooks also have special pages entitled "My Self-Development Goals — Method, Tools, and Investment" to be filled in by the worker.

Appendix G gives more details on how the Canon Production System encourages KAIZEN. ∎

5

KAIZEN Management

Cross-functional management and policy deployment are two key management concepts supporting the TQC strategy. As mentioned earlier, in TQC thinking, management's job is broken down into two areas: (1) "maintenance-managing" current business performance for result and profits and (2) "KAIZEN-managing" for improving processes and systems. KAIZEN-managing relates to both cross-functional management and policy deployment.

Cross-functional management relates to coordinating the activities of different units for realizing the cross-functional goals of KAIZEN, and policy deployment to the implementing policies for KAIZEN.

At many companies, managing primarily means getting top management policy filtered down to the line organization, as illustrated in the maintenance side of Figure 5.1. If there is an inter-unit conflict on such issues as quality and cost, it is often settled by internal politics. In TQC, the cross-functional goals of QCS (Quality, Cost, and Scheduling) are clearly defined as superior to such line functions as design, production, and marketing. Therefore, the positioning of cross-functional goals as superordinate goals necessitates a new systems approach to decision making. It is this need that the concept and practices of both cross-functional management and policy deployment have been developed to meet. Within this context, "quality" is concerned with building a better system for quality assurance; "cost" is concerned both with building a system for identifying cost factors and with reducing costs; "scheduling" refers to building a better system for both delivery and quantity.

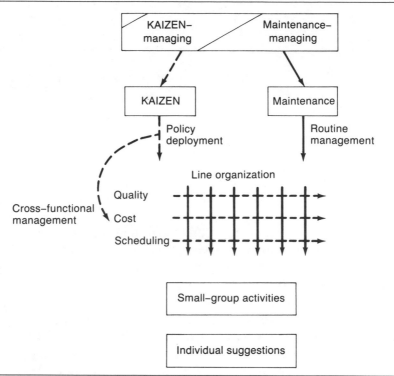

FIGURE 5.1   *KAIZEN-Managing vs. Maintenance-Managing*

As shown in the KAIZEN side of Figure 5.1, the KAIZEN target is conveyed to line (functional) organizations through policy deployment in two ways: directly through line managers and indirectly through cross-functional organizations.

Both small-group activities (such as QC circles) and schemes for encouraging individual suggestion support KAIZEN activities at the workplace level, and the goals of these activities are set through policy deployment.

Management's commitment to the key management concepts of cross-functional management and policy deployment is expressed in directions provided by top management. Top management usually formulates its annual policies or goals at the beginning of the year on the basis of long-range plans and strategies. Such formulations encompass, again, two major goals categories: (1) goals relating to such factors as profit, market share, and products, and

(2) goals relating to overall improvements in the company's various systems and cross-functional activities.

In Japan, the term "policy" is used to describe long- and medium-range management orientations as well as annual goals or targets. Therefore, the word policy as used in TQC refers to both longer-range and annual goals.

Another important aspect of policy is that it is composed of both goals and measures, both ends and means. Goals are usually quantitative figures established by top management, such as targets for sales, profit, and market share. Measures, on the other hand, are the specific action programs to achieve these goals. A goal that is not expressed in terms of such specific measures is merely a slogan. It is thus imperative that top management determine both the goals and the measures and then "deploy" them down throughout the organization.

Although achieving result targets usually takes priority as the primary goal for managers, the goal of strengthening and improving the organization and its systems is no less important. The former generally is a corporate response to external requirements such as stockholder pressures for profits; the latter usually is a self-generated move for improvement in corporate culture, chemistry, and overall competitiveness. In TQC strategy, these two major goals of profit and KAIZEN are interwoven, and the PDCA cycle is applied in carrying out both policy deployment and cross-functional management. Both of these management concepts are formulated (planned), deployed (done and checked), and audited (acted upon for improvement).

Cross-Functional Management

An enterprise is organized by vertical functions, such as R&D, production, engineering, finance, sales, and administrative services. Through such functional organization, responsibilities are delegated and profit goals pursued.

Among the objectives of TQC are not only enhanced profits but also general improvements in such areas as employee education, customer satisfaction, customer service, quality assurance, cost control, volume, delivery control, and new-product development. These objectives call for cross-functional efforts cutting horizontally across the whole organization. Today, it is almost a cliché to say that the quality-control or quality-assurance department alone cannot obtain the desired quality. All functional departments must be involved. Cross-functional management is thus a major organizational tool to realize TQC's improvement goals.

Many top managers say that their company's mission is to provide quality products to meet the needs of their customers. Yet even if we accept this at face value, how high should quality stand in the hierarchy of various corporate goals? The corporation has many goals to pursue, such as maximizing shareholders' profits, providing employment for employees, producing goods or services to satisfy customers' needs, and serving the community in which it works. On the internal side, line managers and staff are held responsible for carrying out the missions of their respective departments, such as engineering, production, marketing, and administration.

Where should quality place among these sometimes conflicting external and internal goals? The hierarchy of various management goals vis-à-vis cross-functional goals was clearly described by Shigeru Aoki, senior managing director at Toyota Motor, when he explained Toyota's corporate philosophy:

> The ultimate goal of a company is to make profits. Assuming that this is self-evident, then the next "superordinate" goals of the company should be such cross-functional goals as quality, cost, and scheduling (quantity and delivery). Without achieving these goals, the company will be left behind by the competition because of inferior quality, will find its profits eroded by higher costs, and will be unable to deliver the products in time for the customers. If these cross-functional goals are realized, profits will follow.
>
> Therefore, we should regard all the other management functions as existing to serve the three superordinate goals of QCS (Quality, Cost, and Scheduling). These auxiliary management functions include product planning, design, production, purchasing, and marketing, and they should be regarded as secondary means to achieve QCS.

Figure 5.2 shows the relationship among cross-functional and other functional activities. As this diagram shows, we are dealing with a PDCA wheel for improvement, turning forever with QCS* in the center. Corporate strategy and planning precede cross-functional

---

*In Japan, the term QCD is often used instead of QCS. The D in this case stands for delivery, but the volume commitment to customers is often included in delivery to make the two terms virtually interchangeable. Although the terms are equally valid, QCS is used throughout this book to avoid confusion.

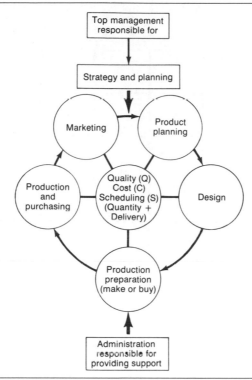

FIGURE 5.2 *The QCS Wheel*

goals, and other functional activities are carried out to serve these goals. Another aspect of the QCS wheel is determining criteria for solving cross-functional management problems.

Toyota's Zenzaburo Katayama says:

Meeting both volume and delivery schedule targets is just as much a part of management as are people, capital, and production facilities.

If customers cannot get the products they need in the volume they need when they need them, the system has broken down. This is the whole meaning of "scheduling," and yet it requires tremendous cross-functional efforts to meet scheduling targets. Only after scheduling problems have been solved should the company worry about such competitive factors as quality and costs.

Just as quality must be maintained throughout product development, production preparations, purchasing, production, marketing, and servicing, scheduling must be maintained throughout all processes within the company.

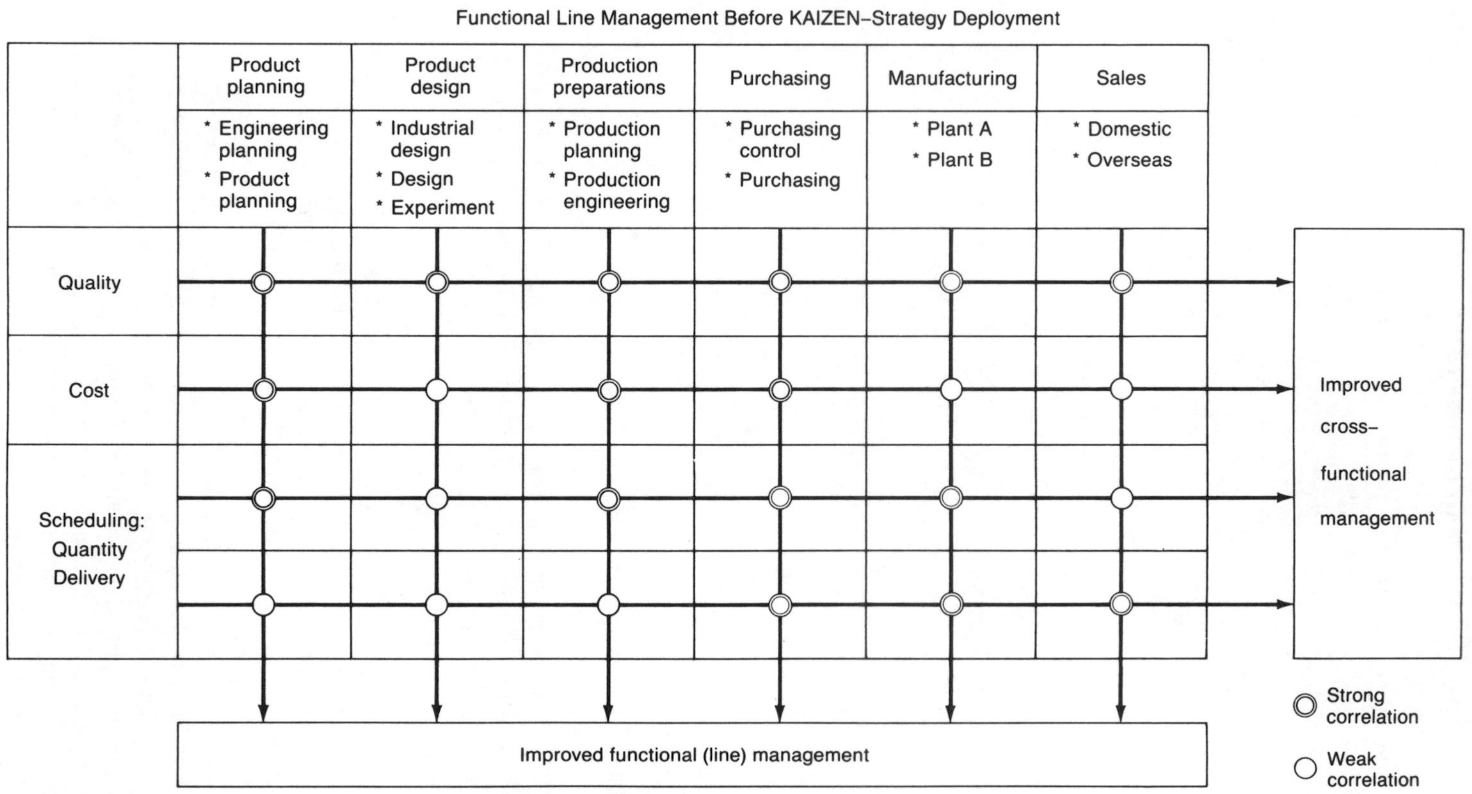

Functional Line Management Before KAIZEN–Strategy Deployment

	Product planning * Engineering planning * Product planning	Product design * Industrial design * Design * Experiment	Production preparations * Production planning * Production engineering	Purchasing * Purchasing control * Purchasing	Manufacturing * Plant A * Plant B	Sales * Domestic * Overseas	
Quality	◎	◎	○	○	○	◎	→ Improved cross-functional management
Cost	◎	○	○	○	○	○	→
	○	○	○	○	◎	○	→
Scheduling: Quantity Delivery	○	○	◎	○	◎	◎	→

Improved functional (line) management

◎ Strong correlation

○ Weak correlation

FIGURE 5.3 *Functional vs. Cross-Functional Matrix*

130

The job of administration is to see that all these cross-functions and functions are carried out properly. Aoki asserts that the roles of each functional (line) department in meeting the QCS targets should be well defined. Further, he says the kinds of activities and functions needed by each line department to achieve these goals should be clarified.

The relationship between functional and cross-functional organizations may be better understood with the matrix in Figure 5.3. The vertical lines represent various functional (line) departments, starting with product planning and including design, purchasing, manufacturing, and sales. The horizontal lines represent the major cross-functional goals of quality, cost, and scheduling. These cross-functional activities cut across all the line departments with varying degrees of impact.

Department managers naturally tend to place the priority on their own department's functions. Without cross-functional goals, the departments with the loudest voices tend to win interdepartmental negotiations, regardless of the impact on company-wide goals. In the case of introducing a new product, for instance, the engineering people prepare specifications and drawings based on information obtained from their marketing people (if not from their own imaginations) and then "dump" them on the production people, who say that they cannot make such a product. A long period of in-fighting and adjustment then ensues before the production starts, based on the revised requirements. Figure 5.4 shows the typical movement of information among different functional departments.

The ideal situation for new-product development is shown in Figure 5.5, where there is overlapping of various functions at every stage (prepared by Toshio Iwahashi of Kubota, Ltd.). Cross-functional management has been born of the need to break the interdepartmental communication barriers. In order for this to happen, however, there must be a system for quality assurance and supporting rules, regulations, formats, and procedures.

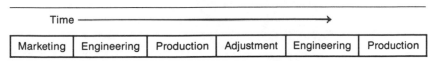

FIGURE 5.4 *Product Development in a Typical Company*

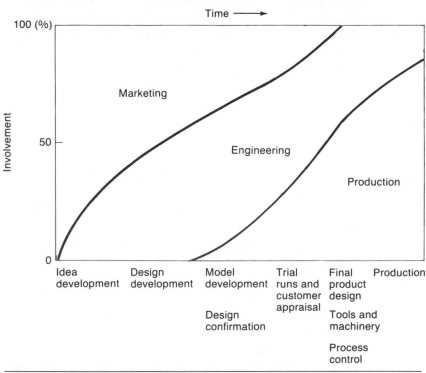

FIGURE 5.5 *Product Development at Ideal Company*

The introduction of cross-functional goals thus helps managers maintain a proper balance in their work, with the ultimate goal of QCS in mind. If cross-functional goals are established as the superordinate goals at the company, it follows that the various goals of the company should be determined in the following order:

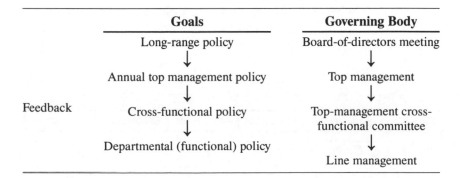

Cross-functional goals should be determined *prior to* the determination of departmental goals. Either top management or the cross-functional committee should determine the goals for each cross-function of quality, cost, and scheduling. This committee is organized at the top-management level, and its role is to establish cross-functional goals and measures. Such subjects as new product development, facilities, production, and sales are also discussed as they relate to QCS.

At Toyota, all members of the cross-functional committee are board members representing the departments involved in a particular cross-function, such as quality. The goals and measures determined at the committee meeting carry almost the same weight as those coming out of the board meeting, since the cross-functional committee is second in importance only to the board. There are about 10 members on each committee, and each committee is headed by a senior officer appointed by the president.

In other companies, the cross-functional committee is often headed by the president or his second or third in command. Meetings are usually held monthly. Depending on the size of the company and the number of board members, the cross-functional committee is sometimes composed of both board members and department managers. Often, the TQC department or quality assurance department acts as secretariat for the cross-functional committee.

Cross-functional management is concerned with building a better system for quality, cost, and scheduling. Scheduling refers to meeting the volume and delivery targets. It is the job of each functional department to work in accordance with the goals established by the cross-functional committee.

Because policy consists of the two components of goals and measures, cross-functional policy on QCS needs to be established in terms of both goals and measures before being "deployed" to lower levels.

Just as a company's annual performance is audited by a CPA firm, its QCS progress also needs to be audited in what is called a TQC audit. This TQC audit is a very important part of policy deployment. There is, however, one crucial difference between auditing corporate performance and auditing cross-functional goals. Whereas the financial audit is conducted by an independent third party, the cross-functional audit is conducted by line management.

A cross-functional audit starts top management auditing the divisions, after which division managers audit their subordinates. This process of auditing the progress made in achieving cross-functional goals should take place at every level throughout the organization.

Cross-functional management has become an integral part of TQC in Japan and is actively promoted in all Japanese companies that have introduced TQC. Basically, the raison d'être for cross-functional management is to look for ways to improve corporate activities, both vertically and horizontally.

CROSS-FUNCTIONAL MANAGEMENT AT TOYOTA

Toyota was first in Japan with cross-functional management, which emerged in 1962 from the following two needs: (1) a need for top management to clarify its quality goals and deploy them to all employees at every level and (2) a need to establish a system of close coordination among different departments.

Toyota's Shigeru Aoki says:

> The concept of statistical quality control is something which can be applied independently within each department, such as the inspection department and the manufacturing department. However, TQC is a company-wide campaign, involving every department within the company to realize its goals across the board. In the case of quality, for instance, the sales department clarifies the quality which satisfies the customers. The design department incorporates the quality in the design, and then the job of actualizing the quality goes through such stages as production preparation, purchasing, and manufacturing. In other words, all these functional departments are coordinated in order to realize the cross-functional goal of quality. The purpose of cross-functional management is to achieve these goals effectively.

At Toyota, both quality and cost are regarded as the primary targets of management. As tools for cross-functional activities, Toyota has developed detailed rules for both quality assurance and cost control.

Toyota divides the flow of cross-functional activities from product planning to sales into the following eight steps:

1. Product planning
2. Product design
3. Production preparation
4. Purchasing
5. Full-scale production

(Toyota — continued)

6. Inspection
7. Sales and services
8. Quality audit

At each of these eight steps, the rules spell out which functional (line) departments are involved and which people are responsible for cost control or quality assurance at that particular stage. The rules also list specific items to be assured and designate specific activities to be followed for cost control or quality assurance.

How these rules are used is explained below, drawing examples from quality assurance. So that everyone in the company has the same understanding, the rules define quality assurance as "assuring that the quality of the product is satisfactory, reliable, and yet economical for the customer." Toyota has developed a list of QA activities to be carried out within each functional department (see Figure 5.6). Figure 5.7, which is attached to the rules, gives a sample list of quality-assurance activities at the product-planning stage. Notice that both the people in charge of each stage and the items to be checked are listed. The overriding goal is to never inconvenience downstream customers.

There is an underlying belief at Toyota that any serious defects in the management system tend to show up in quality. Other cross-functional problems, such as cost, can be concealed for some time before they surface. However, there is no way to hide poor quality resulting from poor management.

According to Aoki, each functional department has several cross-functional responsibilities, and each cross-function runs through several departments. Similarly, as a rule, several board members are involved in the same cross-functional activities, and each board member in charge of a particular function has several cross-functional responsibilities.

The cross-functional committees of the directors in charge are the nucleus of cross-functional management at Toyota. In fact, these are the only official organizations dealing with cross-functional management, and they deal only with the planning (the actual implementation being the responsibility of each line department).

Each committee has about 10 members and is headed by the senior director most closely concerned with the particular cross-function. For instance, the cross-functional committee on quality is headed by the director in charge of quality assurance.

Typically, cross-functional targets are set after annual corporate targets have been determined for such items as the number of cars to be produced and the profit ratio.

The main subjects discussed at the committee include:

1. Goal setting
2. Planning measures for achieving the goal

(Toyota — continued)

Step	Person Responsible for QA	Major QA Activities	Contribution to Quality
Product Planning	General Manager, Sales Dept.	Forecast of demand and market share	*
	Engineer, Product Planning Office	Secure quality required by market • Establish and allocate optimum quality and cost targets • Prevent recurrence of major quality problems	***
Product Design	General Manager, Product Planning Office	Trial design • Evaluate adaptability to quality goals	***
	General Managers, Engineering Depts.	• Test and study performance, function, and reliability	**
	Chief Engineer, Product Planning Office	• Production design (confirm necessary conditions for QA)	**
Production Preparation	Production Engineering Manager	Formulate processes which satisfy design quality	***
	QA General Manager	Prepare optimum automobile testing	**
	Inspection Managers (Plant)	Evaluate trial model	**
	Production Dept. Managers	Study and suggest initial and routine process-control plan	*
		Secure process capability	***

FIGURE 5.6 *List of Cross-Functional QA Activities for Each Department*

(Toyota — continued)

Step	Person Responsible for QA	Major QA Activities	Contribution to Quality
Purchasing	Purchasing Managers	Confirm qualitative and quantitative capability of vendors	*
	QA General Manager		
	Inspection Dept. General Manager (Plant)	Check action of manufacturing quality by testing initial supplies	*
	QA General Manager	Assist vendors in strengthening their QA systems	*
Production	General Manager, Production Dept.	Maintain optimum level of manufacturing quality to meet quality standards	**
	Manager, Plant General Affairs	Secure process control under optimum level	**
		Maintain process and machine capability	**
Inspection	QA General Manager	Check manufacturing quality by testing initial products	**
	Plant Inspection Managers	Determine whether or not to deliver vehicle	***
	QA General Manager		
Sales and Services	General Manager, Sales Dept.	Packaging, maintenance, prevention of quality deterioration during shipment	**
	General Manager, Service Dept.	Education and PR on proper use and maintenance	*
		Testing of new vehicles	*
		Analysis and feedback of quality information	***

***Critical importance, and downstream alteration impossible
** Influential, but downstream alteration feasible
* Of little consequence

FIGURE 5.6 *(continued)*

(Toyota — continued)

Step: Product Planning (I)	Quality- Assurance Items	Operations for Quality Assurance	Person Responsible for Quality Assurance
I-1 Overall planning	Overall effectiveness of new-product planning	1. Projection of demand and share	General Manager, Sales Dept.
		1. Projection of competitors' strategies 2. Planning and evaluation of long-range corporate plans	General Manager, General Coordination Office
I-2 Overall long-range new-product planning	Overall effectiveness of product-line planning	1. Study the propriety of product line against demand projections and need for new product	General Manager, Sales Dept.
		1. Coordination between technological projections and R&D items	General Manager, Engineering Planning Office
		2. Study effect of model change on current market share	Chief Engineer, Product Planning Office
		3. Study overall balance of new-product-development capabilities	
I-3 Individual new-product plan	Propriety of aim to the demand fluctuation	1. Confirm adaptability to demand fluctuations	General Manager, Sales Dept.
		2. Confirm price competitiveness	General Manager, Engineering Planning Office
		1. Study technological competitiveness	General Manager, Engineering Planning Office

FIGURE 5.7   *List of QA Activities at the Product-Planning Stage*

(Toyota — continued)

Step: Product Planning (I)	Quality-Assurance Items	Operations for Quality Assurance	Person Responsible for Quality Assurance
I-3 (cont.)		2. Confirm results of R&D 3. Confirm new-product-development capabilities 4. Confirm propriety of targeted useful life 5. Establish cost goals	Chief Engineer, Product Planning Office
I-4 Basic plan for individual new products	Secure quality required by market	1. Establish optimum quality targets 2. Confirm R&D and production capabilities 3. Plan development schedule 4. Distribute targeted costs 5. Prevent recurrence of important quality problems (same or similar line of vehicles)	Chief Engineer, Product Planning Office

FIGURE 5.7 *(continued)*

3. Planning new products, facilities, production, and sales
4. Other important subjects raised for the committee's attention

Aoki points out that the board members must study very seriously before they can participate actively in the discussions on cross-functional subjects, and that their participation in the conference gives them an excellent opportunity to understand the implications of quality, cost, and scheduling for the company. Often a member of the board representing only one particular division or department of the company has a narrow perspective, and the discussion on cross-functional subjects is eye-opening.

Professor Masao Kogure of the Tamagawa University engineering

(Toyota — continued)

department says that in a company where TQC has just been started, an influential member of the management who has not yet been "turned on" to TQC should be appointed to head one of the cross-functional committees. He points out this will prove to be an excellent TQC education, and that the person will probably become an enthusiastic supporter of the movement as he becomes involved in the implementation of TQC concepts. ■

CROSS-FUNCTIONAL MANAGEMENT AT KOMATSU

At Komatsu, cross-functional committees are placed under the TQC Committee and divided into the three areas of profit (cost) management, quality assurance, and quantity (volume) management. The role of the cross-functional committee on quality assurance at Komatsu is defined as follows.

1. This committee is intended to improve the *system* of quality assurance from product planning to sales and services, and thus to upgrade the level of quality assurance.
2. In order to achieve the above goal, this committee studies items and reports on the following to the TQC Committee:
   a. Planning for company-wide quality assurance
   b. Determination of the following items:
      i. Systems improvement plans
      ii. Items for systems improvement and the departments responsible for them

The quality-assurance committee is headed by the board member in charge of quality assurance, and its members are appointed by the president. Other committee members are board members representing various related functions, but the committee also includes one or two board members who are not directly concerned with quality assurance. Depending on the nature of the subject, working teams are also organized at the lower levels, such as at the plants, to assist the committee.

Since each cross-functional committee deals with the improvement of the system, it tries to identify any malfunctioning in the system and to make recommendations for improvements. For instance, the committee may find that the malfunction arises from inappropriate rules. In that case, the committee makes recommendations to the departments concerned on reviewing and revising the rules.

When the profit-management committee finds that the profit target has not been achieved, it studies why the initial target was not achieved and

(Komatsu—continued)

identifies the areas for improvement. Although it is the job of each line department to achieve the profit target, the cross-functional committee reinforces the efforts of line departments by providing direction for the system improvement.

One project recently taken up by Komatsu's quality-assurance committee was to review current quality-assurance control points and to revise the list of control points. The committee established criteria for control points so that (1) their effect is measurable in the marketplace in terms of customer satisfaction and quality and (2) the criteria make it possible to manage quality assurance activities at each step.

As a result of this review, the committee first identified 119 control points. It then reduced the number to 41 on the basis of importance, ease of problem identification, and ease of data acquisition. The committee further decided that semi-annual spot checks should be conducted in all business units to study the degree of accomplishment, problems encountered, and specific countermeasures adopted. It was also decided that the results of these spot checks would be reported to the committee, and that the results of the spot checks on the 16 most important items would be reported to the board meeting.

As a result of these measures, it has become easier for management to understand the current problems and to adopt quality-assurance measures. Perhaps more important, everyone in the company, from top management down to shop-floor workers, has come to a common understanding of quality assurance.

At Komatsu, the planning and coordination office at each plant takes care of cross-functional coordination for that plant, and the head of this office is second in command at the plant. Three managers report to him: the managers in charge of quality assurance, cost, and scheduling.

When an important quality issue is raised by the quality-assurance committee, the quality-assurance manager at the head office conveys the message to the plant's planning and coordination office, and the planning and coordination manager is empowered to act right away through the quality-assurance manager reporting to him. Thus the plant's quality-assurance manager does not suffer status problems in talking to other managers in the plant.

Every month, the plant manager presides over day-long meetings on quality assurance, cost, and scheduling. Each meeting is attended by *all* managers to review progress in their cross-functional activities.

Figure 5.8 shows the organization of TQC activities at Komatsu. The TQC Committee is chaired by the president, and other members of the executive board automatically become members of this committee. As a rule, TQC Committee meetings are held monthly. The TQC Committee establishes annual plans for activities based on annual policy, checks on the level of progress in each department, and determines the schedule of the audit. It also supervises other committees' activities.

(Komatsu — continued)

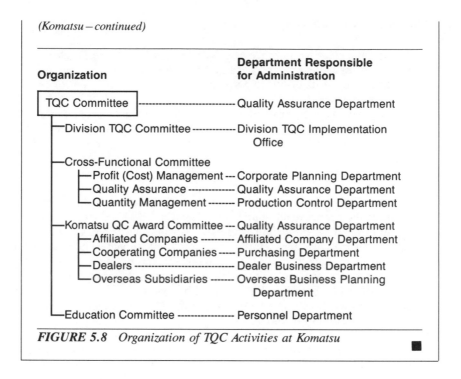

Organization	Department Responsible for Administration
TQC Committee	Quality Assurance Department
Division TQC Committee	Division TQC Implementation Office
Cross-Functional Committee	
Profit (Cost) Management	Corporate Planning Department
Quality Assurance	Quality Assurance Department
Quantity Management	Production Control Department
Komatsu QC Award Committee	Quality Assurance Department
Affiliated Companies	Affiliated Company Department
Cooperating Companies	Purchasing Department
Dealers	Dealer Business Department
Overseas Subsidiaries	Overseas Business Planning Department
Education Committee	Personnel Department

FIGURE 5.8 *Organization of TQC Activities at Komatsu*

Policy Deployment

Policy deployment refers to the process of internalizing policies for KAIZEN throughout the company, from highest to lowest level. As mentioned before, in Japan the term policy describes both annual and medium- to long-range targets or orientations.

Annual goals for profit and KAIZEN are established on the basis of long-term and medium-term corporate goals. Several months before top managers meet to formulate these annual goals, there is preliminary vertical consultation between top management and division managers and between division and department managers. Information goes back and forth among the parties concerned until the details have been worked out. Needless to say, the past year's performance and the yardsticks for measuring improvement are taken into consideration in formulating the new goals.

Another important aspect to be considered before new goals and measures are established each year is the list of all current problems at every business unit. The degree of success in fulfilling the previous year's goal is evaluated in light of the existing problems before the new goals are determined.

Once top management's annual goals have been determined, they are "deployed" throughout the lower levels of management. The goals that were stated as abstracts by top management become increasingly concrete and specific as they are deployed downward. Unless top-management policies (goals) are put to practical use by lower-level managers, they will be of no use. No matter how beautifully drawn, the policies artfully composed at the top management level are often no better than castles in the air.

One important aspect of policy deployment is prioritization. Prioritization is an inherent part of the Pareto diagram often used in QC-circle activities, and this same concept is applied in the deployment of goals as well.

Because the resources that can be mobilized are limited, it is essential that priorities be assigned. Once this has been done, an increasingly specific and clear list of measures and action plans can be deployed at the lower levels of management.

Typically the policy statement is formulated differently at different management levels:

Top management:	General statement of direction for change (qualitative)
Divsion management:	Definition of top-management statement (quantitative)
Middle management:	Specific goals (quantitative)
Supervisors:	Specific actions (quantitative)

As the goals work their way downward, top management's general policy statements are restated as increasingly specific and action-oriented goals, eventually becoming precise quantitative values. Thus policy deployment is a way for top management's commitment to be internalized by the lower ranks.

There are several prerequisites for policy deployment:

1. There must be a clear understanding of the role of each manager in achieving the predetermined business result and improving the processes (KAIZEN).

2. Managers of different ranks must have a clear understanding of the control points and check points established to realize the goals.

3. The system of routine management (maintenance) must be well established in the company.

While management policy at most Japanese companies is categorized into the two areas of KAIZEN (cross-functional) policy and departmental (functional) policy, management policy at Japan Steel Works is categorized into three areas:

1. Product policy: The target is strategic deployment of the products and relates to KAIZEN in quality, cost, and delivery of major products, as well as the development of new products.

2. KAIZEN (cross-functional) policy: The target is KAIZEN in the corporate culture, which relates to cross-functional tasks such as QA (Quality Assurance), cost reduction, meeting the delivery target, and vendor management.

3. Functional (departmental) policy: The target is what each department should do and achieve based on product policy and KAIZEN policy. Functional policy is closely geared to meeting financial targets.

To illustrate the need for policy deployment, let us consider the following case: The president of an airline company proclaims that he believes in safety and that his corporate goal is to make sure that safety is maintained throughout the company. This proclamation is prominently featured in the company's quarterly report and its advertising. Let us further suppose that the department managers also swear a firm belief in safety. The catering manager says he believes in safety. The pilots say they believe in safety. The flight crews say they believe in safety. Everyone in the company practices safety. True? Or might everyone simply be paying lip service to the idea of safety?

On the other hand, if the president states that safety is company policy and works with his division managers to develop a plan for safety that defines their responsibilities, everyone will have a very specific subject to discuss. Safety will become a real concern. For the manager in charge of catering services, safety might mean maintaining the quality of food to avoid customer dissatisfaction or illness.

In that case, how does he ensure that the food is of top quality? What sorts of control points and check points does he establish? How does he ensure that there is no deterioration in food quality in-flight? Who checks the temperature of the refrigerators or the condition of the oven while the plane is in the air?

Only when safety is translated into specific actions with specific control and check points established for each employee's job may safety be said to have been truly deployed as a policy. Policy deployment calls for everyone to interpret policy in light of his own responsibilities and for everyone to work out criteria to check his success in carrying out the policy.

This may be explained in an ends/means chart such as Figure 5.9. For top management, policy is an end. At the same time, an end calls for specific means to realize it. Such means become the ends for the next-level managers, who in turn have to develop means to accomplish their ends. Both ends and means differ at each management level, and what is a means for one person becomes an end for another.

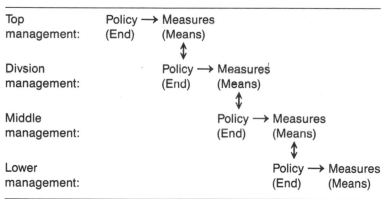

FIGURE 5.9 *Ends/Means Chart for Policy Deployment*

Control Points and Check Points

The concept of policy deployment has its parallels in statistical QC. And because statistical QC activities have their roots in the use of control charts, it may be well here to try to define the role of management in the context of the control chart.

The starting point is the concept of a *manageable margin*. In his *Guide to Quality Control* Kaoru Ishikawa states:

> The purpose of making a control chart is to determine, on the basis of the movements of the points, what kind of changes have taken place in the production process. Therefore, to use the control chart effectively, we have to set the criteria for evaluating what we consider an abnormality. When a production process is in a controlled state, this means that:
>
> **1.** All points lie within the control limits, and
> **2.** The point grouping does not form a particular form
>
> We would therefore know that an abnormality has developed if (a) some points are outside the control limits, or (b) the points form some sort of particular form even though they are all within the control limits.*

When we find points outside the specified margins, we must seek out the factors responsible for the abnormalities and correct them so that the same problems do not recur. (See Figure 5.10.) In other words, the control chart is useful to check *with* the results, identify the causes of abnormalities, and then work out ways of eliminating these causes. In using control charts in statistical quality control, we go from the result back to the source and correct or eliminate the factors that have caused the problems.

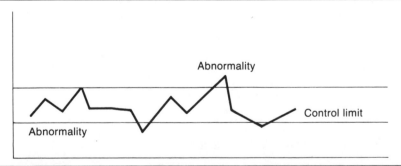

FIGURE 5.10   *Use of Control Charts to Check Abnormalities*

---

*Asian Productivity Organization, Tokyo, 1976, p. 76. Reprinted by permission of the publisher.

By analogy, control points and check points can also be used in management. Professor Yoji Akao of Tamagawa University's engineering department uses the following example to explain control points and check points in management. In heat-treating a metal in oil, it is important to maintain a given temperature range in order to ensure the metal's post-treatment properties. This means the oil temperature must be checked to see that it stays within the prescribed range. There may be several factors affecting oil temperature, including oil volume and the flow of gas from the burner nozzle. If we assume that it is the job of the foreman at the heat treatment shop to control the temperature level of the oil, that the oil volume and the gas flow are the two major factors affecting temperature, and that these two latter jobs are his workers' job, the foreman has only to check the oil volume and the gas flow to know whether the job is being done right.

From the standpoint of the foreman, the temperature level represents his control point. The control point is something he checks with the result. He checks the control chart showing the fluctuations of the temperature level. He checks the result to see whether the required conditions are being maintained in the production processes. In order to do this, he must manage the activities of his subordinates. On the other hand, the oil volume and the gas flow represent the foreman's check points. These are the factors he checks for their effect on the results. To put it another way, the control point is something he manages with the data, and the check point is something he controls through his subordinates. For instance, he can see the temperature level from the control chart. When he finds an abnormality, he can take corrective action by adjusting a check point—for example, by having his subordinate tighten the nozzle. The foreman must look at his check points from time to time to maintain his control point.

By this time, the reader may have realized that the control point represents an R criterion and the check point a P criterion. (See Figure 5.11.)

This same concept can be extended to the role of the manager. Each manager has both control points (R criteria) and check points (P criteria) on his job. At the higher management level, the control points are policy goals and the check points policy measures. When these specific control points and check points are established between

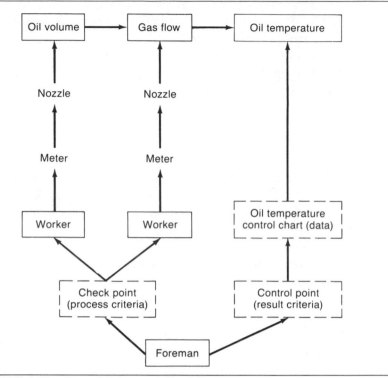

FIGURE 5.11   *Control Points and Check Points*

superiors and subordinates, a series of goals and measures is established, with linkages between managers at different levels.

It is precisely these control points and check points that are used in the deployment of policies in TQC. For such a system to work effectively, it is essential that each manager know exactly what his R criteria (control points) and P criteria (check points) are and that his check points be clearly understood as his subordinates' control points.

Every goal must be accompanied by measures to realize it. Without such measures, all a manager can say to his subordinates is "I trust that you will do your best" or "Work harder!" When manager and subordinates have developed specific measures to achieve the goal, he can be much more specific than just "Do your best!" or "Work harder!"

Here, "goal" refers to the control point and "measures" to the check points. The goal is result-oriented, and the measures are process-oriented. In the process of policy deployment, every manager works on policy-deployment form, on which he specifies goals and measures. He discusses this form with both his superiors and his subordinates. Typically, such a form will include the following points:

Top management's long-range policy and strategy

Top management's annual policy

Last year's departmental policy

Degrees of success in previous year's policy deployment

This year's policy (goals)

This year's measures

Major activities

Major control points and check points expressed numerically

Schedule

In the West, planning is often regarded as an inseparable part of a manager's job. If a manager does not plan, he is not doing his job right. At the same time, if a subordinate joins in the planning phase, he may be seen as infringing on the manager's turf.

Policy deployment is a revolutionary breakthrough in that it invites the participation of the lower-level managers in setting up and deploying the goals. This is done in the belief that joint work is essential to building a commitment to fulfilling the goal.

Management at the head office sometimes maintains a complete list of such policy-deployment forms presented by all managers. Often, the division manager has a matrix form on his desk, showing the various activities to be conducted by his subordinates as agreed upon through the process of policy deployment. Sometimes, major top management policies are listed with serial numbers so lower level managers can relate what they are doing to the top management policies with the same serial number.

Since top-management policies have such a direct bearing on what each manager should be doing, top management makes a great effort to convey its message to all managers. This is done through the process of policy deployment to the next-level managers.

Policy Audit

Policy deployment, we have seen, represents the deployment between goals (control points, or R criteria) and measures (check points, or P criteria), starting from top management and going down to the supervisors and workers in the workshop. As the mesh joining result-oriented and process-oriented management, policy deployment offers opportunities for meaningful discussions between managers of different levels and ensures that every manager clearly understands the goals to be reached and is committed to them. Whenever an abnormality occurs (in the form of a deviation from the agreed-upon target), the causes can then be sought in a *policy audit* and corrective action taken.

Since the term "audit" has the connotation of "inspection," some people prefer the term "policy diagnosis." Although the TQC audit associated with the Deming Prize is well known, there are TQC audits at all levels of management in Japan, starting with the audits performed by top management and going down to the division manager's audit. These audits are conducted to check whether the policies (or goals) that have been deployed between the different levels of management have been properly executed.

The audits or diagnoses are conducted not to criticize the result but to point out the processes that have led to the result and thus to help people recognize the shortcomings in their efforts. In other words, the audits are conducted to identify *what* is wrong, not *who* is wrong.

The president of a company that has introduced TQC conducts audits once or twice a year at all major divisions of the company. When he visits a plant, he typically spends the morning with the plant managers going over the progress made in implementing the cross-functional policies deployed. In the afternoon, he will walk through the workshops, seemingly at random, and talk with foremen, supervisors, and workers to check their understanding of TQC as it relates to their jobs. Often, he will ask to see the reports and charts so essential to TQC.

All deviations, both positive and negative, are handled with equal zeal and their causes studied in the audit process. In the case of negative deviations, such as not meeting the production norm or turning out more defective parts than anticipated, it is understandable that management would make every effort to find the causes. But even when production exceeds the target or the sales figures are far better than expected, management tries to identify the causes for such pleasant surprises, since, in the TQC way of thinking, they represent deviations. In this case, however, the causes for the deviation must be identified not so that corrective measures can be taken but rather so that the causes for the positive deviation can be applied in subsequent operations.

POLICY DEPLOYMENT AND AUDIT
AT KOMATSU

At Komatsu, a manufacturer of industrial vehicles and construction machinery, every employee is provided with a small, pocket-size notebook at the beginning of each year. The first page of this notebook carries the president's policy for the year. The president's 1983 policy states, among other things, that Komatsu should develop its overall capabilities for producing cost-competitive products equipped with unique features, using the latest production techniques and know-how.

The policy goes on to emphasize that if Komatsu's overall capacity to plan and develop new products is to be enhanced, customer needs must be identified through the sales department and new ideas must be hatched and developed through R&D efforts. Such departments as sales, R&D, design, and production must improve their expertise in order to advance the state of the art in construction machinery, prepare for the market entry of new products, and develop qualified human resources to support a strong system of new product development.

The second page of this notebook is reserved for the policy of the division manager. In the plant, for example, the plant manager's policy is distributed to employees on adhesive-backed sheets that can be stuck onto the blank second page. In his policy, the plant manager has broken down the president's policy into about a dozen specific goals to be achieved at the plant. The requirements for building a system of new product development spelled out in the president's policy are "translated" into specific subgoals, such as more precise allocation of cost items in developing new products, the introduction of new production technology for designing drawings, and paying close attention to customer requirements when developing new products.

The third page of the notebook is again blank, except for the heading "Department Manager's Policy." Here, the department manager's policy is further "deployed" to each department level and spelled out in even more specific terms. Specific tasks are set forth for each department, corresponding to the plant manager's policies for realizing more accurate cost allocations for new products.

In the Procurement Department, for instance, measures to achieve the plant manager's policy to attain a more accurate cost breakdown for new product development include: (1) establishing a VT (value target) to use in conceptualizing and designing a new product and showing this

(Komatsu—continued)

target to subcontracting firms, (2) identifying and using the technologies developed by subcontractors, and (3) joining with the subcontractors in studies that focus on analysis of the VT and productivity. Each department devises its own specific measures to realize the goals spelled out in the plant manager's policy.

The fourth page of the notebook is reserved for each plant worker to use for noting down his immediate supervisor's policy. This policy is decided upon in private consultations between each worker and his supervisor.

Thus, the top-management policy is first handed down to the division manager and then to the middle and lower managers. As it goes down the line, it is transformed into very specific and concrete measures. Policy is spelled out throughout the organizational hierarchy in a systematic manner. The system allows each manager to quickly identify what needs to be done for each goal corresponding to the policy he laid out. ■

POLICY DEPLOYMENT AND AUDIT
AT KOBAYASHI KOSE

At Kobayashi Kose, a manufacturer of cosmetics, the plant manager's policies are broken down into four major categories: (1) quality assurance, (2) volume and delivery, (3) cost reduction, and (4) training and education. Each of these items is further broken down into specific items, such as, in the case of quality assurance: (a) improved production processes, (b) improved quality of supplies, (c) improved reliability, and (d) improved inspection procedures for quality assurance.

In September, each department starts working out basic plans for the next year. Plant managers coordinate the department plans by November in order to formulate an overall plant management policy, which is passed up to top management. Top management's policies, which have already been worked out, are coordinated with the plant-management policy into a final policy draft. The specific measures from each department serve as guidelines for the department's performance.

In order to audit the deployment and implementation of policies at Kobayashi Kose, the policy deployed at each level is put on the vertical axis of a matrix. On the horizontal axis of this matrix are listed measurement criteria such as the number of customer complaints, supply shortages, and per-capita productivity.

Every manager or supervisor at Kobayashi Kose has a checksheet in his pocket entitled, "My Criteria Indices." A female supervisor who has a dozen workers reporting to her at the production line, for instance,

(Kobayashi Kose — continued)

has a checksheet that states such criteria as the ratio of defective parts produced, the absenteeism rate, the production index on the production line, and the number of suggestions made by the workers.

Although the audit preliminary to the awarding of the famous Deming Prize is perhaps the most famous, every Japanese company that has started vigorous TQC uses policy deployment and internal audits as inseparable parts of its TQC activities.

Typically, such audits start with an audit by top management. The president and other directors visit each division and spend the whole day meeting with the plant management to discuss the progress of the policies at the plant level. Specialists from the leading universities may also be invited to join the audit. The president also uses part of his time to listen to presentations on various KAIZEN activities in this particular plant. A plant manager's audit is conducted following this twice-yearly top-management audit. The audit is repeated at every organizational level to evaluate performance with regard to the policies, measures, and control points that have been agreed upon.

One plant manager told me, "Audit meetings are very blunt, and many managers are loathe to attend, but in the end we find them quite effective." Experiences at such audit meetings are taken into account when the manager starts working on next year's plans, and as he becomes used to policy deployment and audit, the quality of his planning is also said to improve; namely, his planning becomes increasingly closer to reality year after year. Thus, both policy deployment and audit are believed to be an excellent opportunity to train people's planning and management skills. ■

Quality Deployment

One of the problems of management today is that employees have come to accept lower standards for the products they make. This happens because workers work on parts and components far removed from the final product and the customer. A prize-winning slogan by Mark Basich, a worker at Matsushita's Quasar Plant in the United States is indicative of this trend: "Are you proud enough to buy what you build?"

The concept of planned obsolescence has often been abused to the extent that factory people begin to accept a lower level of quality in the name of AQL (Acceptable Quality Level). Even worse, the salespeople in some companies have been reduced to selling products they know to be defective, and when their sales efforts are unsuccessful, they are accused of not working hard enough.

I recently visited the quality assurance manager at a European telecommunications equipment manufacturer, who told me that his problems were not those of the 1980s but of the 1970s. In explaining what he meant by the problems of the 1970s, he said that most of his staff's time was taken up in handling customer complaints and identifying causes of problems in the production stage. Since the firm's equipment was designed to last for many years, most of these complaints hark back to production problems encountered in the 1970s.

For instance, one of the most common causes was nonconformance to specifications, and the QA people are now trying to find why specifications were not followed. They are finding that different materials were sometimes used because they cost less, or that design specifications were arbitrarily changed in the workshop. What is worse, the standards and specifications used to produce the equipment are often missing, and there is nobody in the company today who knows what the situation was in those days. The problems' solutions must often be painstakingly put together like a jigsaw puzzle.

This is in sharp contrast to the approach of many Japanese companies. Today, the main emphasis in TQC is on building quality into design and production when new products are being developed. This starts with obtaining market information and identifying customer needs and involves deploying these findings into engineering and design requirements, production preparations, purchasing, and so on. Since it takes many years to develop new products, it is safe to say that many Japanese companies are now trying to deal not with the problems of the 1970s but with the problems of the late 1980s and 1990s.

According to Tamagawa University professors Masao Kogure and Yoji Akao, there are two approaches to satisfying customer requirements in quality control:

> The traditional method has been to look for the causes of problems and then to try to prevent the causes from recurring. . . .
>
> This method is called the analytical approach. In TQC, this approach has been firmly established, as is evident in the widespread use of tools like the Pareto analysis and the cause-and-effect diagram.
>
> However, [these tools] may not be effective in developing new

products—a process that requires a different approach. For new products, a design approach is needed to find means to achieve specific product objectives.

This design approach requires companies to work back from objectives to means of achieving those objectives.*

The problem in developing a new product is that design engineers sometimes do not understand the market requirements, since engineers and customers often speak different languages. For instance, when a housewife says, "I want a facial cream that doesn't melt when I go outside in the hot summer weather," she uses her own language to express her desire. However, the customer language itself is not enough to develop a new product, since it has to be "deployed" into technical language the design engineers can understand. For instance, "a facial cream that doesn't melt in Japan's summer heat" must be translated into a specific melting point for the facial cream, which may require a specific property for the clay used as the base.

In their article, Professors Kogure and Akao cite the example of Dynic Corporation's quality deployment for the connection between cars on the Japanese National Railways' *shinkansen* "bullet train." One of the customer requirements is to protect the passengers. This may be deployed into such secondary requirements as (a) does not leak, (b) does not undergo change in atmospheric pressure in tunnels, (c) does not tear under pressure, and so on. If necessary, the secondary requirements may be further deployed into tertiary requirements. These requirements are then deployed into counterpart characteristics the engineers can understand, such as tensile strength, tear strength, extension ratio, and anti-crumple strength. (See Figure 5.12.) Thus the customer-required quality characteristics are deployed into counterpart characteristics on the matrix form. Then the counterpart characteristics are further deployed into engineering and production requirements.

Through this process, it is possible to identify various engineering bottlenecks that exist at the time of developing new products. Dealing with these bottlenecks is called bottleneck engineering. If the bottlenecks are identified when the new product is being developed, and if coping with them calls for a high-level corporate strategy,

---

*Quality Progress Magazine, October 1983, published by ASQC (American Society for Quality Control).

Stage	No.	Primary	No.	Secondary	No.	Tertiary	Importance	Thickness	Weight	Tensile Strength	Tear Strength	Extension Ratio	Anti-crumple Strength	Water-pressure Resistance
Sewing	1	Easy to sew	11	Easy to stitch and cut	111	Light	C		O					
					112	Does not stick	B							
			12		121	Easy to work on sewing machine	B							
					122	Surface coating does not fall off	B							
			13	Can use adhesives	131	Withstands organic solvent	C							
Usage	2	Protect passengers	21	Does not let rain seep	211	No hole, no tear	A							O
			22	No change in atmospheric pressure in tunnel	221	Air-tight (no pinhole)	A							
			23	Does not tear under pressure	231	No tear under air pressure	A			O	O		O	
					232	No tear from poking from inside	A			O	O	O		
					233	No tear from shocks of starting or stopping	A			O	O	O		

Required Quality | Counterpart Characteristics

Copyright American Society for Quality Control, Inc., *Quality Progress Magazine*, October 1983. Reprinted by permission of publisher.

FIGURE 5.12   A Chart Showing Deployment of Quality Requirements at JNR

management can decide whether it should make the investment needed to solve these problems or resort to other alternatives, such as compromising on the quality of the product.

One of the benefits of quality deployment is improved communication among sales and marketing people and design and production people. Typically, sales and marketing people, despite their first-hand knowledge of the customer requirements, do not understand the technical language. On the other hand, engineers are concerned with sophisticated engineering applications and do not understand the customer needs. Thus, after the product has been produced and customer complaints start pouring in, the design engineer says, "I never dreamed that the product would be used that way."

As mentioned earlier, it may also happen that the design engineers do not care whether the company is capable of producing the product they design. After they have spent years developing a new product, they may be told by the production people that they cannot make it. With the quality-deployment tables at hand, however, the engineer can maintain better communication with the sales and marketing people as well as with the production people. Design engineers can even visit customers and discuss their requirements. Similarly, the purchasing people can maintain better communication with the vendors. Today, Japanese companies are trying to deploy the counterpart characteristics as well as cost factors and component factors together with the quality-deployment tables. With these latest tools for new-product development, Japanese companies have been able to develop competitive products with much shorter lead time than their competitors.

While Kogure and Akao maintain that the system of quality deployment works only if it is used as part of TQC, quality deployment has been regarded as the most significant development to come out of TQC in the last thirty years. According to Hisashi Takasu of Kobayashi Kose's TQC planning and coordination department, quality deployment yields the following benefits:

- It facilitates identification of the causes of customer complaints and makes it easier to take prompt remedial action
- It is a useful tool for improving product quality
- It is a useful tool for competitive analysis of product quality
- It stabilizes quality

- It cuts down on rejects and rework at the production site
- It decreases claims substantially

Another benefit of quality deployment is that it reduces the time required for developing a new product—sometimes by one-third to one-half.

Total Productive Maintenance

Although the term TPM (Total Productive Maintenance) is not as well known outside of Japan as TQC is, TPM is now practiced at a considerable number of Japanese manufacturing companies and is being vigorously promoted by the Japan Institute of Plant Maintenance. Whereas the major thrust of TQC is to improve overall management quality, TPM is directed at equipment improvements. Thus TPM is more hardware-oriented and TQC more software-oriented. As defined by the Japan Institute of Plant Maintenance, "TPM aims at maximizing equipment effectiveness with a total system of preventive maintenance covering the entire life of the equipment. Involving everyone in all departments and at all levels, it motivates people for plant maintenance through small-group and voluntary activities."

Training is an important part of TPM, just as it is of TQC, and TPM training is conducted with the emphasis on such basics as how the machines work and how to maintain them in the workshop.

Just as TQC has the Deming Prize and the Japan Quality Control Prize for companies that successfully introduce TQC, the Japan Institute of Plant Maintenance gives out the PM (Plant Maintenance) Distinguished Plant Award and other awards to companies that have successfully introduced TPM.

So far, most of the companies that have introduced TPM have been automobile or automobile-parts manufacturers. Since TQC and TPM emphasize different aspects in the quest for overall improvement, many of these companies have introduced both TQC and TPM at different times in their effort to improve corporate performance.

Topy Industries' Ayase Works, a medium-size factory with 660 employees and about 800 machines manufacturing automobile wheels, decided to introduce TPM in 1980. Until then, management efforts had been directed at improving worker performance and efficiency, allocating resources better, and making systems improvements.

However, management realized that further improvements would be difficult unless equipment productivity itself were dealt with. In this era of slower economic growth, better equipment utilization had become just as important as manpower and system improvements.

Topy's top management had declared that the Ayase Works should make an effort to remain profitable even if it had to operate at less than 80 percent of capacity. TPM was introduced as a means to this end.

There were three major parts to TPM at this factory: (1) establishing a system in which everybody was personally involved in voluntary PM activities and working to eliminate the four main causes of inefficiency (equipment breakdowns, mold troubles, tool-replacement time, and defectives); (2) improving the maintenance crew's problem-solving skills and engaging in KAIZEN activities aimed at zero breakdowns; and (3) improving production-engineering capabilities in such areas as tools and dies, tool-replacement time, tool design, and defectives and repairs.

The Japan Institute of Plant Maintenance helped the Ayase Works introduce TPM. In-house instruction was provided for 70 foremen and other leaders in basic maintenance skills. These courses included lubrication, how to tighten nuts and bolts, basic electricity, hydraulics and pneumatics, and drive mechanisms. Four hours were spent on each topic to ensure that these people had a firm grounding in maintenance. For example, they learned why applying too much oil sometimes causes the machine to overheat. Then these foremen and shop leaders went on to train the workers in the workshop.

TPM at the Ayase Works was a seven-step process, with workers involved in voluntary small-group activities at every stage.

Step 1: Housekeeping (with everybody participating in keeping the Works clean)

Step 2: Identifying problem causes and hard-to-clean places and taking the necessary countermeasures

Step 3: Drawing up standards for cleaning and oiling

Step 4: Reviewing the total system

Step 5: Setting standards for voluntary checking procedures

Step 6: Making sure everything is in order and in place

Step 7: Policy deployment

Mikiro Kikuchi, Ayase Works Manager, believes that sweeping, cleaning, and other housekeeping chores should be the starting point for all improvement activities. While housekeeping may look easy, it is the most difficult hurdle. Housekeeping is a way of eliminating unnecessary substances, and it is easier to identify trouble spots on machines that are kept clean. For instance, it is easier to identify such developing irregularities as cracks when the surface is clean. In fact, housekeeping is popularly perceived to be a process of checking for trouble spots.

Once the workers are in the habit of sweeping and cleaning their workplace, they have acquired discipline. During the first months of TPM, everyone in the Works, manager and worker alike, swept and cleaned the workplace every other Friday afternoon. At the time, the plant was operating at less than capacity, and employees had ample time to devote every other Friday afternoon to housekeeping. As the shop got cleaner, neater, and safer, workers developed a greater respect for their equipment, and they even volunteered to come in during the summer vacation to do cleaning. When the Works became busier and most housekeeping operations had to be conducted after working hours, management paid for this overtime.

In step 2, workers went around looking for trouble spots and distinguishing between those that they could take care of themselves and those that needed expert attention. In the past, the practice had been to leave all trouble spots to the maintenance crew. Now the workers were trained and motivated to do the easier repairs themselves. Also at this stage, workers identified many lubricating spots that had never been noticed before.

The workers checked a total of 240,000 nuts and bolts in the Works, tightened them, and then marked them with a line of white paint on both nut and bolt. Today, when every worker spends a few minutes housekeeping before he finishes up, he has only to look at the line on the nuts and bolts to see if they are aligned (that is, if the bolt is properly tightened).

In three years, they identified 9,000 trouble spots on the machines and added 130 foolproof devices at the Ayase Works. Although limit switches had been used before, there had been no standards for their installation or use. Today, 1,467 improved limit switches have been installed throughout the Works. The number of machinery breakdowns (defined as any breakdown that causes the line to stop for three minutes or more) was reduced from 1,000 per month before TPM to only 200 per month now. Likewise, oil leakage was reduced from 16,000 liters per month to 3,000 liters per month.

Far from being put out of business, the maintenance crew saw its job transformed into one of doing equipment diagnostics, working on more sophisticated maintenance jobs, and training machine operators to do simple maintenance work themselves.

The workers pride themselves on their neat, clean work environment. Morale is higher, and they have a much stronger attachment to the equipment with which they work. One of the unexpected side benefits of TPM has been that Topy's salespeople are now eager to bring customers to the plant and employ plant tours as a marketing tool.

TPM has clearly been good for Topy. By the time the company was awarded the PM Distinguished Plant Award three years later in 1983, it had achieved improvements in virtually every measure:

Labor productivity:	up 32%
Number of equipment breakdowns:	down 81%
Tool-replacement time:	down 50%–70%
Equipment operating ratio:	up 11%
Cost of defectives:	down 55%
Inventory-turnover ratio	up 50%

6

The KAIZEN Approach to Problem Solving

The Problem in Management

KAIZEN starts with a problem or, more precisely, with the recognition that a problem exists. Where there are no problems, there is no potential for improvement. A problem in business is anything that inconveniences people downstream, either people in the next process or ultimate customers.

The problem is that the people who create the problem are not directly inconvenienced by it. Thus people are always sensitive to problems (or inconveniences created by problems) caused by other people, yet insensitive to the problems and the inconveniences they cause other people. The best way to break the vicious circle of passing the buck from one person to another is for every individual to resolve never to pass on a problem to the next process.

In day-to-day management situations, the first instinct, when confronted with a problem, is to hide it or ignore it rather than to face it squarely. This happens because a problem is a problem, and because nobody wants to be accused of having created the problem. By resorting to positive thinking, however, we can turn each problem into a valuable opportunity for improvement. Where there is a problem, there is potential for improvement. The starting point in any improvement, then, is to identify the problem. There is a saying among TQC practitioners in Japan that problems are the keys to hidden treasure. Yet how many people have the courage to admit that they have a problem?

I still vividly recall my first sales call twenty-some years ago. I had just gotten back from a five-year stint with the Japan Productivity Center in the United States, had hung out my shingle as a management consultant, and was enthusiastically calling on prospective clients.

My first call was on Revlon Japan. I had an introduction from an executive at the head office in New York and had been told that their man in Tokyo needed some assistance. So, as a novice in the consulting business, I made a sweeping entrance into the general manager's office and, as soon as I had introduced myself, started with, "With regard to your problems in Japan . . ." The American general manager cut me off with a curt, "We have no problems in Japan." End of interview. I have since become wiser and now never discuss a client's "problem." It is always the client's "opportunity for improvement."

It is only human nature not to want to admit that you have a problem, since admitting to problems is tantamount to confessing failings or weaknesses. The typical American manager is afraid people will think he is part of the problem. However, once he realizes that he has a problem (as most people do), his first step should be to admit it and to "share" the problem. It is particularly important that he share the problem with his superiors, since he usually does not have the resources to solve it alone and will need company support.

The worst thing a person can do is to ignore or cover up a problem. When a worker is afraid that his boss will be mad at him if he finds out a machine is malfunctioning, he may keep on making the defective parts and hope that nobody will notice. However, if he is courageous enough, and if his boss is supportive enough, they may be able to identify the problem and solve it.

A very popular term in Japanese TQC activities is *warusa-kagen,* which refers to things that are not really problems but are somehow not quite right. Left unattended, *warusa-kagen* may eventually develop into serious trouble and may cause substantial damage. In the workplace, it is usually the worker, not the supervisor, who notices the *warusa-kagen.*

In the TQC philosophy, the worker must be encouraged to identify and report such *warusa-kagen* to the boss, who should welcome the report. Rather than blame the messenger, management should be glad the problem was pointed out while it was still minor and should welcome the opportunity for improvement. In reality, however, many opportunities are lost simply because neither worker nor management likes problems.

Another point in *warusa-kagen* is that the problems must be expressed in quantitative, not qualitative, terms. Many people are uncomfortable with the effort to quantify. Yet only by analyzing problems in terms of objective figures can we tackle them in a realistic manner.

When workers are trained to be attentive to *warusa-kagen,* they also become attentive to subtle abnormalities developing in the workshop. In one Tokai Rika plant, workers reported 534 such subtle abnormalities in a single year. Some of these irregularities might have led to serious trouble had they not been brought to management's attention.

Another important aspect of this approach to problems is that most problems in management occur in cross-functional areas. Good Japanese managers who have worked at the same company for years and expect to stay for years more have developed a sensitivity to cross-functional situations. (Promotion to important managerial positions should in part be based on how much sensitivity to cross-functional requirements the employee develops.) Information feedback and coordination with other departments is a routine part of a manager's job.

In many Western companies, however, cross-functional situations are perceived as conflicts and are addressed from the standpoint of conflict resolution rather than problem solving. The lack of predetermined criteria for solving cross-functional problems and the jealously guarded professional "turf" make the job of solving cross-functional problems all the more difficult.

KAIZEN and Labor–Management Relations

This may be an appropriate point at which to consider the role Western trade unions have traditionally played with regard to improvement.

If we take an unbiased look at what unions have been doing in the name of protecting their members' rights, we find that they have, by obstinately opposing change, often succeeded only in depriving their members of a chance for fulfillment, a chance to improve themselves.

By resisting change in the workplace, unions have deprived the workers of a chance to work better and more efficiently on an improved process or machine. Workers should welcome being exposed to new skills and opportunities, because such experience leads to new horizons and challenges in life. However, when management has suggested such changes as assigning workers different jobs, the unions have opposed it, arguing that it would lead to exploitation and would infringe upon the workers' union rights.

Stubbornly preserving the tradition of union membership based upon particular job skills, union members have been confined to their fragmented pieces of work and have forfeited precious opportunities to learn and acquire new skills associated with their work—opportunities to meet new challenges and to grow as human beings. Such an attitude has often been based on the union's fear that improvements may result in a decline in membership or unemployment for its members.

In May 1982, Hajime Karatsu, then managing director of Matsushita Communication Industrial, gave an address in Washington, D.C., explaining Japan's successful TQC practices. After this speech, someone asked him if he thought there was a culture gap between Japan and the United States that made TQC possible in Japan but not in the United States. Karatsu's response was:

> Before coming to Washington, I stopped off in Chicago to see the Consumer Electronics Show. There were many Matsushita products on display at the show. When they arrived packed in crates, it was the work of the carpenters' union to remove nails from the crates. However, simply taking out the nails was not enough to remove the entire wooden frame, since there were some nuts and bolts remaining. The man from the carpenters' union said that it was not his job to remove the nuts and bolts, and that he would not do it. Finally the frames were removed, but again the work stopped because the rest had to be done by a worker from another union. Then we learned that pamphlets ordered from Japan had arrived. I went to see about them, but there was nobody there from the right union to unload the packages. We waited for two hours, but no one showed up. Finally, the truck driver who had delivered the packages gave up and went back, with the pamphlets still in his truck.
>
> It might seem that there is a cultural pattern here that makes it impossible to cooperate to get the job done. However, baseball is a very American game, and I have never seen the first basemen's and second basemen's unions discussing who should field the ball

after the batter hits it. Whoever can do it does it, and the whole team benefits. In Japanese companies, people try to achieve the same type of teamwork as on a baseball team.

In 1965, Isetan Department Store, one of the largest department stores in Japan (6,000 employees), moved to a five-day week for all employees. At the same time, labor and management agreed that one of the days off should be used for rest and the other for self-improvement. In fact, a joint declaration on Isetan's manpower resources development policy was issued by the company president and the union president. It read:

> The Isetan management and union hereby declare that, sharing the same workplace, we will join hands to develop our natural personalities and capabilities to the fullest extent in our daily life and to create an environment conducive to development.

The underlying philosophy of this joint declaration was that (1) an individual's developing and exercising his skills at work benefits both the company and the individual and (2) people are constantly seeking self-improvement, and the real meaning of equal opportunity is to provide opportunities for growth.

Stealing Jobs

People who are interested in improving their work should take a positive interest in the upstream processes that provide the material or semifinished products. They should also take an interest in the downstream processes, regarding them as their customers and making every effort to pass along only good materials or products.

As the old saw goes, "You cannot make a good omelette out of rotten eggs." There is a similar correlation between the individual's job and the jobs of his co-workers: if one worker is interested in making KAIZEN part of his work, his fellow workers must also be involved.

Any job involving more than one worker has gray areas that do not belong to any one individual. Such gray areas must be taken care of by whoever is at hand. When the worker sticks to his own job description and refuses to do any more than what is formally required of him, there is little hope of KAIZEN.

The Japanese worker has been noted for his willingness to take care of such gray areas. Because of the lifetime-employment system, the Japanese blue-collar worker does not feel threatened even when other people pitch in and do part of his job, since it affects neither his income nor his job security. For the same reason, he is willing to teach workers the skills that he has acquired on the job. This smooth transfer of skills from one generation of workers to another has consolidated the solid base of skilled labor in Japanese industry.

In an environment where job descriptions and manuals dictate every action, there is little flexibility for workers to engage in such "gray area" activities. The workers should be trained so that they can work flexibly in these gray areas, even as they strictly follow the established work standards in performing the job. Flexibility is further reduced when several craft unions are involved in the same workplace. In such a case, going too far into a gray area can easily be construed as "stealing the other guy's job." In Japan, this would not be stealing but would be a positive and humane contribution to KAIZEN, viewed as being to everyone's advantage.

There is something dehumanizing about the logic that the only way you can be assured of a job is to refuse to teach anyone else your skills. We must create an environment in which improvement is everybody's business and everyone's concern.

A JOINT COMMITMENT FOR KAIZEN—THE NUMMI STORY

There are several avenues through which KAIZEN activities may be pursued in the plant. The first and most common of them is for the worker to change the way he does his job to make it more productive, more efficient, or safer. This usually leads to a change in the work pace.

The second avenue is to make equipment improvements, such as installing foolproof mechanisms and changing the machinery layout. The third avenue is to make improvements in the systems and procedures, and the fourth is a combination of the other three. All these alternatives should be exhausted before management starts thinking about innovation.

One of the many activities to be conducted at the first stage is reviewing the current work standards to see if there is room for improving performance to meet the standards and then to upgrade the standards. This is the starting point for worker KAIZEN.

Generally speaking, however, labor unions in the West have been very sensitive to such issues as changing the way workers work, since they fear any changes may lead to harder work and exploitation. Consequently,

(NUMMI — continued)

organized labor has shown great reluctance to changing work standards in the West.

NUMMI (New United Motor Manufacturing, Inc.), a joint venture between Toyota and General Motors in Fremont, California, deserves special mention in this respect. At the NUMMI plant, the UAW (United Auto Workers) has negotiated a pact that includes agreement to worker involvement in KAIZEN. (Management and the union have not only agreed to the concept of KAIZEN but even used the Japanese term KAIZEN in the contract in lieu of "improvement," which did not seem to represent the right concept!)

Work standardization is one of the mainstays of the Toyota production system. As Toyota defines it, standardized work is the optimum combination of workers, machines, and material. The raison d'être for standardized work is that it is the best way to ensure such things as quality, cost, and volume. Standardized work is also regarded as the safest way to do the job.

There are three major components of standardized work at Toyota: cycle time, work sequence, and the number of pieces in process. If the worker is unable to do the standardized work, the foreman's concern is to help him do a better job. Once this has been done, the next step is to raise the work standards themselves. The challenge of KAIZEN is constant.

At Toyota, a foreman is expected to do this by involving workers in the KAIZEN process. Thus KAIZEN at Toyota means first improving worker performance to enable the workers to perform up to standard and then raising the standards themselves in a total effort involving the workers.

The experience at NUMMI indicates that the union has accepted management's role in KAIZEN as well as worker participation in KAIZEN, which will lead to upgraded work standards. Practically every worker at NUMMI speaks of KAIZEN today. This is the first instance in Western labor relations where there has been accord on the joint commitment to KAIZEN in the workplace. It should also be added that the NUMMI management has made a commitment to the union to do its best to see that KAIZEN activities in the workplace will not result in a reduced work force.

Many workers at NUMMI had been employed at GM's Fremont plant, which was shut down because it was not competitive. They had no difficulty understanding that they had to produce quality cars in order to keep their jobs viable. If standardized work and KAIZEN are what it takes to produce quality cars, then it follows that they should welcome the opportunity to participate in KAIZEN.

Another development at this plant has been multiple job assignments. Instead of breaking the jobs down into many different categories, labor and management agreed to establish fewer job categories and to encourage workers to engage in multiple jobs. ■

One of the lessons to be learned from the NUMMI story is that organized labor's acceptance is essential if KAIZEN is to succeed. In this context, it may be useful to review KAIZEN from the industrial-relations perspective.

Most activities that take place within a company fall between the two extremes of cooperation and confrontation – cooperation referring to working together to bake a bigger pie and confrontation to fighting over how to divide the pie. Because there is no such thing as 100 percent confrontation between labor and management, thinking of industrial relations as a cooperation/confrontation continuum gives a more positive and realistic picture than the traditional "us–them" stereotype.

It is in the worker's best interests to make his company more competitive and profitable, since this enhances his chances for higher wages and greater job security. Thus, because the thrust of KAIZEN activities is to improve such cross-functional areas as quality, cost, and scheduling, and because improvement in these areas leads to a bigger pie, it is only natural that labor has a stake in promoting KAIZEN.

So far so good. But what if KAIZEN's improvements adversely affect income and job security—for example, by throwing people out of work? Figure 6.1 reviews KAIZEN in terms of income and job security, with organized labor's response shown as either positive or negative.

	Income Potential	Job Potential	Job Allocation
Labor response is:	Positive	Positive if management is flexible.	Positive if labor is flexible.
		Negative if management is not flexible.	Negative if labor is not flexible.
		⬆ Calls for management initiative.	⬆ Calls for labor initiative.

FIGURE 6.1 *Labor Response to KAIZEN Implementation*

"We want more" has long been a rallying cry for organized labor, but it is important that labor and management realize that this "more" can mean not only a bigger share of the existing pie but also a big share of a larger pie. Although less in percentage terms, 55 percent of 120 is still more than 60 percent of 100.

Wages must be carefully weighed against job security, and labor's concern is thus divided into job potential and job allocation where job potential means the potential impact upon the total number of jobs available, and job allocation the actual assignment of manpower within this potential.

Figure 6.1 shows that while organized labor has good reason to be positive about KAIZEN from the standpoint of income potential, labor will not fully accept KAIZEN if the resulting improvements lead to reduced job potential. On the allocation side, labor must be prepared to accept the training needed for the manpower-allocation changes that ensue as a result of KAIZEN.

Large-scale innovation is superficially less complicated, since the decision to innovate is usually made by management, with little worker input or involvement. Yet despite this lack of labor input, innovation is a major labor concern if it adversely affects income or job. Microelectronics are a case in point, and it is easy to see labor's concern in this area.

It is therefore crucial that a joint labor–management commitment be forged, as was done at NUMMI, before introducing KAIZEN. This calls for both parties to be realistic and flexible in approaching KAIZEN. Just as it is essential that management take the initiative in meeting labor's concern about job potential, so are labor initiative and acceptance on job allocation and retraining essential. Job security can happen only when it is accompanied by cooperation on such issues as the demarcation lines between different jobs and the status of workers who do jobs that are "enlarged" and "enriched" as a result of KAIZEN. Where there are a number of unions involved, they have to work together in the best interests of all workers rather than only their own members. It would be ironic indeed if unions, formed to defend the workers' rights, ended up squabbling over turf at the workers' expense.

Does KAIZEN activity automatically lead to job redundancy? Generally speaking, it does not. Even when redundancy ensues, it may well be possible to assign redundant workers to other jobs and to offer them the opportunity to learn new skills. Chapter 4 on suggestion systems explains that the main areas for suggestions for improvement in Japan are the individual's own work; energy and other resource conservation; the work environment; machines and processes; jigs and tools; office work procedures; product quality; new-product ideas; customer services; and customer relations. Few of these activities lead to redundancy.

When management retains the same number of workers despite productivity increases, it can increase production. In addition, the more broadly capable workers are, the more likely they are to see opportunities for additional KAIZEN.

Only when management has succeeded in building a KAIZEN-conscious work force can it tackle the challenge of just-in-time production and the assembly of different models of products on the same line. KAIZEN has been successfully introduced in the Japanese workplace building upon continuous management efforts to secure labor support and a positive and constructive labor response, as shown in the productivity movement and small-group activities that stress voluntary involvement in KAIZEN.

Management and Labor: Enemies or Allies?

I recently had occasion to talk with a Japanese businessman just back from Europe, where he had been the managing director of a Japanese branch office employing about 50 local people. A typical Japanese executive, he would visit his staff members at their desks and chat with them about their families and hobbies. His office was "open," and his employees were free to see him anytime during working hours. During wage negotiations, he took the time to explain the general economic climate and competitive market conditions to help his employees understand and accept their new wage levels.

One of the first steps taken by his European successor was to request that employees wanting to see him make appointments through his secretary. When wage increases were determined, the new manager simply posted a notice on the bulletin board. He also fired several redundant employees outright.

With the world becoming smaller, more and more people of different nationalities, ethnic heritages, and cultural backgrounds have come to work together, and there has been an increasing need for "intercultural understanding and communication." However, a good look inside the company shows that it is the management class that most needs to learn these communication skills. Most managers seem to be at a loss how to relate to their workers. Sharing a common language does not guarantee effective communication. In fact, it might be better if managers regarded their workers as people from a totally different cultural background, since, after all, the working class has values and aspirations different from those of the management class. One should not be fooled by the fact that they both speak the same language.

In the West, it may be that managers do not understand, or do not want to understand, workers' aspirations because of the psychological divisions between labor and management. This problem is compounded where workers literally do not speak the same language as management. Managers in such a situation are truly faced with the need to develop intercultural skills as well as skills to facilitate communication with their compatriots.

What does one usually do on first meeting someone from a foreign culture one knows very little about? The accepted practice is to display gestures of friendship (to assure the other party that one's intentions are not hostile), to pay careful attention to behavioral cues, and to wait patiently until there is an understanding of the other party's actions.

However, the typical Western manager's behavior is every cultural anthropologist's nightmare. His behavior is just the opposite of everything a person wishing to establish rapport with strangers is supposed to do. Since the manager views the workplace as a hostile jungle, his office is a well-fortified, plush outpost where he entrenches himself and shuns communication. If communication exists at all, it is at best one-way. The manager feels protected by walls he builds between himself and the workers. He often flaunts his status and power in the face of the less privileged workers.

I recently heard about a factory in Europe where the blue-collar workers wear blue shirts, the technicians yellow shirts, and the white-collar workers and managers white shirts. Blue-collar workers in the West usually eat in a separate dining room from white-collar workers. I am told that there are four different dining halls in the Soviet Ministry of Foreign Trade to serve four different levels of bureaucrats. Apparently the propensity to divide people into different classes is no monopoly of Western capitalism.

From the color of the shirts they wear to the separate dining rooms they use, workers are constantly reminded that they are a different breed of animal. And yet, management today loves to talk about such ideals as personal fulfillment and the quality of the work environment! In Japan, it is not uncommon for *all* the people to wear identical uniforms, and for everyone to eat together in the common dining room.

There are places where the foreman's effectiveness is measured by the number of punitive actions taken against his workers. The more the better. This kind of relationship is a far cry from the goal of establishing intercultural communication and understanding between the two groups.

One of Japan's advantages has been the homogeneity of its society and the existence of highly motivated workers. However, this does not mean that Japanese management did not have to develop communication skills. The Japanese National Railways (JNR) represents one case where management has failed to build a working relationship with labor, and the result has been the creation of deep-seated antagonism. Absenteeism, for instance, runs as high as 40 percent in some quarters. In most Japanese companies, however, management has succeeded in assuming a supportive role and in building two-way communication.

Both sides must be willing to alter their behavior to change labor–management relations. Management, for example, should develop a more open and supportive style. Although change is not easily effected, it is possible to introduce programs in which both parties are *forced* to work together and to learn from each other.

Along with QC circles and other small-group activities to encourage worker participation, Japanese companies have devised various other programs to improve communication with workers and their families. The following are some examples:

- Plant tours for family members
- Family-directed publicity on company activities
- Company badges for workers
- Citations for outstanding performance, long service, safety maintenance, and the like
- Intradepartmental contests

- Welcome parties for new employees
- Visits to other company plants
- Company bulletins and plant newspapers
- Radio broadcasts of the latest news
- President's message enclosed in pay envelope
- Field-day events
- In-house "Guinness Books"
- Regular meetings with top management

Unless a conscious, pervasive effort is made to neutralize differences of status within the company, class antagonism will poison the atmosphere and doom the most rational of plans. The manager's first job is to learn to communicate with his employees so both workers and the company can achieve their common goal.

Small-Group Activities: Bridging the Labor–Management Gap

Every year, 500 "junior leaders" from Japanese companies attend a 16-day seminar/cruise on the *Coral Princess* that takes them to the Philippines and Hong Kong. A captive audience, they spend their days listening to lectures given by experts on such subjects as leadership development, workshop activation, self-development, and the impact of small-group activities on productivity improvement. At night, they meet informally and discuss work experiences. Selected from companies all over Japan, these junior leaders have all demonstrated leadership skills in small-group activities. They are usually about 27 or 28 years old and are union members.

These "on-board training sessions," which have been held since 1972, are conducted by the Junior Executive Council of Japan, an organization established to develop the young leaders who will eventually form the backbone of Japanese corporate management.

Says Fumio Imamura, managing director of the Council:

> A good piece of fabric is always made of two threads—the warp
> and the woof, the horizontal and vertical threads. Similarly, a
> healthy organization must have both formal and informal threads.
> The vertical threads are the managerial hierarchy, the formal lines
> of communication through which company policy is conveyed.

The informal or horizontal are represented by voluntary participation in the numerous small groups of which the company is comprised. It is at this level that corporate policy is discussed and implemented, and this is why we need to develop junior leaders who can draw out participation and commitment from other group members.

Since the late 1950s, Japanese companies have encouraged the formation of small groups among their workers. These small groups have played a vital role in raising productivity, creating a more pleasant and meaningful work environment, and improving industrial relations. QC circles are a good example of the informal small-group phenomenon. There are many other "circles," active in such areas as the ZD movement, the worker suggestion system, safety groups, and recreational activities.

According to a survey conducted recently by the Japanese Ministry of Labor, about half the companies with more than 1,000 employees have small-group activities. Most of them are employee-initiated with management approval.

The Junior Executive Council of Japan also conducts a number of two- and three-day programs for training informal leaders. These programs provide regular training to some 10,000 leaders annually. Over the years, the Council has trained more than 100,000 such leaders, and these people now spearhead worker groups in production shops. As a further incentive, the Council presents annual awards to leaders who have made outstanding contributions, and junior leaders compete for various trophies and citations.

Small groups also play an important role in resolving conflict and laying the foundation for good industrial relations. Union leaders often take intransigent stances when facing management, refusing to yield on their specific demands. However, workers at the shop floor level are usually more pragmatic and concerned with the day-to-day affairs directly related to their role as employees, not just as union members. It is here that the vertical and horizontal threads cross.

Thus the creation of sound labor–management relations in Japan often depends on building up a small core of workers at the shop floor level who are able to reconcile their dual roles as loyal employees and loyal union members. The loyal employee wishes to work hand in hand with management to create better products and bigger profits. There is no conflict here with management. There is conflict, however, as the loyal union member challenges management regarding the distribution of profits.

Once a new policy has been adopted by management, it is transmitted to shop floors through the normal management hierarchy. However, this process represents communication involving only half of the "threads." At the same time, workers must be brought to a full understanding of management's aims in order to elicit their cooperation and commitment. This is the raison d'être of the small groups led by their informal leaders.

The grass-roots "democratization" process witnessed in postwar Japanese companies has taken the form of worker involvement in shop-floor affairs. By encouraging participation in small groups, management gains worker commitment and consent. Union leadership has also found that communication channels with management are often inadequate without such grass-roots activity. The Japanese model stands in sharp contrast to West Germany, where the so-called *Mitbestimmung* is discussed only by the top levels of management and labor, without inviting the involvement of rank-and-file workers. Shop-floor "democratization" is the result of constant efforts on the part of both labor and management to build small, informal circles.

Another organization involved in the formation of worker circles is the Japan Productivity Center, which conducts productivity seminars for young workshop leaders. These four-day seminars are held several times a year, and participants are selected from both management and labor.

Productivity seminars are included in the annual training programs at major companies such as Nippon Steel Corporation, and some unions also use productivity seminars as part of their leadership training programs. During these seminars, the workers are told that the goal of productivity improvement is to build a better future and greater welfare. They are also taught that nothing will be handed to them on a silver platter but everything will require diligent efforts on everyone's part. Cooperation between labor and management is seen as an essential factor, and mutual trust a must.

However, when it comes to the actual division of the fruits of these efforts, labor and management naturally stand opposed. Collective bargaining and strikes are the tools used in reconciliation.

Previous collaboration with management is not seen as a contradiction of union efforts.

This is the essence of the philosophy taught to the young leaders at these seminars. But they also discuss ways to create a more pleasant and fulfilling work environment and methods of organizing informal circles. Since the Japan Productivity Center first began holding seminars in 1965, nearly 10,000 leaders have attended.

The JPC also has another set of educational programs for union executives called the "University of Labor." This program was initiated in the belief that union leaders must have a sound and broad understanding of business management, including such areas as financial analysis, if they are to deal with management on an equal footing. The union leader who cannot understand financial statements and analyze the company's performance will not be able to negotiate with management on such labor-related subjects as technological innovation, personnel transfers, and the scrapping of facilities. Thousands of union leaders have been "graduated" from this university already.

The Productivity Culture

The Japan–United States Economic Relations Group, a bilateral study team of four "wisemen" each from Japan and the United States, recently submitted a report on factors affecting the two nations' economic relationship and how it can be strengthened.

The report cited the concern in the United States over decline in the rate of annual productivity growth with a special observation on how that decline affected competitiveness in U.S.–Japanese trade.

It also noted increased awareness in the United States for a thorough program to increase productivity. As a part of this growing awareness, the group will also look for areas of cooperation between Japan and the United States in an effort to take advantage of improvements attained by Japan recently.

On reading this interim report, I recalled nostalgically my years in the United States when I was helping Japanese-productivity study missions to look at how labor and management in America were dealing with the problem of productivity, to learn from them, and to discover the "secret" of America's high productivity. Among those with whom I had the pleasure of working were Masumi Muramatsu, now president of Simul International; T. Y. Arai, now president of Tokyu Hotels International; Thomas T. Yamakawa of Price Waterhouse; Masaaki Matsushita, president of Shaklee Japan K.K.; Shoichi Osakatani of Mitsubishi Motors Corporation; and Masao Kunihiro, now a television news anchorman. The organization responsible for these missions on the Japanese side was the Japan Productivity Center, an organization founded in 1955 with the following philosophy:

> We believe that improvement in productivity ultimately leads to expanded employment opportunities. Temporary redundancy should be dealt with to the extent possible by reallocation, thus minimizing the risk of unemployment.
> We believe that specific steps should be studied by joint consultation between labor and management.
> We believe that the fruits of improved productivity should be fairly distributed among management, labor, and consumers.

Yoshisaki Ohta, former managing director of the Japan Industrial Vehicles Association, recalls that the industrial gap between the United States and Japan was so great at the time that some people even argued that it was no use Japan's trying to learn from the United States, since it would be unable to apply any lessons learned anyway. In 1959, when he visited the United States for the first time as a member of a study mission, Japan's total production of fork lifts was 1,600 as against 30,000 for the United States. In 1980, Japan surpassed the United States in fork-lift production. While the Japanese fork-lift industry grew 60-fold from 1958 to 1980, the U.S. industry grew only three-fold during the same 22-year period. In 1959, not a single Japanese company was among the international "big five" fork-lift companies. In 1980, three of the big five were Japanese companies.

The Japan Productivity Center celebrated the silver anniversary of its founding in 1980. During its first 25 years, JPC dispatched 1,468 overseas study missions involving 22,800 executives. Yet today, JPC receives more study missions from abroad than it sends.

JPC's activities now include such diverse fields as executive development, labor–management relations, international exchanges of experts and technology, and management and technical consultation. In addition, it publishes newspapers, manuals, and books on productivity-related subjects. Employing 600 people at 20 regional chapters, it also has overseas offices in Washington, D.C., Frankfurt, London, Paris, and Rome. Clearly, JPC has grown along with Japanese productivity.

Kohei Goshi, who was instrumental in organizing JPC in 1955 and has headed it ever since, said in 1980:

> Twenty-five years ago, we started the productivity movement in the conviction that its ultimate goal should be to improve the welfare of employees. No matter what management may do, physical productivity will not improve unless people working for the company are willing to work and have the feeling that they are doing important work. In those days, Japan was eager to introduce scientific management from the West. But we felt that management involves not only technology but also the human heart.
>
> While the efforts for raising productivity have been mostly directed to the technical side in the West, our efforts have been directed to raising the level of worker satisfaction at the place of work. In other words, it is not enough to simply try to manipulate productivity. We have to deal with the human heart. Thus I believe that the issue of productivity should be introduced with a cultural approach.
>
> With its grounding in this philosophy, the productivity movement in Japan has flourished, making maximum use of the human-centered management techniques such as labor–management cooperation, collectivism, small-group activities, QC circles, and what have you. The "productivity culture" has been one of Japan's greatest postwar achievements, something which we can export to other countries with pride.

A few years ago, Goshi was awarded the First Class Order of the Sacred Treasure. Present at the party celebrating this award were two former Prime Ministers, Takeo Fukuda and Takeo Miki. Said Fukuda, "I have yet to receive this high award just bestowed on Goshi, which means that I shall be seated behind him at Imperial receptions. This is indicative of the Japanese government's appreciation for his contributions to the field of productivity improvement. He obviously outranks me."

THE WELL-ROUNDED WORKER:
EXPERIENCES AT NIPPON STEEL AND NISSAN MOTOR

At Nippon Steel Corporation's Kimitsu Works, six men working on the reheating furnace at the hot strip mill formed a JK group to study how to improve heat-use efficiency. In their studies, they found that the clue was to stop air from getting into the furnace. This led them to the idea of using pressurized air. In order to make the necessary adjustments on the equipment, however, they needed electro-welding and plumbing help from the maintenance department engineers.

When they asked the maintenance department for help, they were told, "Since you're working on a problem with your own equipment, why don't you try to do all the work by yourselves? We'll be glad to help you learn the necessary skills, though."

So these furnace operators set about learning welding and plumbing on holidays and after work under the guidance of maintenance department engineers. Although these skills had nothing directly to do with their jobs, they were willing to make the effort to acquire the new skills. After 20 hours, they were sufficiently skilled to do their own modifications on the reheating furnace. When the adjustments were made, the heating efficiency was improved enough to save 5,000 kilocalories per ton.

As mentioned earlier, JK stands for *jishu kanri,* which might be translated as self-management or voluntary participation. In the framework of permanent employment, Japanese workers are psychologically ready to tackle many different job assignments. When they first join the company, they do not even know what kind of job they are going to be assigned to. When they are assigned to a specific position, such as working on a lathe, management makes sure that they are given enough training. When the company decides to transfer them to a different job, such as a milling machine, management again provides them with the necessary training, and the workers willingly make the switch. So far as the workers are concerned, they are assured of life-long employment with the company, and they are willing to acquire the various skills as part of their ongoing self-development. They regard themselves as vendors of nonspecific skills to be developed during their employment. In turn, management needs this receptiveness to enable the company to respond as scientific advances and environmental changes create new jobs.

This has, for example, helped management to shift the work force between different industry segments. When the Kyushu coal mines were closed in the 1960s, the displaced miners were transferred to the steel industry. Similarly, when the shipbuilding industry was struck by recession, many of its workers were transferred to the automobile sectors of the same corporate groups. Such flexibility and adaptability, and the workers' willingness to tackle any job assignment, are one of the strengths

(Nippon Steel—continued)

of the Japanese economy. This is enhanced by the fact that most of these workers are organized into enterprise unions, not craft unions.

It is ironic that modern science, in fostering specialists and professionals, has tended to strengthen people's class consciousness and the very "caste system" that modern society is trying to get away from. These rapidly multiplying spheres of specialists lose no time in organizing themselves and forming alliances. Sometimes, there are more specialists than there are jobs in a given field, yet they often resist changing jobs out of "professional pride."

This same attitude is evident in business. Coal miners want to remain coal miners, regardless of whether there are enough jobs for all of them or whether there is a need for the coal they mine. When workers in a company begin to assert their coveted "specialties," want to remain in the same job category, and refuse to learn new skills or to take different types of jobs, it becomes a colossal task for management to introduce change. But in Japan, the workers are more than willing to acquire new skills and take new jobs, and there has recently been a conscious effort on the part of Japanese management to train multiple-skill workers.

At Nissan Motor, workers doing manual spot-welding on auto bodies are trained to do the necessary dressing work on the chip when it is worn out. Under normal circumstances, such work would be done by an engineer from the maintenance department. However, says Nissan managing director Shoichi Nakajima, since it is the workers who know their equipment best, they welcome the opportunity to acquire new skills that relate to their work.

Regarding it a challenge to do the maintenance work on their own equipment themselves, they willingly go to the maintenance department every other month to acquire maintenance skills. To them, this is job enrichment and job enlargement of a sort.

According to Nakajima, the worker's job in the mass-production process tends to be simple and single-skilled—particularly in assembly-line operations—which leads to painful monotony. Helping workers acquire multiple skills is a good way to liberate them from monotonous work. Nissan began encouraging multiple-skill workers about the same time as management started to introduce automation and robotization. Work procedures at the body assembly plant have been automated 50 percent, which means that the number of workers has been halved over the last 10 years. Rather than being laid off, redundant workers were assigned to other departments, such as assembly lines, presses, and painting.

At Nissan, there are three main criteria for the training of multiple-skill workers. First, if possible, the worker should be able to perform all types of jobs within a given department. For instance, in the case of the auto-body department, the worker should be able to do spot-welding, soldering, and more. Second, in keeping with the increasingly complex

(Nissan Motor—continued)

requirements of new equipment and systems, the worker should be familiar with such subjects as machining, hydraulics, pneumatics, electricity, and electronics so that he can function knowledgeably in such related nonproduction fields as equipment monitoring, maintenance, and emergency countermeasures. Third, with the introduction of automation and labor-saving devices, workers in a given department are liable to be shifted to other departments, in which case they may have to do totally new work. Workers must therefore be trained so that their skills can be extended to new and unrelated fields. For instance, over the years, workers from the body section have been shifted to such other areas as painting and press operations.

As Nissan tried to improve productivity with the introduction of automation and industrial robots, personnel reassignments were needed. This meant that management had to train the displaced workers in new skills and prepare them for new jobs. Nissan had no choice but to train the workers so that they could become multiple-skill workers. The transition has certainly not been toil-free, but the workers have generally been more than willing to learn new skills.

Nissan has a combination of programs to develop such multiple-skill workers. First, newly hired workers go through an initial orientation program in which they are exposed to the use of machines and equipment. In some cases, this orientation may take several weeks.

Second, the company sponsors annual competitions in technical skills, at both the plant level and the corporate level. Competitors in these "technolympics" undergo intensive training on holidays and after work to be worthy of representing their workshops. In 1978, competitions were held on 42 technical skills.

Third, Nissan evaluates and certifies technical competence levels according to a format developed within the company. Skills are divided into basic skills and applied skills, and each level is broken down into three grades. Before assuming a more difficult job, the worker must prove himself and pass the certification test.

Fourth, production workers are sometimes transferred to the maintenance or inspection departments for three to six months to acquire the necessary skills.

Fifth, workers are rotated both within a given department and among departments, with additional technical training provided whenever necessary. Each worker carries a card showing his training history.

All in all, this extensive program has more than paid for itself in creating a work force at once technically more flexible and psychologically more receptive to automation. If the Nissan experience is any guide, developing multiple-skill workers appears to be a crucial step for today's management to meet the ever-changing requirements of tomorrow. ■

Productivity in Disarray:
The Hard and the Soft Aspects

Several years ago, the New Year's card from Japan Productivity Center chairman and founder Kohei Goshi read, "Productivity is a concept implying continuing progress, both material and spiritual."

This simple but profound statement is an eloquent definition of the nature of productivity, for it calls attention to the spiritual as well as the material aspects of progress. It is becoming increasingly evident that the latest engineering and management techniques are effective only if used in an environment in which employees can adopt these techniques as their own and work hand in hand with management to improve productivity in the workshop.

It is obvious that the first step is to ensure the cooperation and commitment of workers in improving productivity. This is as much of a challenge to management as to labor. Before launching an all-out campaign for productivity improvement, it is important to obtain labor's explicit understanding of and commitment to the idea that productivity improvement is mutually beneficial.

According to Goshi, labor–management problems in the West tend to be solved within the framework of contracts and regulations, while such problems are solved in Japan by mutual trust, compassion, and understanding. Labor–management practices in Japan have been developed over the years through conscious, concerted efforts on both sides to solve individual problems, one at a time. Both labor and management seek agreement through discussion of mutual problems rather than confrontation.

For years, my barber used to ask me if I had itchy places on my scalp. I interpreted his question as meaning, "You have dandruff, so your scalp must be itchy," and my answer was therefore always a categorical "no" in repudiation of my dandruff. It was only some years later that it dawned on me that what he meant was, "If your scalp is itchy, I will be glad to massage it while washing your hair." Since realizing this, I have become more relaxed and have been able to enjoy the barber's extra consideration.

I suspect that this sort of misunderstanding often occurs in labor–management relations. Management puts a proposal to labor that it feels will be mutually beneficial, but if management does not take the time and effort to explain this proposal, its message may be misconstrued. In order to build a more human relationship between the two parties, both should strive to create better lines of communication. In this instance, management must carry a bigger share of the responsibility than before.

I should point out that while it is frequently assumed that all Japanese companies have high levels of productivity, there are cases where the introduction of a productivity movement has ended in outright failure. For instance, labor disputes abound in the Japanese public sector. Needless to say, public-sector workers do not feel that the existence of their organization is endangered by their actions, nor does management feel a need to build effective labor-management relations. As a result, both parties tend to be less concerned with productivity.

In 1970, the Japanese National Railways (JNR) decided to launch a productivity campaign to cope with its perennial deficits and to improve worker morale. The major thrust of the campaign was to provide training programs for managers and workers on such topics as the concept of productivity, "modern" labor–management relations, and supervisor-effectiveness training programs.

Although this campaign appeared to be effective in raising productivity and improving morale in some workshops during the first few months, it soon met with opposition from the union, which claimed that the true objective of the campaign was to destroy the union and exploit the workers by forcing them to work harder.

The following year, the union started a "Down with the Productivity Movement" campaign, which relied heavily on mass-media support. The union also took its case to the Public Corporations and Government Enterprises Labor Relations Commission, charging that the productivity movement was an "unfair labor practice." The union said it would drop the case if management abandoned the productivity campaign. After a number of traumatic events, including the suicides of several executives, management was forced to give up the productivity campaign altogether.

Considering that most private-sector productivity campaigns at the time were successful, the JNR case offers several lessons. First, management was not determined to stand firmly behind the movement. Second, it tried to introduce the campaign too quickly. Apparently, there was no consensus within management on the vital need to improve productivity, and there were few people who really shared the sense of urgency that something had to be done. Third, management did not spend enough time and effort explaining the implications of the movement to workers before it began. Thus the failure of the productivity movement merely served to poison JNR labor–management relations.

In those workplaces where the campaign was initially success-ful, workers claimed that they made a new discovery: it is possible to cooperate with management. They came to realize that they share basic interests that transcend the division between labor and management, and that cooperation with management is not necessarily class betrayal. Although the question of how to divide profits still remained unresolved, the workers were in general agreement with the need to cooperate in order to make a larger amount to be divided. As a result of the initial campaign, some workers have come to believe in the possibility of labor–management cooperation.

As one executive who was deeply involved in the JNR campaign later recalled, the productivity campaign should have been directed first toward obtaining the workers' understanding and commitment. Having failed to reach the workers, management inevitably failed to achieve its productivity goals.

SOLVING PROBLEMS TOGETHER:
THE INTRODUCTION OF TQC AT KAYABA

Identifying problems was the starting point for TQC at Kayaba, a manufacturer of shock absorbers, hydraulic equipment, marine equip-ment, special-purpose vehicles, and aircraft components.

According to executive managing director Kaisaku Asano, Kayaba's 1976 decision to introduce TQC was prompted by the severe external pressures in the wake of the oil crisis, including increasingly strict qual-ity requirements and strong price competition.

Kayaba started its TQC activities by identifying all the major quality assurance problems, both current and past. (See Figure 6.2.) These problems were listed by department and analyzed in terms of the fol-lowing questions:

1. Did they happen because of a lack of a system?
2. Did they happen because of inadequate training and education?
3. Did they happen because there was no applicable rule?
4. Did they happen because nobody followed the applicable rule?

(Kayaba – continued)

Step	Problems prior to introduction of CWQC	Activities	Schedule (1976, 1977, 1978, 1978, 1979)	Responsibility	Documents (Guidelines and standards)
Product planning	1. Insufficient grasp of market requirements	• Strengthen system for gathering technical data to obtain accurate grasp of market quality requirements	1978 → 1979	Engineering division	• Guidelines for new product development • Data collection manual • Quality table manual • Production engineering manual
	2. Inappropriate goals in quality and engineering	• Establish goals anticipating market requirements • Highlight correlation between quality and engineering	1978 → 1979 1978 → 1979		
	3. Inadequate cost correlation of quality and engineering	• Establish cost control system coordinated with QA system and use it to implement cost planning	1978 → 1979	Cost control division	• Cost control guidelines
Product design	1. Inadequate model for basic engineering	• Improve theoretical analysis of engineering • Improve correlation between theoretical and experimental work	1977 → 1979 1976 → 1979	Engineering division	• Quality table manual • Production engineering manual
	2. Insufficient quality deployment and evaluation	• Make use of quality deployment techniques • Improve FMEA and DR • Develop methods for evaluating trial products under conditions analogous to actual use	1978 → 1979 1978 → 1979 1978 → 1979	Engineering division	• DR implementation

FIGURE 6.2 *Outline of QA (Quality Assurance) Implementation (cont'd on next two pages)*

Step	Problems prior to introduction of CWQC	Activities	Schedule (1976–1979)	Responsibility	Documents (Guidelines and standards)
Production preparation	1. Problems in the introduction of new products	• Improve process planning • Introduce and use FMEA for processes	1978–1979	Production engineering division	• Production engineering manual • Process FMEA manual • Control guidelines for initial production lot • Inspection planning manual
	2. Insufficient quality evaluation of initial production lot	• Improve control and evaluation of initial production lots	1978	Manufacturing division, QA division	
Production	1. Lack of systematic process control (sacrificing quality to quantity)	• Review process control • Improve control of key processes • Improve quality recording	1977–1979	Manufacturing division	• Control guidelines for key processes • Problem–prevention system diagram • Guidelines for irregularity control • QA essentials for customers
	2. Frequent recurrent complaints (weak response to complaints and process defects)	• Promote measures for preventing problems • Improve control of irregularities • Furnish QC guidance to key supplier plants	1977–1979	Manufacturing division, Purchasing division	
	3. Halfhearted approach to study and analysis of process capability	• Step up efforts for equipment improvement • Study process capability • Do more process analysis	1976–1979	Manufacturing division	• Study manual for process capability
	4. Inadequate inspection system (leading to customer problems)	• Clearly define authority for suspending shipments • Carry out priority inspections • Improve trial production to confirm processes	1977–1979	QA division	• Rules for shipment suspension • Essentials of inspection standardization

FIGURE 6.2 (continued)

188

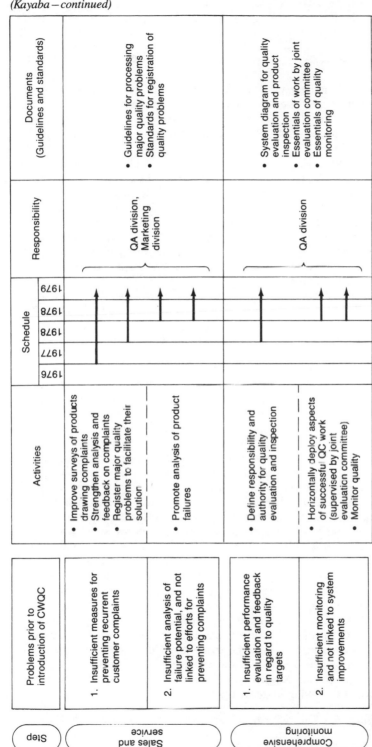

Step	Problems prior to introduction of CWQC	Activities	Schedule					Responsibility	Documents (Guidelines and standards)
			1976	1977	1978	1978	1979		
Sales and service	1. Insufficient measures for preventing recurrent customer complaints	• Improve surveys of products drawing complaints • Strengthen analysis and feedback on complaints • Register major quality problems to facilitate their solution						QA division, Marketing division	• Guidelines for processing major quality problems • Standards for registration of quality problems
	2. Insufficient analysis of failure potential, and not linked to efforts for preventing complaints	• Promote analysis of product failures							
Comprehensive monitoring	1. Insufficient performance evaluation and feedback in regard to quality targets	• Define responsibility and authority for quality evaluation and inspection						QA division	• System diagram for quality evaluation and product inspection • Essentials of work by joint evaluation committee • Essentials of quality monitoring
	2. Insufficient monitoring and not linked to system improvements	• Horizontally deploy aspects of successful QC work (supervised by joint evaluation committee) • Monitor quality							

FIGURE 6.2 (continued)

189

(Kayaba — continued)

After identifying the underlying cause of each problem, Kayaba devised an implementation plan for each step from product planning to customer monitoring. This plan indicates the problem, the countermeasures to be taken, the schedule, the department responsible, and the support documentation.

Also in 1976, Kayaba inaugurated an all-out effort to promote the TQC concept. Asano says that it is absolutely essential that the president or number-two person be determined to introduce TQC. Because division heads and plant managers should also be 100 percent committed, these people were sent to TQC seminars for top management and were encouraged to visit other companies that had already introduced TQC. Efforts were also made to activate participation at the grass-roots level, including suggestions from QC circles. Figure 6.3 shows the Kayaba schedule for QC training.

Since one of the major objectives was to create a QA system to ensure that quality targets were fulfilled at each stage, Kayaba developed a series of tools to ensure the match between quality and technology at every stage from product development through manufacturing, sales, and customer service. Figures 6.4 and 6.5 show some of the tools and how they were used at Kayaba.

Figure 6.6 shows the Kayaba quality assurance systems diagram. In preparing this diagram, Kayaba first tried to modify other companies' quality assurance systems diagrams to fit its own situation, but it soon found that business patterns and reporting procedures are so different from company to company that it would have to start from scratch. This systems diagram shows how each department is involved in each stage from product planning through sales, service, and monitoring.

In reviewing current practices preparatory to developing its systems diagram, Kayaba found that there was very little coordination among different departments and that there were no clear-cut reporting channels or responsibility assignments in moving from one step to the next. After the systems diagram, a table of quality assurance activities was needed. This is shown in Figure 6.7. This QA table helps each employee understand what he should be doing in order to assure quality. It also shows the documentation and reports needed to support these activities, as well as the regulations and standards to be followed.

Figure 6.8 shows the relationships among the various departments in dealing with major customer complaints. Once these systems are prepared, says Asano, it is essential that everybody understand how very important it is that the systems and procedures be observed.

So successful was Kayaba in introducing TQC in 1976 that the company won the Deming Prize in 1980.

(Figures 6.3, 6.4, 6.5, 6.6, 6.7, and 6.8 follow on pages 191–201.)

Participant level	Course	Site	Before CWQC	1976	1977	1978	1979	Target group	Participation	Participation rate
Top management	Special course for directors	Public courses	5	1	2			3	3	100
	Special management course	Public courses			8	5	5	27	23	85
	Director training	In-house				16		18	16	89
Middle management	Department and section manager's course	Public courses	45	30	65	64	23	289	227	89
	Manager training	In-house	59			307		311	307	99
	Basic QC course	Public courses	30	10	16	9	3	128	97	76
	Introductory QC course	Public courses	60	21	44	22	4	152	121	80
	Foremen's courses (including correspondence courses)	Public courses	14	11	33	147	9	271	260	96
Supervisors	Basic reliability course	Public courses	14	5	8	20	5	54	52	96
	SQC seminars (introductory course on statistical QC)	In-house			⎫	114	125	290	239	82
	SQC seminars (introductory course on planning techniques)	In-house			⎬	(114)	80	245	194	79
	SQC seminars (Basic reliability course)	In-house			⎭	(114)	102	245	216	88
QC circle staff	QC circle leaders' course	Public courses	11	9	7	6	1	36	34	94
	QC circle cruising university	Public courses				7	5	12	12	100
Management at cooperating plant	Cooperating plant managers' seminars	In-house				76		76	76	100

FIGURE 6.3 QC Training

(Kayaba — continued)

Tool	Use
Basic quality table	Identification and analysis of market quality requirements, competing product costs, available technology, and technical bottlenecks for each product group
Basic production engineering tables	Identification and analysis of existing technology, technical bottlenecks, and technology needs for meeting the quality requirements in the basic quality table
Individual quality tables	Evaluation of quality requirements, quality of competing products, and patent rights, as well as identification and analysis of available technology for achieving quality goals (all data needed to set targets for a given product)
Individual production engineering tables	Identification and analysis of available manufacturing technology, manufacturing technology needs, and technical bottlenecks showing up in the individual quality tables
QA table	Listing of important characteristics and parts, along with notes on process capability, assembly and processing, and functions
Inspection planning table	Planning and implementation of inspection and testing, as well as quality evaluation, in line with the QA tables
Process planning table	Comprehensive process design as needed for incorporating the quality requirements indicated in the QA table
QC process table	Identification of control characteristics, items, and methods for each process as needed for QA
Work standardization sheet	Standardization of process factors and establishment of appropriate work procedures for incorporating quality in processes
Quality survey table	Evaluation of quality characteristics from quality and QA tables in terms of market data, complaints, etc., and applications of the findings to future product planning

FIGURE 6.4   *Outline of Tools*

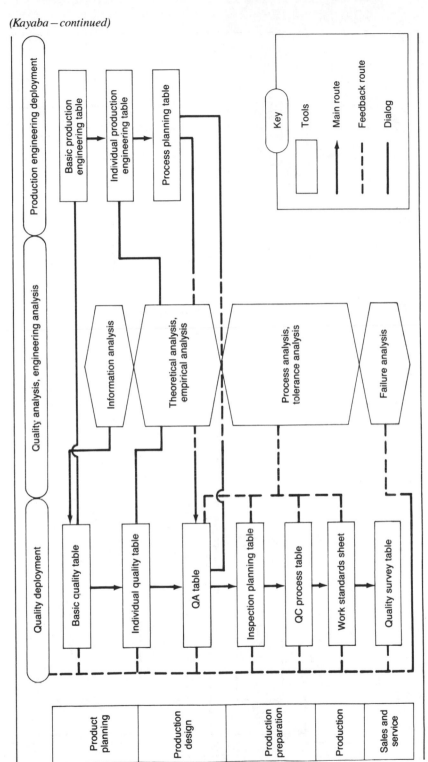

FIGURE 6.5 Tool Utilization

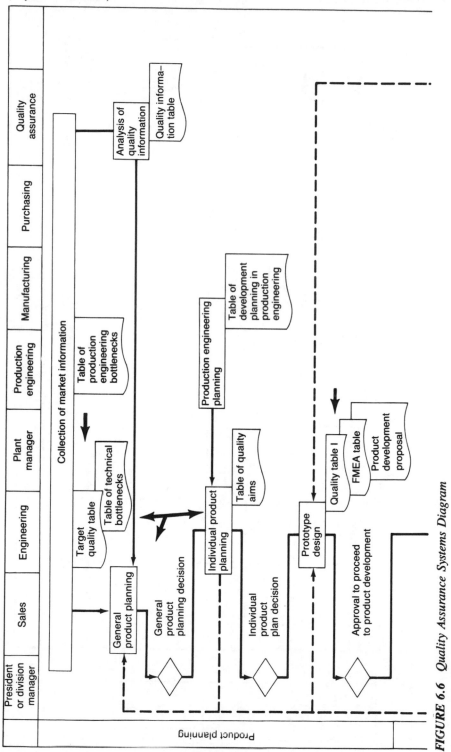

FIGURE 6.6 Quality Assurance Systems Diagram

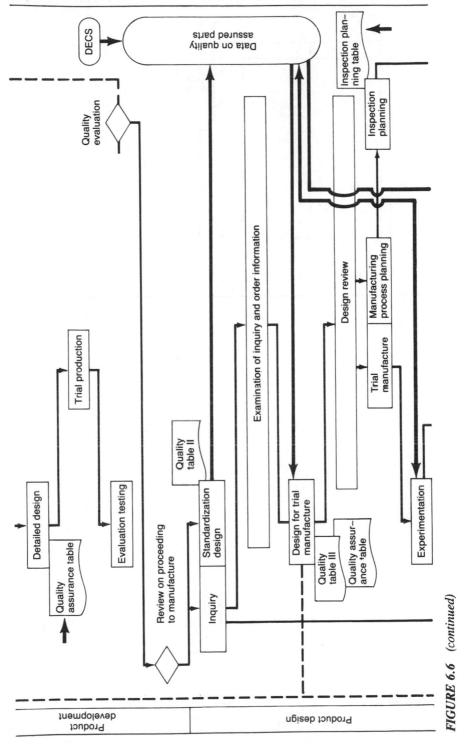

FIGURE 6.6 *(continued)*

195

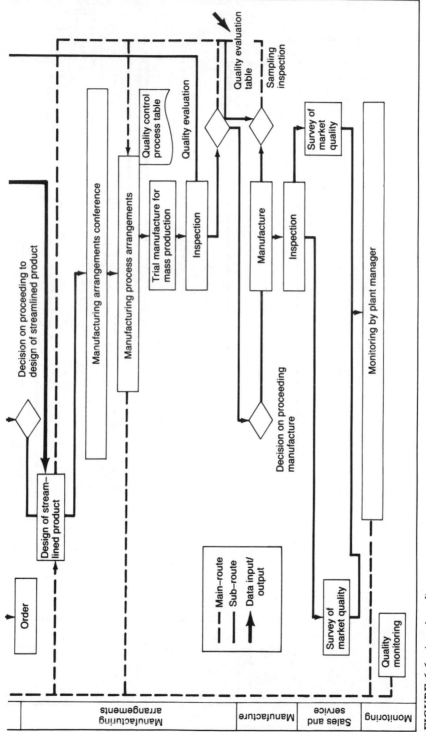

FIGURE 6.6 *(continued)*

196

Symbol

Symbol	
◉	Responsible department
○	Collaborating department
△	Information–receiving department

Classification

Classification	
New product	ABC
Product improvement	BC
Others	C

Assurance item: Product planning — Collection of information — Propriety of market information

Assurance activity	Classification	President or division manager	Sales division	Engineering division — Design section	Engineering division — Development section	Engineering division — Experimentation section	Quality assurance department	Inspection section	Quality assurance section	Pump quality assurance section	Manufacturing department	Quality control documents	Regulations or standards
1. Collection, analysis and survey of market information	A	◉		○	◉				○	○		Product development information table	Product development administration regulations
2.	A	△			◉							Quality information table	
3.	A	◉			△							Quality table (listing quality aims) / Table of technical bottlenecks	

FIGURE 6.7 Quality Assurance Activity Table (Example)

			Summary of product plan	Detailed estimate of development budget	Concept drawing	Quality table 1	Product development administration regulations	Quality table manual

General product planning — Propriety of general product planning
- 1. General product planning — A
- 2. Approval of general product plan — A

Individual product planning — Propriety of individual product planning
- A
- 3. Approval of individual product plan — A

Adaptability to user needs
- 1. Basic design — B
- C

FIGURE 6.7 *(continued)*

198

Process		Internal defect / Important quality problem processing rules	Complaint investigation report	Critical quality problem registration instructions	Critical quality problem control table	Complaint recurrence prevention measures	Complaint evaluation report	Important quality problem processing rules	Critical quality problem control table	Monthly quality report	Inspection and check table
Complaint processing and recurrence prevention — Sales and service	1. Urgent complaint report	C	○	○		○						
	2. Investigation of	C	○	●		●	●	●			○	○
	3. Registration of critical quality problem	C	○	○		○	●	●			○	○
	4. Instruction of complaint recurrence prevention	C	○	●		●					○	○
	5. Accumulation and analysis of complaint data	C			●							
	6. Evaluation of critical quality problem	C										
Product quality evaluation — Evaluation	Registration of critical quality problem	C							●	●	●	
	Inspection of quality assurance system	C								○	○	
	Periodic quality inspection/evaluation	C								○	○	

FIGURE 6.7 (continued)

199

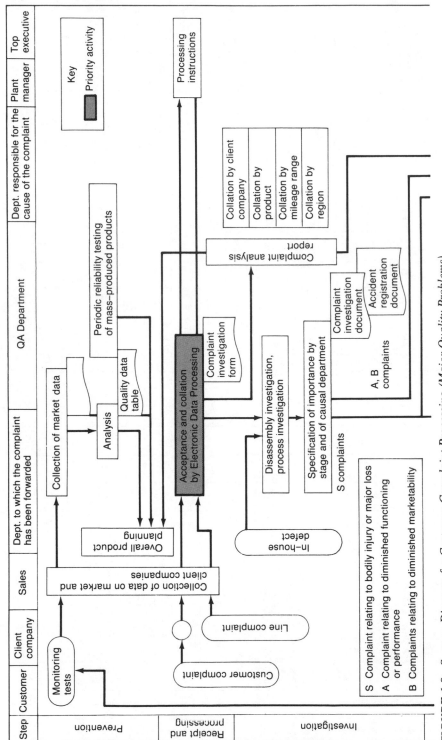

FIGURE 6.8 Systems Diagram for Customer Complaint Processing (Major Quality Problems)

200

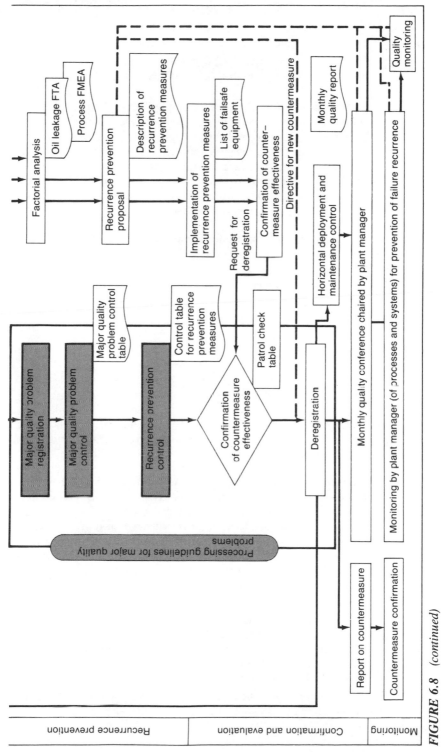

FIGURE 6.8 (continued)

201

INTRODUCTION OF TQC
AT KOBAYASHI KOSE

In 1980, Kobayashi Kose received a Deming Factory Prize. Kobayashi Kose is the fourth largest manufacturer of cosmetics in Japan. In the early 1970s, a series of production problems in its plant led to returned products, which harmed both the company's reputation and employee morale. Management was forced to take a hard, critical look at the business.

Vowing never again to deliver defective products to its customers, the management of Kobayashi Kose decided in January 1977 to introduce TQC. The five major targets established at the time were:

1. To improve management effectiveness using QC statistical techniques
2. To introduce quality assurance and establish a system for producing good products
3. To get employees behind the "customer-first" philosophy
4. To train and develop the company's human resources through QC groups or circles that learn and challenge
5. To win a Deming Prize by 1981

Although nobody used the term "strategy" at the time, it is clear that the company's TQC campaign was a classic example of strategic planning. Hisashi Takasu, manager of Kobayashi Kose's TQC Planning and Coordination Department, believes that TQC is an endless process of improvement that includes the following three prerequisites for its successful implementation:

1. Top management must make a firm commitment. Since the introduction of TQC concepts challenges existing ways of doing business, such an effort may meet resistance from some executives in the company who are used to their own ways of doing business. Unless top management is firmly committed and endorses it, TQC strategy implementation is doomed to fail shortly after it is started. There must be a serious commitment by managers at all levels in every plant or division.
2. It is imperative that the best available people be mobilized and allocated to work on the implementation of TQC strategy at crucial positions in the company. There may be a time when they must "push" by exercising the authority top management has given them, while at other times they may have to "appease" resistance. They must be good at internal politics.
3. A special group must be created within the company to spearhead the movement by serving as an example for other groups.

(Kobayashi Kose — continued)

Before the formal start of Kobayashi Kose's TQC movement, the managers concerned thoroughly discussed the company's problems in order to come to a common understanding. Then they devoted themselves to learning the techniques of quality control. All key managers and engineers were sent to TQC courses sponsored by JUSE and other organizations. Upon their return to the company, these key employees were assigned to the following tasks:

1. To serve as instructors within the company
2. To participate in special task forces to improve particular aspects of production-related problems and, where such task forces do not exist, to create them
3. To serve as quality-circle leaders helping other circle members apply the statistical techniques of TQC to specific problems

One of Kobayashi Kose's goals was to win a Deming Prize by 1981. Introducing TQC to achieve this goal required reforms in the way business was conducted. What might otherwise take 10 years to do had to be done in four years. This provided a clear target for everyone.

Takasu recalls that the Deming Prize effort was like preparing for a difficult examination. No matter how hard you worked, it was never enough. It was an endless cycle of studying and practicing. As the date of the Deming Audit approached, few managers were able to go home before 11 P.M. They even put in several days of work during the New Year holidays. On the average, they worked 28 days a month. Typically, managers had to start their work on quality control after 5 P.M., as they were fully occupied with their normal business routine in the daytime. But they enjoyed a great sense of satisfaction and achievement when they finally won the Deming Factory Prize. Unless managers are prepared to meet such challenges, says Takasu, they should not even contemplate vying for the Deming Prize. ■

Top Management's Commitment

Whereas quality is regarded as the line manager's responsibility in Japan, quality has often been regarded as the quality control manager's responsibility in the West. It is almost as if quality were an entirely separate issue in management, one to be dealt with by the quality control manager alone. Whenever a serious quality problem arises, it is the line manager who is held responsible in Japan. In the West, it is the quality manager who is sacked. Unfortunately, this practice only reinforces the Western line manager's feeling that he is not responsible for quality problems. Let there be no mistake: quality is management's responsibility, and poor quality is the result of poor management.

If the benefits of KAIZEN come gradually and its effects are felt only on a long-term basis, it is obvious that KAIZEN can thrive only under top management that has a genuine concern for the long-term health of the company.

It has often been pointed out that one of the major differences between Japanese and Western management styles is their time-frames. Whereas Japanese management has a long-term perspective, Western managers tend to look for shorter-term results. This difference is also manifested in the way management approaches improvement. Western management is reluctant to introduce improvement gradually and tends to favor innovation, which provides a more immediate return on investment.

It is one of the ironies of Western management that the higher up the manager is in the hierarchy, the more preoccupied he is with short-term results. When a worker or lower-level manager thinks of an improvement with potential long-term benefits, the idea is usually rejected by higher-ups whose perspective and criteria are shorter-term.

Unless top management is determined to introduce KAIZEN as a top priority, any effort to introduce KAIZEN into the company will be short-lived. In most KAIZEN-oriented Japanese companies, the KAIZEN strategy was introduced by top management.

When Komatsu started its TQC activities under the Maru-A campaign name in 1961, Shoji Nogawa was put in charge of TQC implementation. Ever since, he has been involved in TQC activities, even though he was promoted to production manager, plant manager, and then production division manager. When Nogawa was nominated for the Komatsu presidency in 1982, Ryoichi Kawai, outgoing president and now chairman, said that Nogawa was chosen because of his involvement in TQC. Today, Nogawa is "Mr. TQC" at Komatsu — and with good reason: Komatsu was awarded the Deming Prize in 1959 and the Japan Quality Control Prize in 1981, and is thought to have one of the best TQC programs in Japan. So ingrained is TQC at Komatsu that board directors have been known to oppose something because it "doesn't sound like TQC."

Komatsu's chairman Kawai recently said, "In TQC strategy, the job of the salespeople is to identify customer needs. Then the engineers should develop product designs that maintain a proper balance between quality and cost, and the manufacturing people should make the product as designed. It is management's job to provide the services needed to make this system work."

A "Mr. TQC" is needed at any company to build a climate for KAIZEN. At Yokogawa-Hewlett-Packard, Kenzo Sasaoka is Mr. TQC. With a TQC program started in 1977, Yokogawa-Hewlett-Packard won the Deming Application Prize in 1982, and its outstanding performance has caused its U.S. parent, Hewlett-Packard, to take a positive interest in TQC activities. Today, Sasaoka visits Hewlett-Packard in the United States regularly to explain TQC activities.

Sasaoka maintains that the Japanese industrial revolution is a direct challenge to conventional wisdom in the following three areas.

Conventional Wisdom	Japanese Revolution
Higher quality leads to higher costs.	Higher quality leads to lower costs.
Larger lots lead to lower costs.	Smaller lots lead to lower costs.
Workers do not need to be taken into account.	A thinking worker is a productive worker.

KAIZEN's introduction and direction should be top-down. But the suggestions for KAIZEN should be bottom-up, since the best specific suggestions for improvement usually come from the people closest to the problem. The KAIZEN strategy therefore calls for both top-down and bottom-up approaches.

Over the past few years, I have had the opportunity to speak with a great many Western executives who have come to Japan to learn TQC practices. Many of them left Japan convinced that something should be done when they got back. And yet, in almost all cases, their personal commitment failed to spark a company-wide movement, because the message never got through to top management. In fact, people who come to Japan to learn TQC often say, "My boss should see this." If management is to introduce the KAIZEN strategy on a company-wide basis, it is absolutely essential that the initiative come from the top. Without an unwavering commitment by the company executive officers, the board, and the rest of top management, KAIZEN will never get off the ground as a company-wide campaign.

On a short-term basis, management should be interested in performance as expressed in profit terms. These results are evident and may be easily measured in the P/L statement, per-share earnings, and ROI. On a long-term basis, management should be interested in overall improvement for enhanced competitive strength. However, improvement is slow, and the measures' success at best ambiguous. Thus top management often feels that it has very little to gain even if it launches an ambitious program for improvement. Yet it is precisely because improvement is needed in so many different areas, including productivity, labor-management relations, quality control, participative management, new-product development, and supplier relations, that a commitment by top management is essential to building a climate for improvement.

How long does it take for KAIZEN's benefits to show up? According to Kaoru Ishikawa, it is usually three to five years from the time TQC is introduced until there is marked improvement in corporate performance. Kenzo Sasaoka is more optimistic. He says that if Western companies follow through seriously and are willing to learn from the Japanese experience, it should take them only two years to do what it has taken Japanese companies a decade to do.

When KAIZEN is directed to a specific target, such as improved product quality or enlarged market share in a given area, says President Yotaro Kobayashi of Fuji-Xerox, it is not difficult to obtain positive results within several months. However, Kobayashi maintains that a system should be instituted to assure continuous improvement and spread KAIZEN's benefits throughout the company. He says management should not be content simply to see improvement but should stress that the goal of KAIZEN is to be better than the competition. Achieving such a goal obviously takes more than several months.

Management may be tempted to forego the long-term opportunity for improvement in favor of short-term profit goals, but how long can companies maintain even their short-term profits if their competitors in the world market are working at KAIZEN day in and day out with carefully planned and meticulously executed strategies?

7

Changing the
Corporate Culture

The Customer: The Ultimate Judge of Quality

All of management's efforts for KAIZEN boil down to two words: customer satisfaction. No matter what management does, it is of no avail if it does not lead to increased customer satisfaction in the end. However, it is not easy to define customer satisfaction. Which aspects of customer satisfaction should management address?

In KAIZEN, customer satisfaction is measured in such terms as quality, cost, and scheduling. It is management's job to establish priorities among these goals and to deploy the goals down throughout the organization.

Take, for example, the case of a manager who puts in a request for a new carpet in his office. He says that he receives many important customers and that the new carpet will add to customer satisfaction. How is management to judge such a proposition? If management has made cost reduction its number one priority, the manager has no place making such a request. If, on the other hand, management's priority is on providing better personal service to the company's more important customers, then the request for a new carpet may not be so far out of line after all.

I have often wondered why Japanese management has felt so compelled to adopt TQC. There have been many factors, such as the oil crises, but one of the overriding factors has been the rigorous requirements imposed by Japanese customers. In the final analysis, it is the customers who set the standards for quality, and they do this by deciding which products to purchase and whom to buy them from. In this respect, it appears that Japanese customers often impose more rigorous requirements on the product or service than customers in other countries do. For better or worse, their attention to (or obsession with) detail has forced management to develop a system for building in quality.

The following story is about some Japanese customer characteristics and the harsh demands they often make on suppliers.

The Eye of the Needle

Why doesn't Japan buy more products from us? There has recently been a mounting chorus of protest from businessmen and politicians all over the world. A trade mission that recently visited Japan concluded, among other things, that more imported goods should be sold through Japanese department stores.

There is no doubt that introducing a new product to the market through a well-known department store is one of the best ways to start doing business in Japan, since the association with the department store brings the prestige and volume turnover that no other retail outlet could possibly bring. However, there appear to be many overseas exporters who believe that they can start doing business with Japanese department stores simply by sending the stores their product brochures and catalogues. I should like to describe briefly what it takes to deal with a Japanese department store.

The power balance between the department store and the hundreds of wholesalers it deals with has always been overwhelmingly in favor of the department store. As far as the department store is concerned, it is a buyer's market. Only those wholesalers who have "accounts" with the department store are able to deal with it. Therefore, manufacturers wanting to place their merchandise in a given department store can do so only through a wholesaler who has such an account there.

In the past, there have been cases in which foreign companies wishing to sell their products in Japan tried to bypass the wholesaler and deal directly with the department store. These people have almost invariably failed, since their attempt ran against established practices. No matter what kind of new product a company wants to market through the department stores, chances are the stores already carry many similar products. Since space at the store is booked to capacity, any new product means less space for the others, and competitors will do everything they can to thwart the interloper.

The selection of new merchandise for a particular sales floor is entrusted to the *shunin* or "chief" in charge of that floor. As a result, the *shunin* is constantly deluged with myriad supplicants seeking to have their merchandise carried—this on top of his dealings with the regular wholesalers with whom he does business. Faced with this situation, his main job seems to be not so much to discover promising new products as to screen out the ones that do not have the popular appeal to contribute to his floor's sales.

The *shunin* thus wields absolute authority, not only over people wishing to do business with him for the first time but also over wholesalers he deals with on a regular basis. Everybody wants to stay in his good graces, and there have been reports in the past that this power has brought the *shunin* truckloads of gifts in the summer and winter gift-giving seasons. Indeed, it used to be said that a man would be able to buy a new house after a few years as *shunin*.

Little wonder, then, that the Tokyo sales manager for an American beverage company that had just started selling in Japan, a man I shall call Yamada, had such a hard time dealing with the *shunin* at a leading department store where he wanted to start doing business. As a newcomer in the business, he found the first hurdle was the seemingly simple one of getting an appointment with the *shunin*.

The *shunin,* who was responsible for several hundred brands of beverages of all kinds, was extremely busy meeting with salesmen and managers from both wholesalers and manufacturers, and had no time to meet this stranger. Having failed to see the *shunin* during the week, Yamada decided to go see him on Sunday, when people from other wholesalers were not calling on him. Finally, he was able to corner the *shunin* and discuss the feasibility of having the department store carry his company's beverage. Although the beverage was a well-known brand abroad, the *shunin* was very reluctant to carry it, since he already had several competitive lines that were selling well. Finally, since he was not sure the new beverage would bring enough sales and hence profits to the department store, he requested a rebate on top of the normal commission.

After this was granted and the *shunin*'s approval obtained, Yamada had to see the *kacho* (or section chief) to get his consent on the deal. Again, it was impossible to make an appointment beforehand.

Every time Yamada called, he found that the section chief was out. So he left his name card as evidence of his having called. After the cairn of cards on the *kacho*'s desk was sufficiently high to show his "sincerity," he was finally awarded an "audience" and the opportunity to show his wares. By this time, six months had passed.

After the section chief's consent was obtained, Yamada had to go through this entire process again with the department manager. Thus it was that, a full year afer his first contact with the department store, Yamada was able to win his company's beverage a place on the shelves.

But the story does not end there. Once the product is on the department-store counters, it is closely monitored with regular sales accounting. Merchandise with a slow turnover is subject to reevaluation every six months, with the threat that it may be dropped from the lists if it does not earn its space. Therefore, the salesmen handling this beverage for Yamada's company had to make every effort to maintain a satisfactory turnover, sometimes even by buying the products themselves with company money.

There are many trade practices unique to Japan that reflect the overwhelming dominance of the department store over wholesalers and, indirectly, even manufacturers. First of all, merchandise is often carried at the store on consignment, which means the department store can send merchandise back to the wholesaler and does not actually have to pay for anything until it has been sold. Second, the department store often requests wholesalers to provide sales clerks for the floor. Third, the department store expects the wholesalers to cooperate on the occasion of special sales, such as those during the summer and winter gift seasons. For instance, the layout of the sales floors for special sales promotions is usually done after the store closes.

This preparation for the new layout, called *tachiagari* or "standing up," usually starts at 10 P.M. and ends at 3 A.M. — and Yamada's salesman is usually there to help. Although such cooperation is never formally requested, it has become more or less mandatory, since the salesmen from other companies are there too; and if Yamada's man is not there, he may well find his products "displayed" in a far-off corner of the floor the next day.

It is said that the more alert salesmen go back to the floor again very early the next morning before the store opens to move their products to slightly more advantageous locations.

Sometimes, the salesmen stay in the department store during the special promotions to assist sales clerks on the floor, to work at the cashier's counter, and generally to get a better feel for how their products and their competitors' products are selling.

On top of this, during the busy shopping seasons, Yamada goes to the store's delivery center in suburban Tokyo where part-time students and housewives are hard at work packing and sorting merchandise for delivery. There he compliments them on how hard they are working, thanks them for their efforts, and leaves them snacks of *onigiri* (rice balls) and *senbei* (rice crackers). This he does to maintain amicable relations with the department store and remain in their favor.

The department store closes at 6 P.M., after which it takes three hours in the peak season for the clerks to check the sales figures and inventories. Therefore, it is usually not until 9 P.M. or 10 P.M. that replacement orders are phoned to the wholesaler. This means that the salesmen at the wholesaler must stay at the office, standing at the ready for an order, until late at night. It also means that Yamada and his salesmen have to wait in their office so that products can be delivered at a moment's notice.

The Tokyo Branch of Yamada's company keeps two delivery trucks standing ready to leave at any moment. When neither truck is available, the salesmen often make deliveries to the stores themselves.

All these stories may sound unbelievable to many foreign executives, and there is no doubt that these trade practices are a formidable hurdle to the newcomer of whatever nationality who wishes to do business with the department store. However, the existence of these trade practices is hardly grounds for concluding that the Japanese market is closed to Western products. It is easy to blame strange trade practices, but it is more useful to make an effort to understand them and work within them.

As one successful marketing expert in Japan said: "There are many trade practices and customs unique to Japan. Yet if these are unmovable givens, we have no choice but to learn to live with them."

Supplier Relations

One of the fundamental principles of TQC is that product or service quality downstream is best assured by maintaining quality upstream. This concept extends even to relations between the plant and its suppliers.

The April 2, 1984 *Fortune* carried an article by Jeremy Main in which he wrote:

> The essence of just-in-time is that the manufacturer does not keep much inventory on hand—he relies on suppliers to furnish parts just in time for them to be assembled. U.S. companies, by contrast, have traditionally employed what is sometimes called the "just-in-case" system—fat inventories that ensure production won't be interrupted.

Improving supplier relations has become one of the top-priority areas of management-oriented KAIZEN in Japan. Guided by the plant manager's policy, which has been deployed from top management, the purchasing people constantly work on improvement issues in their relations with suppliers. Such issues usually include:

- Establishing better criteria to measure optimum inventory levels
- Developing additional supply sources that can ensure faster delivery
- Improving how orders are placed
- Improving the quality of the information provided to suppliers
- Establishing better physical distribution systems
- Understanding the suppliers' internal requirements better

One of the purchasing agent's jobs is to develop criteria for checking the relative strengths of the suppliers in terms of price, cooperation, quality, delivery, technology, and overall management competence.

Komatsu provides special awards to its suppliers and distributors. The awards to suppliers (whom Komatsu calls "cooperating companies") are based on such factors as the supplier's policies and management system, quality assurance, cost control, delivery, technology development, education, safety, and environmental control.

Japanese manufacturers have made considerable efforts in such areas as assisting suppliers to initiate TQC programs, helping them introduce various KAIZEN programs such as suggestion programs and small group activities, and maintaining better communication on product quality, quantity, and delivery schedules. As a result, suppliers have been able to improve their working procedures, often at little or no cost, and this has led to such achievements as improved yields, better identification of new materials, and lower break-even points.

Most manufacturers of passenger cars, industrial machines, or electronic products hold annual or bi-annual meetings to present awards to suppliers who have met their quality requirements or delivery schedules. Japanese companies have a vested interest in helping their suppliers do the best they can, and supplier and purchaser work together to satisfy their shared need. As a result of such shared efforts for improvement, Honda's suppliers were able to achieve the following results between 1974 and 1978.

Average sales:	Up 60 percent to 80 percent
Number of employees:	Almost the same or fewer
Per-capita added value:	Up 60 percent to 70 percent
Breakeven point:	Down more than 15 percent

Honda meets with suppliers every month to study such subjects as employee education, new materials, physical distribution systems, improved production lines, and better QA systems.

More recently, manufacturers and suppliers have been forming joint project teams to work on such issues as new-product development, resource saving, and energy conservation. It is not uncommon for the president of a manufacturing company to visit his major suppliers annually to discuss key policy issues.

Supplier relations are also a crucial part of the just-in-time system, since this system demands not only consistent quality but precision delivery. Close communication and a joint commitment are both essential.

Kaoru Ishikawa says that there are three stages in manufacturer–supplier relations. In the first stage, the manufacturer checks the entire lot that is brought in by the supplier. In the second stage, the manufacturer only sample-checks. In the final stage, the manufacturer accepts everything without checking the quality. Only in the third stage may it be said that a truly worthwhile relationship has been established.

When Yoshisaki Ohta first visited the United States in 1959 to study the American industrial-vehicle industry, he noticed that there were many parts suppliers serving the various industrial-vehicle manufacturers. In those days, Japanese manufacturers were obsessed with "integrated" production, believing that it was the most efficient way to make industrial vehicles. This U.S. experience was therefore very revealing to Ohta.

Since then, Japanese manufacturers have chosen to outsource most of their parts and components, and this change has been possible only because of the appearance of reliable subcontractors in such specialty fields as hydraulic components. In the last 30 years, Ohta notes, Japan has developed many reliable specialty subcontractors, and manufacturers have become more like assemblers, free to concentrate on finding more efficient assembly methods.

On a recent visit to the United States and Europe, however, Ohta was surprised to note that some large manufacturers of industrial vehicles have reverted to the "integrated production" myth. This, he says, accounts for much of the productivity gap between Japan and the West.

Even with Western companies engaged in "integrated production," their divisions appear to lack the level of liaison and trust that exists between a Japanese manufacturer and its suppliers. Many Western companies are having a hard time establishing relations of trust among their different business units. Worse yet, a factory that purchases supplies from another factory in the same group is unable to exercise the same level of control as it would over an outside supplier, since it does not have the option of turning to another supplier.

There are several features distinguishing Japanese factories from Western factories. The first, as noted above, is their heavy dependence on outside contractors. As much as 50 percent of the parts and components are contracted out. One of the first decisions faced by Japanese management in developing a new product is thus that of whether to "make or buy." Another feature of the Japanese factory is the use of part-time employees (up to 50 percent of the total employment in some industries).

This dual dependence on outside contractors and part-time employees helps Japanese management better cope with business fluctuations.

SUPPLIER RELATIONS AT RICOH

Ricoh's Atsugi plant relies heavily on the just-in-time and *kamban* concepts in its manufacture of office equipment and copying machines. According to Katsumi Yoshida, general manager for the Reprographic Products Division's purchasing department, the Ricoh equivalent of the

(Ricoh — continued)

just-in-time system is called STF (speedy and timely flow), and Ricoh's *kamban* system is called RP (real-time plate). Both of these systems are vital to maintaining product quality and productivity while keeping the production areas neat and well organized.

The Atsugi Plant has a minimum of inventory space, and parts and components are generally delivered by outside suppliers for assembly within hours. As is the case at Toyota, several types of equipment are assembled on the same assembly line.

Close relations with suppliers are essential to this system. Ricoh suppliers are divided into "designated" and "nondesignated" suppliers. Once a year, Ricoh reviews the performance of all suppliers. When a particular supplier is felt to be reliable in terms of product quality and delivery terms, he is eligible to become a "designated" supplier.

Designated suppliers enjoy first priority on Ricoh orders and are entitled to special incentives and favorable payment terms. Currently, Ricoh has about 70 designated suppliers, and this group accounts for the majority of its suppliers.

In an effort to improve the designated suppliers' technical capabilities, Ricoh invites designated suppliers' technical personnel to work on solving problems together with Ricoh technicians. Ricoh also sends its technical experts to the suppliers to help them implement various KAIZEN activities. In addition, employees at designated suppliers are entitled to participate in Ricoh's various in-house training programs.

Ricoh's ordering schedule is also designated to facilitate cooperation between Ricoh and its supplier. At the end of every month, Ricoh places a firm order for the entire next month. RP parts are an exception, however. In light of the greater precision of the RP system, RP parts are ordered daily, for delivery at a specified hour three days hence. Ricoh also tells suppliers what it expects to need during the first, second, and last ten days of the month after next, and gives order estimates for each of the next two months after that. So by the end of every month, suppliers are able to estimate their required production levels for the following three months and can plan their production schedules accordingly.

Because parts are brought into the factory by the suppliers and fed to the assembly line through a conveyor system, it is crucial that quality, quantity, and delivery schedule be strictly observed.

When parts made to new specifications are brought in for the first time, the supplier is also expected to provide a list of quality assurance tables used in production. In addition, the supplier's box sizes and labeling, including numbering, must follow Ricoh's standards perfectly, or the whole lot may be rejected. For instance, when a lot of 10 boxes is brought in, each box must be marked 1/10, 2/10, 3/10, and so on to show its order in the ten-box lot. If even one box is missing a number, the whole lot is rejected, since these boxes have to be fed to the conveyor system in order and any misfeed could lead to serious trouble further down the line.

(Ricoh—continued)

Often, Ricoh engineers will visit their suppliers and ask them to write out the production processes or show them the tools and molds they would be using if they got a particular order. When a supplier's processes appear too complicated, Ricoh will recommend that the processes be simplified to cut costs.

Every year, Ricoh holds a company-wide purchasing managers' convention. One of the highlights of this convention is the awards ceremony for outstanding suppliers. These suppliers are selected by the purchasing managers, and the certificates are personally presented by Ricoh's president.

The certificate is a much-coveted mark of excellence for the supplier, and it is recognized both by the financial community and by other manufacturers as a certificate of quality and reliability. With the certificate in hand, the supplier can negotiate new bank loans at more favorable terms or get new customers more easily.

While manufacturer and supplier interests diverge on pricing, Ricoh believes a manufacturer and its suppliers have a common interest in serving customer needs and should therefore work together for constant KAIZEN and cost reduction. ■

Changing Corporate Culture: Challenge to the West

"The front line in the 'semiconductor war' today is the battle of TQC," says Matsushita's Hajime Karatsu. In Japan, we have come to the point where executives are now discussing defective rates in terms of "ppm" (parts per million). Some TQC enthusiasts say that the executive who still thinks of defective rates in terms of percentages belongs in a museum, and his company is on its way to extinction.

Michael Haley, a professor at Vanderbilt University's Owen Graduate School of Management, recently visited Japan to observe TQC at work. He came to the conclusion that TQC is applied in Japan as a corporate strategy:

To be implemented, the strategy must become concrete to everyone in the organization. Therefore, long-run strategies must be translated into short-run plans and objectives which are clear and actionable.

The principles of total quality control provide the necessary structural framework to help both the employees and management communicate and decide how to improve the quality and productivity of work.

Thus, total quality control as a corporate strategy inevitably involves such areas as improving communication and labor–management relations, as well as revitalizing organizational structures.

But above all, most importantly, total quality control as corporate strategy must deal with *people*. Its net results are more productive workers, more efficient managers, improved communication, and more effective organization. Better and competitive products are the result of better people and better management, and not vice versa.

Corporate strategy should not be monopolized by a handful of top management executives. It must be spelled out in a form that can be understood, interpreted, and carried out by everyone in the company. As Haley stated, "It must be a basis of communication between all individuals of a business organization. The strategy must relate to their needs and motivate their performance."

Getting everyone to participate in KAIZEN has become a crucial part of staying competitive today. However, getting everyone to participate positively needs the right climate or corporate culture. For instance, it will be difficult to get everyone's cooperation if there are serious confrontations between labor and management. Thus management must constantly apply the KAIZEN concept to its industrial relations if it wants to apply the KAIZEN concept to overall corporate activities.

Creating a cooperative atmosphere and corporate culture has been an inseparable part of KAIZEN programs. All the KAIZEN programs implemented in Japan have had one key prerequisite in common: getting workers' acceptance and overcoming their resistance to change. Achieving this has necessitated:

1. Constant efforts to improve industrial relations
2. Emphasis on training and education of workers
3. Developing informal leaders among the workers
4. Formation of small-group activities such as QC circles
5. Support and recognition for workers' KAIZEN efforts (P criteria)
6. Conscious efforts for making the workplace a place where workers can pursue life goals
7. Bringing social life into the workshop as much as practical

8. Training supervisors so that they can communicate better with workers and can create a more positive personal involvement with workers

9. Bringing discipline to the workshop

Figures 7.1 and 7.2 may help explain the relations between corporate culture and profit. The corporate objective of maximizing profits may be attained by (1) increasing the sales and/or (2) lowering both fixed and variable expenses. Assuming that there are two companies making identical products, the ultimate difference in their competitiveness may be expressed in terms of their breakeven point.

Between Figure 7.1 and Figure 7.2, it is quite clear which company is more profitable and more competitive. And it is the different corporate cultures within these companies that account for the difference. KAIZEN strategy aims to maximize profits, both by lowering variable and fixed expenses and by increasing sales. This can be done only by improving the way business is done at all levels, including the executive suite and the shop floor.

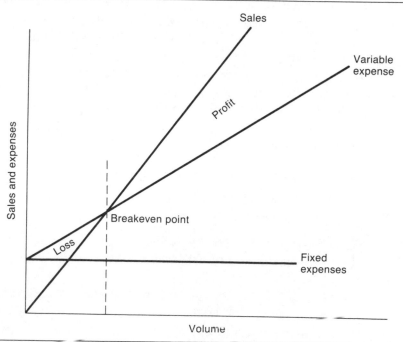

FIGURE 7.1   Breakeven Point and Profit for Company A

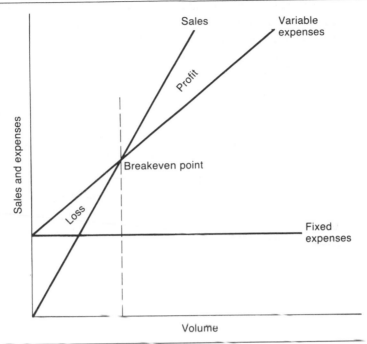

FIGURE 7.2 *Breakeven Point and Profit for Company B*

During my twenty-odd years as a management consultant I have observed many expatriate managers in Japan and have come to realize that their mode of decision making is distinctly different from the Japanese mode. In making decisions, expatriate managers tend to employ criteria different from those of Japanese managers.

For instance, the incoming top manager at a foreign-affiliated company often institutes new policies. Most Western companies in Japan have reputations for suddenly changing their marketing practices, much to the annoyance of their Japanese customers and distributors. This includes such practices as pricing, discounting, and abruptly switching from one wholesaler to another. Such changes have always been motivated by one consideration only—to improve the bottom line in the next quarter.

On the other hand, Japanese managers are usually reluctant to introduce any abrupt changes in business practices for fear they might have a negative impact on the organization and the market. The Japanese manager is more likely to place his priority not on profit but on culture. The term "culture" is rather vague, but I am using it here to mean factors of industrial structure and psychology that determine the company's overall strength, productivity, and competitiveness in the long term; such factors include organizational effectiveness, industrial relations, and the capacity to produce quality products economically.

If we single out profit and KAIZEN as two criteria affecting managerial decisions, we find that the relative weight given these criteria differs for Japanese and foreign managers. Most Western management is distinctly oriented toward short-term profits whereas the Japanese corporate culture is KAIZEN-oriented. The problem is that these two criteria are often seen as mutually exclusive and contradictory: the manager who decides to use one often has to sacrifice the other, and vice versa. Yet, every manager has both of these yardsticks in mind when making decisions, although the considerations for culture are often subtle and latent and most managers do not even realize that they are using such yardsticks.

If management is successful in improving the culture of the organization, the company will be more productive, more competitive, and more profitable in the long run. However, the full impact of the effort management makes to improve the culture will not be felt until years later. If managers are concerned primarily with immediate profit, they will be reluctant to spend time and effort on improving the culture, and over the long run the organization may fail to become more competitive. Thus, when Western managers try to improve productivity, they usually attempt to do so without hurting short-term profitability. On the other hand, when Japanese managers take measures to improve the corporate culture, they often do so with the knowledge that they risk hurting short-term profitability in order to pursue the long-term goal of creating a more competitive organization.

Figures 7.3 and 7.4 show the trends in customer complaints and production costs after the concept of company-wide quality control was introduced at Kobayashi Kose. As can be seen, both the number of complaints and the production costs increased immediately after TQC was introduced. This is understandable, however, because it always takes some time before a new measure brings about a positive result. If management's only criterion is profit, the manager will get cold feet as soon as the production performance starts deteriorating, and he may wish to abandon the TQC program altogether.

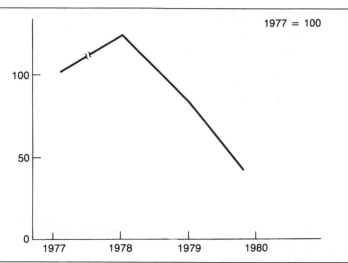

FIGURE 7.3 *Number of Customer Complaints at Kobayashi Kose After Introducing TQC*

This is why efforts to introduce TQC into Western companies have often been fragmentary and have seldom succeeded in improving the corporate culture. The only way Western companies can become internationally more competitive is to begin employing the

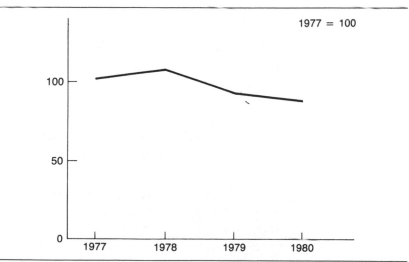

FIGURE 7.4 *Production Cost at Kobayashi Kose After Introducing TQC*

two-sided yardstick of profit and KAIZEN in measuring their top managers' performances.

Such an initiative should begin in the boardroom. If the board uses profit as the only criterion to measure top management performance, managers will be reluctant to initiate P criteria improvements that risk hurting short-term profits, even if the long-term benefits of such changes are obvious.

The board should establish a budget for changing the culture over a period of five or ten years so that top management can devote its efforts to building KAIZEN *along with* its normal duty of realizing a profit. Naturally, there must be an equilibrium between profit and KAIZEN. The board must therefore seek to convince its investors as well as the community and the public of the importance of KAIZEN.

Furthermore, the board should establish top management's P criteria to measure the level of KAIZEN. Just as profit is measured in specific terms such as the bottom line, ROI, and per-share earnings, KAIZEN must be measured in clear, preestablished terms.

Changing the corporate culture to become more productive and competitive while maintaining a balance between profit and KAIZEN —this is the challenge facing Western companies today.

In this connection, if Western management is to introduce KAIZEN in its management systems, the following items should be taken into consideration.

- Is top management committed to the introduction of KAIZEN as a corporate strategy? Is it committed to spending enough time to really understand KAIZEN's implications?

- Is top management committed to such cross-functional goals as quality, cost, and scheduling? Is it committed to deploying the necessary resources, including training programs for all employees? Is it committed to following through and auditing its progress?

- Do the existing systems and corporate structures support the fulfillment of such goals? If they are found inappropriate for meeting the cross-functional goals, is top management prepared to make the necessary changes—even if this means changes in such areas as organization, structure, planning and control, and even in personnel practices, including compensation and personnel reallocation?

The corporate structure or organization should serve the cross-functional goals. Sometimes people speak of organizational strategy as if the organization dictated the strategy. This is fallacious. Strategy should dictate the organization, and not vice versa.

What structure will be appropriate for achieving cross-functional goals may differ from company to company and from industry to industry, and may also depend on the size of the company. Many multidivisional companies have adopted the so-called matrix organization. Again, the effectiveness of the matrix organization should be reviewed from the standpoint of whether it satisfies the cross-functional goals.

- Is top management committed to making cross-functional improvement an ongoing program involving everybody in the organization? Cross-functional improvement is often dealt with in Western companies as a one-shot effort by a project team.

One of the underlying tenets of cross-functional management is that most vital problems in management occur in cross-functional areas and thus often involve interdepartmental (intersectional or interdivisional) activities. The problems that arise within a given department (or function) are relatively easy to handle, since the managers concerned usually have the authority and resources to handle them. However, implementing cross-functional improvements necessitates dealing with the crossover areas between departments. Who should have this responsibility? Any particular manager's job description usually confines responsibility to his function or department. The more precise the job description, the less freedom the manager has in addressing cross-functional and interdepartmental issues.

Job descriptions must include cross-functional responsibilities. If they do not, they should be revised. The internal reporting relationships among the different departments should also be reviewed at the same time.

Each function in the typical Western company is staffed with proud professionals who have received extensive education in their professions and have taken many years to attain professional standing. The prouder they are, the more difficult it is for them to communicate effectively with people from other functional areas on cross-functional matters. Effective cross-functional communication is impossible in such an atmosphere, and profound attitude changes are needed. It may even be necessary to offer optional courses encouraging cross-functional thinking in the curricula of business schools and other educational institutions. In addition, management may find it necessary to transfer professionals in a particular function (engineering, for example) to other functions such as production and sales.

■ How can the company encourage engineers to get more involved in production-related activities? The use of engineering resources is particularly important to Western management. Traditionally, engineers have taken pride in working on projects far removed from the plant site. Engineering jobs at the plant are often regarded as lower status than those at the head office, and this is reflected in their lower salary schedules. The typical engineer dreams of "making it" to the central research laboratory with higher social status and more pay. The system as it exists in the West thus encourages the better engineers to move out of production.

Given that cross-functional liaison between the engineering office and the plants is essential, the system should be revised to put better engineering resources at the plants. In the framework of Japan's seniority-based wage system, an engineer assigned to the plant has no trouble accepting the assignment because he knows he is getting the same compensation package as engineers his age working at the head office.

■ KAIZEN starts with the identification of problems. In the Western hire-and-fire environment, identification of a problem is often tantamount to a negative performance review and may even carry the risk of dismissal. Superiors are busy finding fault with subordinates, and subordinates are busy covering up problems. Changing the corporate culture to accommodate and foster KAIZEN— to encourage everybody to admit problems and to work out plans for their solution—will require sweeping changes in personnel practices and the way people work with each other.

■ Last but not least, Western management will be required to introduce process-oriented criteria at every level, which will necessitate company-wide retraining programs as well as restructuring of the planning and control systems.

TAKING THE CHALLENGE:
TQC AT PHILIPS

An increasing number of Western companies are now introducing TQC programs with determined support from the top. Philips is one multinational company where top management has made a firm commitment to introducing what it calls company-wide quality improvement (CWQI). In October 1983, Philips president Dr. W. Dekker proclaimed the following company-wide quality policy:

> The quality of products and services is of the utmost importance for the continuity of our Company.
> By adopting a quality policy aimed at complete control of every activity, maximum quality, productivity, flexibility and a reduction in cost prices will be achieved. Every employee must be imbued with an attitude directed towards a continuous striving for improvements.
> The Board of Management has decided to give vigorous direction to a Company-wide approach to quality improvement.
> Further shape and content will be given to this initiative in the coming months. The main points of our quality policy are:

1. Quality improvement is primarily a task and responsibility of management as a whole.
2. In order to involve everyone in the Company in quality improvement, management must enable all employees — and not only the employees in the factories — to participate in the preparation, implementation and evaluation of activities.
3. Quality improvement must be tackled and followed up systematically and in a planned manner. This applies to every part of our organization.
4. Quality improvement must be a continuous process.
5. Our organization must concentrate more than ever on its customers and users, both outside and inside the Company.
6. The performance of our competitors must be known to all relevant units.
7. Important suppliers will have to be more closely involved in our quality policy. This relates to both external and internal suppliers of goods as well as of resources and services.
8. Widespread attention will be given to education and training. Existing education and training activities will be assessed, also with regard to their contribution to the quality policy.
9. Publicity must be given to this quality policy in every part of the Company in such a way that everyone can understand it. All available methods and media will be used for internal and external promotion and for communication.

(Philips — continued)

10. Reporting on the progress of the implementation of the policy will be a permanent point on the agenda in review meetings.

The Quality Steering Group, under the direction of the Board of Management, together with the Corporate Quality Bureau, will provide support and coordination at corporate level.

Accordingly, Philips has organized a series of seminars for some 400 Philips top managers from all over the world. At these seminars, Dekker has said:

What matters to us as the Board of Management is that we can do very much better if we really want to. And we *must* want to in order to survive. . . .

The importance of the seminar lies in the fact that it is concerned with a new management concept, the concept of *continuous improvement*.

You should be aware of the fact that we are aiming to instill into the total organization not only the importance of company-wide quality improvement but even more the importance of the need for you, together with the employees entrusted to you — and I repeat *together* — to create the conditions for achieving quality objectives. . . .

After this seminar, you should concentrate even more intensely on this problem and provide your staff with the tools they need and teach them how to use them so as to achieve the required improvement in quality.

Not only will you have to apply the *quality audit,* but you will also have to undergo that quality audit yourselves. The Board of Management has already placed the quality audit high on the agenda in all review meetings and will take quality into account in personal appraisals.

What we want to achieve is nothing less than a complete change in mental attitude. ■

Summing Up

So far, I have tried to explain KAIZEN — what it is, how it works, and what it does. The benefits of KAIZEN are obvious to those who have introduced it. KAIZEN leads to improved quality and greater productivity. Where KAIZEN is introduced for the first time, management may easily see productivity increase by 30 percent, 50 percent, and even 100 percent and more, all without any major capital investments. KAIZEN helps lower the breakeven point. It helps management to become more attentive to customer needs and build a system that takes customer requirements into account.

KAIZEN is a humanistic approach, because it expects everybody —indeed, everybody—to participate in it. It is based on the belief that every human being can contribute to improving his workplace, where he spends one-third of his life.

Finally, KAIZEN makes the business more competitive and profitable. For the last 30 years, Japanese management has followed the policy of constant improvements without officially calling it KAIZEN. Today, for the first time, non-Japanese companies can trace the development of KAIZEN, see the total perspective, and start planning the implementation of a KAIZEN strategy.

The KAIZEN strategy strives to give undivided attention to both process and result. It is the effort that counts when we are talking about process improvement, and management should therefore develop a system that rewards the efforts of both workers and managers. This recognition of efforts should not be confused with recognition of the results.

The introduction of a KAIZEN strategy calls for both top-down and bottom-up approaches. It should be noted in this connection that the top-down management style usually calls for a design approach and the bottom-up style for an analytical approach. Thus, at the lower levels of the management hierarchy, both workers and managers need to be trained in the use of analytical tools. On the other hand, at the higher levels, the design approach (for instance, policy deployment, quality deployment, and the use of the New Seven) is more useful, since these levels are more concerned with setting goals and deploying the means to achieve them.

Whereas the analytical approach tries to learn from past experience, the design approach tries to build a better future with predetermined goals. Although the design approach has traditionally been used in such limited fields as industrial engineering and architecture, its application to management issues deserves serious attention. (For a brief description of the design approach and its tools, see Appendix E.)

When these two approaches are combined with the decision-making and problem-solving functions of managers at every level, they will become powerful tools for implementing the KAIZEN strategy. Management should keep both of these requirements in mind in developing training and educational programs for the introduction of KAIZEN concepts.

Many useful concepts and tools have been developed in Japan in implementing KAIZEN strategy, and I believe that most of them are valid in other countries as well. These include the customer-oriented philosophy, the PDCA cycle, cross-functional management, policy deployment, and such tools as systems diagrams and quality tables.

According to Osaka Electronics Communication University professor Yoshinobu Nayatani, KAIZEN strategy and TQC management bring about the following effects:

1. People grasp the real issues more rapidly
2. More emphasis is placed on the planning phase
3. A process-oriented way of thinking is encouraged
4. People concentrate on the more important issues
5. Everybody participates in building the new system

My belief that the KAIZEN concept is valid not only in Japan but also in other countries is based on my observation that all people have an instinctive desire to improve themselves.

Although it is true that cultural factors affect an individual's behavior, it is also true that the individual's behavior can be measured and affected through a series of factors or processes. Thus it is always possible, regardless of the culture, to break behavior down into processes and to establish control points and check points. This is why such management tools as decision making and problem solving have a universal validity. While the impact of cultural factors does need to be considered in applying process-oriented thinking, it does not in the least negate the validity of process-oriented thinking.

KAIZEN does not replace or preclude innovation. Rather, the two are complementary. Ideally, innovation should take off after KAIZEN has been exhausted, and KAIZEN should follow as soon as innovation is initiated. KAIZEN and innovation are inseparable ingredients in progress.

Says Fuji Xerox's Yotaro Kobayashi, "KAIZEN improves the status quo by bringing added value to it. It is bound to yield positive results if efforts are continued toward a clearly defined goal.

"However, KAIZEN is limited in that it does not *replace* or fundamentally *change* the status quo. As soon as KAIZEN's marginal value starts declining, one should turn to the challenge of innovation. Top management's job is to maintain a balance between KAIZEN and innovation, and it should never forget to look for innovative opportunities."

Lastly, while I have confined myself in this book to the impact of KAIZEN strategy on the business community, I believe that KAIZEN strategy is widely applicable in such nonbusiness sectors as government services, schools, and other institutions, and that it would be useful even in the controlled-economy countries. These institutions may lack the profit motive, but the KAIZEN concept remains a valid criterion for checking progress.

In this context, it may be fitting to quote Claude Lévi-Strauss on the concept of progress. In a remark made at the 1983 International Symposium on Productivity in Japan, he said:

> *We call some societies primitive because of their desire to remain in the same state* in which gods or ancestors created them at the beginning of time, with a demographic balance which they know how to maintain and *an unchanging standard of living* protected by their social rules and metaphysical belief. [Italics added.]

It is my sincere hope that we will be able to overcome our "primitive" state and that the KAIZEN strategy will eventually find application not only in the business community but also in all institutions and societies all over the world.

Appendix A
3-MU Checklist of
KAIZEN Activities

A number of KAIZEN check-point systems have been developed to help both workers and management be constantly mindful of the areas for improvement. The following is a widely-used example utilizing three checkpoints:

Muda (Waste)	Muri (Strain)	Mura (Discrepancy)
1. Manpower	1. Manpower	1. Manpower
2. Technique	2. Technique	2. Technique
3. Method	3. Method	3. Method
4. Time	4. Time	4. Time
5. Facilities	5. Facilities	5. Facilities
6. Jigs and Tools	6. Jigs and Tools	6. Jigs and Tools
7. Materials	7. Materials	7. Materials
8. Production Volume	8. Production Volume	8. Production Volume
9. Inventory	9. Inventory	9. Inventory
10. Place	10. Place	10. Place
11. Way of Thinking	11. Way of Thinking	11. Way of Thinking

Appendix B
The Five-Step
KAIZEN Movement

*T*he 5-S movement takes its name from the initials of five Japanese words that start with *s: seiri, seiton, seiso, seiketsu,* and *shitsuke.* As part of the visual management of an overall program, signs that repeat the steps are often posted in the workshop.

Step 1 *seiri* (straighten up)

- Work-in-process
- Unnecessary tools
- Unused machinery
- Defective products
- Papers and documents

Differentiate between the necessary and the unnecessary and discard the unnecessary.

Step 2 *seiton* (put things in order)
Things must be kept in order so that they are ready for use when needed. An American mechanical engineer recalls that he used to spend hours searching for tools and parts when he worked in Cincinnati. Only after he joined a Japanese company and saw how easily the workers were able to find what they needed did he realize the value of "seiton."

Step 3 *seiso* (clean up)
Keep the workplace clean.

Step 4 *seiketsu* (personal cleanliness)
Make it a habit to be clean and tidy, starting with your own person.

Step 5 *shitsuke* (discipline)
Follow procedures in the workshop.

Appendix C
The Five Ws and
the One H

Who	What	Where
1. Who does it?	1. What to do?	1. Where to do it?
2. Who is doing it?	2. What is being done?	2. Where is it done?
3. Who should be doing it?	3. What should be done?	3. Where should it be done?
4. Who else can do it?	4. What else can be done?	4. Where else can it be done?
5. Who else should do it?	5. What else should be done?	5. Where else should it be done?
6. Who is doing 3-MUs?	6. What 3-MUs are being done?	6. Where are 3-MUs being done?

When	Why	How
1. When to do it?	1. Why does he do it?	1. How to do it?
2. When is it done?	2. Why do it?	2. How is it done?
3. When should it be done?	3. Why do it there?	3. How should it be done?
4. What other time can it be done?	4. Why do it then?	4. Can this method be used in other areas?
5. What other time should it be done?	5. Why do it that way?	5. Is there any other way to do it?
6. Are there any time 3-MUs?	6. Are there any 3-MUs in the way of thinking?	6. Are there any 3-MUs in the method?

Appendix D
The 4-M Checklist*

A. *M*an (Operator)
   1. Does he follow standards?
   2. Is his work efficiency acceptable?
   3. Is he problem-conscious?
   4. Is he responsible? (Is he accountable?)
   5. Is he qualified?
   6. Is he experienced?
   7. Is he assigned to the right job?
   8. Is he willing to improve?
   9. Does he maintain good human relations?
   10. Is he healthy?

B. *M*achine (Facilities)
   1. Does it meet production requirements?
   2. Does it meet process capabilities?
   3. Is the oiling (greasing) adequate?
   4. Is the inspection adequate?
   5. Is operation stopped often because of mechanical trouble?
   6. Does it meet precision requirements?
   7. Does it make any unusual noises?

---

*Sometimes "Measurement" is added as a fifth checklist category, in which case the list is called the 5-M Checklist.

    8. Is the layout adequate?

    9. Are there enough machines/facilities?

   10. Is everything in good working order?

C. *Material*

    1. Are there any mistakes in volume?

    2. Are there any mistakes in grade?

    3. Are there any mistakes in the brand name?

    4. Are there impurities mixed in?

    5. Is the inventory level adequate?

    6. Is there any waste in material?

    7. Is the handling adequate?

    8. Is the work-in-process abandoned?

    9. Is the layout adequate?

   10. Is the quality standard adequate?

D. Operation *Method*

    1. Are the work standards adequate?

    2. Is the work standard upgraded?

    3. Is it a safe method?

    4. Is it a method that ensures a good product?

    5. Is it an efficient method?

    6. Is the sequence of work adequate?

    7. Is the setup adequate?

    8. Are the temperature and humidity adequate?

    9. Are the lighting and ventilation adequate?

   10. Is there adequate contact with the previous and next processes?

Appendix E
KAIZEN Problem-
Solving Tools

The Seven Statistical Tools

There are two different approaches to problem solving. The first approach is used when data are available and the job is to analyze the data to solve a particular problem. Most problems that occur in production-related areas fall into this category. The seven statistical tools* used for such analytical problem-solving are:

1. **Pareto diagrams.** These diagrams classify problems according to cause and phenomenon. The problems are diagrammed according to priority, using a bar-graph format, with 100 percent indicating the total amount of value lost.

2. **Cause-and-effect diagrams.** These diagrams are used to analyze the characteristics of a process or situation and the factors that contribute to them. Cause-and-effect diagrams are also called "fishbone graphs" or "Godzilla-bone graphs."

3. **Histograms.** The frequency data obtained from measurements display a peak around a certain value. The variation of quality characteristics is called "distribution," and the figure that illustrates frequency in the form of a pole is referred to as a histogram. This is used mainly to determine problems by checking the dispersion shape, center value, and nature of dispersement.

4. **Control charts.** There are two types of variations: the inevitable variations that occur under normal conditions and those

*The description of the seven statistical tools is adapted from The Quest for Higher Quality: The Deming Prize and Quality Control, RICOH Company, Ltd., with permission.

that can be traced to a cause. The latter are referred to as "abnormal." Control charts serve to detect abnormal trends with the help of line graphs. These graphs differ from standard line graphs in that they have control limit lines at the center, top, and bottom levels. Sample data are plotted in dots on the graph to evaluate process situations and trends.

5. **Scatter diagrams.** Two pieces of corresponding data are plotted in a scatter diagram. The relation between these plotted dots illustrates the relationship between the corresponding data.

6. **Graphs.** There are many kinds of graphs employed, depending on the shape desired and the purpose of analysis. Bar graphs compare values via parallel bars, while line graphs are used to illustrate variations over a period of time. Circle graphs indicate the categorical breakdown of values, and radar charts assist in the analysis of previously evaluated items.

7. **Checksheets.** These are designed to tabulate the results through routine checking of the situation.

These tools are widely used by QC circles and other small groups, as well as by staff engineers and managers, for identifying and solving problems. They are all statistical and analytical tools, and employees at companies active in CWQC are trained to use these tools in their routine activities.

The New Seven

In many management situations, not all the data needed for problem solving are available. New-product development is illustrative. The ideal way to develop a new product would be to identify the customer requirements, translate these requirements into engineering requirements, and then translate the engineering requirements into production requirements. Likewise with developing a new manufacturing method for better productivity. In both cases, the necessary data are not always available—and what data are available are often available only in the minds of the people concerned, and expressed in language and not in mathematical figures. Such verbal data must be rearranged into meaningful form so that a reasonable decision can be made.

Many problem-solving situations in management call for collaboration among people from different departments. Here too, hard data are scarce, and the available data are likely to be highly subjective.

In all these cases, it is necessary to go beyond the analytical approach and to use a design approach to problem solving. The seven new QC tools (commonly referred to as the New Seven) used for this design approach have proved useful in such areas as product-quality improvement, cost reduction, new-product development, and policy deployment. The New Seven are among the most effective tools for today's managers, staff people, and engineers.

The design approach is a comprehensive systems approach to problem solving characterized by attention to detail. Another feature of the design approach is its involvement of people from different backgrounds, which makes it effective in solving interdepartmental or cross-functional problems.

The New Seven tools are:

1. **Relations diagram.** This diagram clarifies the interrelations in a complex situation involving many interrelated factors and serves to clarify the cause-and-effect relationships among factors.

2. **Affinity diagram.** This is essentially a brain-storming method. It is based on group work in which every participant writes down his ideas and the ideas are then grouped and realigned by subject matter.

3. **Tree diagram.** This is an extension of the value engineering concept of functional analysis. It is applied to show the inter-relations among goals and measures.

4. **Matrix diagram.** This format is used to clarify the relations between two different factors. The matrix diagram is often used in deploying quality requirements into counterpart (engineering) characteristics and then into production requirements.

5. **Matrix data-analysis diagram.** This diagram is used when the matrix chart does not provide sufficiently detailed information. This is the only method within the New Seven that is based on data analysis and gives numerical results.

6. **PDPC (Process Decision Program Chart).** This is an application of the process decision program chart used in operations

research. Because implementation programs to achieve specific goals do not always go according to plan, and because unexpected developments are likely to have serious consequences, PDPC has been developed not only to arrive at the optimum conclusion but also to avoid surprises.

7. **Arrow diagram.** This is often used in PERT (Program Evaluation and Review Technique) and CPM (Critical Path Method). It uses a network representation to show the steps necessary to implement a plan.

The list of New Seven applications for improvement-related activities is almost endless. While the list below shows the major application fields in Japan today, it is by no means an exhaustive listing. Not all of the New Seven are used in every project, but one or more are used, depending on the project requirements.

Typical Applications for New Seven QC Tools

R&D

Development of new technology

New-product development

Quality deployment

Improvement of analytical and diagnostic skills

Production scheduling

Production management

Productivity improvement

Introduction of automation

Quality improvement

Cost reduction and energy saving

Safety improvement

Competitive analysis

Claim analysis

QA-systems improvement

Pollution prevention

Sales management

Analysis of market information

Supplier management

Policy deployment

Appendix F
Deming Prizes

*T*he Deming Prizes were initially started with funds contributed by W. Edwards Deming from the proceeds of his early Japanese lectures on quality control and the royalties from the sale of his lecture texts and translations of his book. Today, the Deming Prize costs are borne by JUSE.

There are three categories of Deming Prizes: the Deming Prize, which is awarded to individuals, the Deming Application Prize, which is awarded to companies, and the Deming Factory Prize.

The Japan Quality Control Award, added in 1970 as the highest award, is given only to companies that have demonstrated a sustained high level of TQC practices at least five years after receiving a Deming Prize.

The checklist for the Deming Prize examination is indicative of the range of activities conducted in Japan in the name of total quality control. It shows that a QC audit in Japan is actually an audit of the overall management system.

Audit Checklist for the Deming Application Prize

1. **Corporate Policy**

   What is the corporate policy for TQC? What goals and measures are employed in order to plan, design, produce, sell, and assure good products or services? How successful is it, and how is it checked? (Policy formation, deployment, implementation, and audit)

2. Organization and Administration

What kind of organization is employed to carry out and administer statistical quality control? Other issues to be studied include clarity in authority and responsibility and coordination among divisions, committee activities, and small-group activities. (Cross-functional organization)

3. Education and Extension

What kind of education programs are routinely provided, such as seminars on SQC (Statistical Quality Control), both within and without the company? To what extent are the concepts and methods of SQC understood? How is the effectiveness of these programs confirmed? What education is provided to vendors and subcontractors? How is the suggestion system carried out?

4. Implementation

What kind of activities are conducted to assure TQC in such fields as R&D, design, purchasing, manufacturing, inspection, and sales? For instance, the following items must be checked:

  i. Profit management
  ii. Cost control
  iii. Purchasing and inventory control
  iv. Production-process control
  v. Facility management
  vi. Instrumentation control
  vii. Personnel administration
  viii. Labor relations
  ix. Education programs
  x. New-product development
  xi. Research management
  xii. Vendor relations
  xiii. Grievance procedures
  xiv. Use of consumer information
  xv. QA (Quality Assurance)
  xvi. Customer services
  xvii. Customer relations

(a) **Collection and use of quality information**
How is the information transmitted from the head office and distributed among plants, sales offices, and departments?

(b) **Analysis**
How are important quality problems defined, and how are statistical methods used for problem solving?

(c) **Standardization**
How are standards established, used, and revised? How is standardization maintained, and how is consistency maintained among standards?

(d) **Control**
How are control points established? How are counter-measures adopted? What is the control system for emergency measures, and how is it administered? How are various tools such as control charts used? Are the production processes under control?

(e) **Quality assurance**
How is the quality-assurance system administered and diagnosed? What is the system for new-product development? How are quality functions deployed? What preventive measures exist in the safety and product-liability areas? What measures are employed for process control and improvement? How are process capabilities managed?

5. **Effect**
What impact has TQC's introduction had on product quality? What impact has it had on service, delivery, cost, profits, safety, and the environment? Does the company manufacture and sell top-quality products? What intangible benefits has it gained?

6. **For the Future**
Does the company recognize its current strengths and weaknesses? Are there plans to carry the TQC program forward? How do these plans, if any, relate to corporate long-range policy?

Some of the tangible and intangible effects reported by companies that have been awarded Deming Prizes are:

Tangible Effects

Increased market share
Increased sales volume
Increased production volume
Successful development of new products
Shortening of product development time
Development of new markets
Improved quality
Fewer complaints
Reduced defect costs
Fewer processes
More employee suggestions
Fewer industrial accidents

Intangible effects

Increased awareness and involvement in management by
everybody
Increased quality-consciousness and problem-consciousness
Better communication both horizontally and vertically
Improved quality of work
Improved human relations
Improved information feedback
Improved managerial skills
Permeation of market-in concept
Clear delineation between responsibility and authority
More confidence in new-product development
Conversion to goal-oriented thinking
Improved standardization
More active use of statistical quality control

Appendix G
KAIZEN Activities at
Canon: A Case Study

Canon manufactures cameras, copying machines, and office computers. Its KAIZEN activities are centered in its CPS (Canon Production System). As is shown in the CPS diagram (Figure G.1), the objectives are to manufacture better-quality products at lower cost and deliver them faster. In order to achieve these objectives, Canon has developed the following three systems: QA (Quality Assurance), PA (Production Assurance), and PT (Personnel Training).

The first of CPS's basic structures is the QA system. Quality excellence is critical to gaining worldwide respect for the products. Accordingly, Canon tries to ensure the best quality in all stages of development, production, and sales.

The second basic structure in CPS is the PA (Production Assurance) System. Canon has devised two subsystems to attain the PA goals of fast delivery and low cost: Canon's HIT System (equivalent to just-in-time) and Signal System. The HIT System means making parts and products only when needed and only in the quantity needed. Canon uses either HIT cards or signals for this purpose. These subsystems are designed to achieve just-in-time manufacturing while adopting the "visual control" philosophy.

The third basic structure in CPS is the PT (Personnel Training) System, under which Canon's employees are continually educated through a life-long educational program.

The other crucial instruments for realizing the CPS objectives are the "four investments" and the "elimination of nine wastes."

247

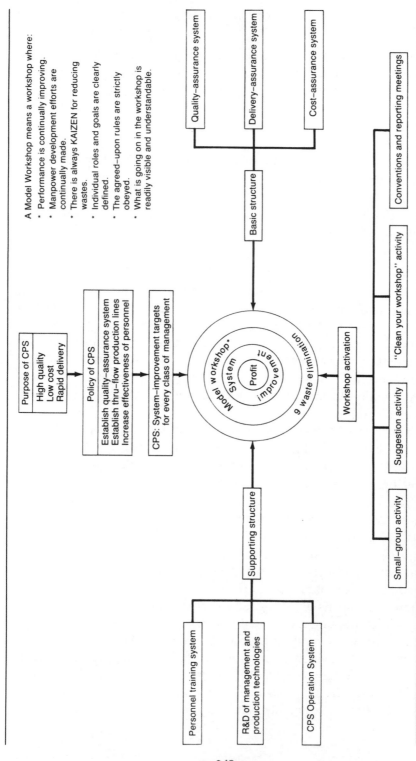

FIGURE G.1 CPS (Canon Production System) Structure Chart

The four investments are directed at technologies, human resources, facilities, and welfare. Canon believes that neglect of any of these investments will eventually lead to corporate failure.

As to the waste, it is not always obvious and is often camouflaged within the daily routine. Without a clear-cut framework, it is difficult to tell whether one should take the trouble to eliminate a particular kind of waste or not. CPS therefore categorizes waste into nine types, shown in Figure G.2.

Waste Category	Nature of Waste	Type of Economization
Work-in-process	Stocking items not immediately needed	Inventory improvement
Rejection	Producing defective products	Fewer rejects
Facilities	Having idle machinery and break-downs, taking too long for setup	Increase in capacity utilization ratio
Expenses	Overinvesting for required output	Curtailment of expenses
Indirect labor	Excess personnel due to bad indirect labor system	Efficient job assign-ment
Design	Producing products with more functions than necessary	Cost reduction
Talent	Employing people for jobs that can be mechanized or assigned to less skilled people	Labor saving or labor maximization
Motion	Not working according to work standard	Improvement of work standard
New-product run-up	Making a slow start in stabilizing the production of a new product	Faster shift to full line production

FIGURE G.2 *Canon's Nine Waste Categories*

CPS activities are judged by the nine wastes removed. Canon management believes that using this nine-part classification for dealing with waste (1) helps employees become problem-conscious, (2) helps them move from operational improvement to systems improvement, and (3) helps employees recognize the need for self-development. Figure G.3 shows the systems diagram for the nine wastes in production as perceived by Canon.

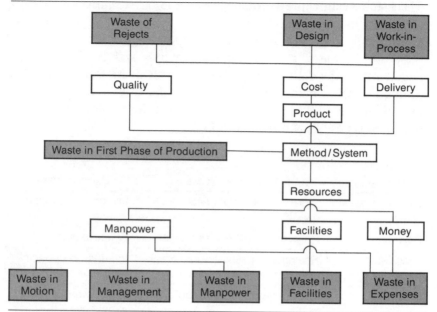

FIGURE G.3 *Nine Wastes in Production*

Canon management estimates that the companywide efforts for reducing waste through CPS saved ¥24 billion (U.S. $100 million) in 1983. The success of Canon's CPS system has given their factory people great confidence and pride in contributing to the corporation's earnings.

The ultimate goal of reducing waste is deployed from top management down to the workshops, and targets are established each year at each level. In one of Canon's plants, a project called "Improvement Project 100" is under way. Figure G.4 shows the sheet used in this project.

Category of Waste	Plan	Countermeasures		Person in Charge		Schedule	Projected Effect
	Problem	5M No.	Actions for improvement	Line	Report		

FIGURE G.4 *KAIZEN Project 100*

The following explains what to write in the sheet.

1. **Waste:** Designation of one of the nine wastes
2. **Problem:** The problem corresponding to each waste is listed, together with the ideal situation to identify the gap between "should be" and "is."
3. **5Ms:** Relate the cause to one of the 5Ms: machine, material, man, method, and measurement.
4. **No.:** Serial numbers
5. **Actions for improvement:** Countermeasures to realize the ideal state (consultations with other related departments are welcome)
6. **Person in charge:** The person's name
7. **Schedule:** Deadline for completion of the project
8. **Projected effect:** An effect projection (serves as a guide to priority)

In this project, the managers are told to think of more than 200 tasks for improvement, and the target for foremen is 100. Each supervisor is handed a "KAIZEN Project 100" sheet to post on the wall in the workshop. Every time he thinks of a new improvement, he writes it down on the sheet. This list serves as a useful guide in planning the workshop's monthly activities.

In some other plants, the foremen are told to set aside the half-hour between 11:30 A.M. and 12:00 noon as KAIZEN time—time to do nothing but think about improvement in the workshop. Foremen should not even answer the telephone or attend meetings during this 30-minute period, and the factories are advised not to hold meetings then. The foremen use this period to identify problems and work on KAIZEN programs.

Figure G.5 lists Canon's annual awards. It should be noted that awards are provided for individuals, small groups, and workshop units, and that the awards are intended to show management's appreciation for the efforts and the results. (Figure G.5 follows on the next two pages.)

Name	Given to	Contents	Award ¥ ($)	Award (Other)	Recipients per Year	Awarded at
Model Workshop Award	Section	Workshop that has realized 30% improvement for 3 consecutive years and is exemplary in Canon	200,000 (900)	Overseas study tour for section manager, Gold Eaglehead for the section	1–2	CPS Convention
Runner-up Model Workshop Award	Section	Same as above, and is representative of Canon	100,000 (450)	Eagle Shield (Silver)	10–20	CPS Convention
Award for Eliminating Nine Wastes	Block	Workshop or team that has made remarkable improvement in reducing waste	50,000 (225)		50	CPS Convention
CFS Performance Award	Supervisor, Assistant section manager, Senior engineer	Those who have conceived unique concepts in reducing waste and succeeded in managing the workshop		Overseas study tour	3	CPS Waste-Elimination Convention, CPS Convention
Excellent Small-Group Activities Award	Small group	Group that has shown outstanding performance in small-group activities	50,000 (225)		2	All-Canon Small-Group Activities Convention
Cumulative-Point Presidential Award	Individual	Top 20 in cumulative points for suggestions	300,000 (1,350)	Gold Medal	20	Work-Improvement Suggestion Conventions

FIGURE G.5 List of Annual Awards Provided at Canon

Name	Given to	Contents	Award ¥ ($)	Award (Other)	Recipients per Year	Awarded at
Annual-Points Presidential Award	Individual	Top 30 in points for suggestions	100,000 (450)	Silver Medal	30	Work-Improvement Suggestion Conventions
Presidential Award	Individual, group	Outstanding suggestions above B level	100,000 (450)		10–20	Work-Improvement Suggestion Conventions
Special Presidential Award	Individual, group	Most outstanding among those who received Presidential Awards		Overseas study tour to the leader	2	CPS Convention
Gold Award	Supplier	Cooperating company that has built promising systems for Quality, Cost, and Delivery	300,000 (1,350)	Eagle Shield (Gold)	1	Cooperating Companies' Executive Meeting
Silver Award	Supplier	Cooperating company that has built promising systems for Quality, Cost, and Delivery	200,000 (900)	Eagle Shield (Silver)	1–2	Cooperating Companies' Executive Meeting
Special Award	Supplier	Cooperating company with high achievement in production engineering, productivity, or quality improvement	100,000 (450)		1–2 per category	Cooperating Companies' Executive Meeting

FIGURE G.5 (continued)

Index

About the Author

Masaaki Imai has helped more than 200 non-Japanese and joint-venture companies rethink their organizations and introduce Japanese management approaches. Mr. Imai is Chairman of the Cambridge Corporation, an international management consulting and executive recruiting firm which he founded in 1962 and is based in Tokyo.

For five years in the 1950s, Mr. Imai, a graduate of the University of Tokyo who majored in American Studies, lived in the United States, working for the Japan Productivity Center in Washington, D.C. (His principal responsibility: escorting groups of Japanese businessmen through major U.S. plants so they could study "the secret of American productivity.")

Today, Mr. Imai writes and teaches the Japanese business philosophy that step-by-step improvement in the nature of "refinements" or "enhancements" are equally as important as "break-through" innovations. His seminars are presented under the KAIZEN service mark. He is the author of *Never Take Yes for an Answer* and *16 Ways to Avoid Saying No.*

A Note on the Type

*T*he text of this book was set in a computer version of a type face called Times Roman, designed by Stanley Morison (1889–1967) for *The Times* (London) and first introduced by that newspaper in 1932.

Among typographers and designers of the twentieth century, Stanley Morison was a strong forming influence—as a typographi cal advisor to The Monotype Corporation, as a director of two distinguished English publishing houses, and as a writer of sensibility, erudition, and keen practical sense.

Text/jacket design: M.R.P. Design
Composition: Arkotype Inc.
Production Managers: Della Mancuso and Valerie Sawyer
Printer/binder: Halliday Lithographers